STRIKE A BLOW
TO CHANGE
THE WORLD

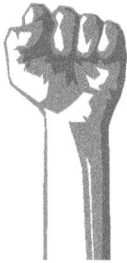

Eknath Awad

Translated by **JERRY PINTO**

SPEAKING
TIGER

SPEAKING TIGER PUBLISHING PVT. LTD
4381/4, Ansari Road, Daryaganj
New Delhi 110002

Originally published as *Jag Badal Ghaaluni Ghaav* in
Marathi by Samakaleen Prakashan in 2012
Published in English by Speaking Tiger in paperback 2018

ISBN: 978-93-88070-40-9
eISBN: 978-93-88070-00-3

10 9 8 7 6 5 4 3 2 1

Typeset in Adobe Garamond Pro by SÜRYA, New Delhi
Printed at Sanat Printers, Kundli

EKNATH AWAD (1956–2015) was a prominent Dalit activist from Maharashtra. He was an active member of the Dalit Panthers and later joined the Vidhayak Sansad in 1981, where he worked to organize the Adivasi groups in Thane. He joined CASA in 1983 and helped established programmes against caste-based practices, and for literacy and women empowerment. He founded the Rural Development Centre in 1985 and the Maanavi Haq Abhiyaan in 1990.

JERRY PINTO is the author of the novels *Murder in Mahim* (2017) and *Em and the Big Hoom* (2012; winner of the Hindu Prize and the Crossword Book Award), and the non-fiction book *Helen: The Life and Times of an H-Bomb* (2006; winner of the National Award for the Best Book on Cinema). He has also translated Daya Pawar's

autobiography, *Baluta*; the memoirs *I Want to Destroy Myself* (*Mala Udhvasta Vhachay*) by Malika Amar Shaikh, and *I, the Salt Doll* (*Mee Mithaachi Baahuli*) by Vandana Mishra; Baburao Bagul's short-story collection *When I Hid My Caste* (*Jevha Mee Jaat Chorli Hoti*); and the novels *Cobalt Blue* by Sachin Kundalkar and *Half-Open Windows* (*Khidkya Ardhya Ughadya*) by Ganesh Matkari. Jerry Pinto is the recipient of, among other honours, the Sahitya Akademi Award and Yale University's Windham-Campbell Prize.

'This is an inspiring book by an inspiring man and deserves to be widely read. The book offers a vivid and engaging insight into processes of social change in Maharashtra. Born into a Dalit (ex-untouchable) family, Eknath Awad offers a detailed—and deeply felt—account of the everyday humiliations and vicissitudes of caste. We see first-hand how caste is structured into daily interactions and institutions. There are some searing details of caste oppression here, but this is most definitely not a story of victimhood. Drawing on a lifetime of activism and grass-roots organizing Eknath Awad offers rich insights into how structures of dominance may be revealed, challenged and, ultimately, overturned. A must-read for all those interested in Dalit politics and caste change.'

—Hugo Gorringe,
author of *Untouchable Citizens*

'This autobiography presents the struggle of an unusual individual against the most oppressive features of our society—exclusion and discrimination, and violence—the quality of which is shockingly cruel and inhumane. A man free of fear who brought hope among the most oppressed, untouchables living in an utterly hopeless social situation. This unique book is factual, but also philosophical and reflective. Therefore, it will serve as a perennial source of inspiration to the exploited Dalits everywhere.'

—Sukhdeo Thorat, Professor Emeritus,
Centre for the Study of Regional Development

STRIKE A BLOW TO CHANGE THE WORLD

My Father, Our Jija

I started calling my father Jija, senior uncle, not because I was taught to do so by my mother, but because that is what everyone called him. They called him Jija because it summed up their feelings for him: the elder statesman of the family to whom everyone could turn in a crisis, knowing that he would come through with a solution that was in equal parts pragmatic, dramatic and effective.

Years after his passing away, it makes me very emotional to remember Jija and to write this introduction to his autobiography.

These memories are also intertwined with memories of my childhood. We were always hearing stories of caste atrocities and tense situations that had arisen in villages out of some imagined infarction of the rules governing caste behaviour. Perhaps all Dalit families heard those stories; certainly many of them lived through those stories. But the Awad household was where they were retold and discussed, and where Jija would sit, listening intently and then work out a plan to tackle them. I do not think it is possible to over-estimate the impact this had on my childhood. The people, activists and various incidents which Jija mentions in his autobiography were all part of my growing-up years. As you will read in his autobiography, Jija became a public figure early in life, almost without willing it; boys in his college started calling him their leader. And he remained a public figure until his last moment.

To better his understanding of his social situation, Jija sought out rigour by studying for a Masters degree in Social Work, then for a law degree. But he waited to complete his law degree until his certificate could bear the name of the man whose example he followed, Dr Babasaheb Ambedkar.

In many cases, ideology and college degrees can turn a man into an ideologue. This was never the case with Jija. His lived experience of poverty, of caste injustice, of the everyday humiliations of being a Mang, leavened his ideological positions so that emotion was never far from the surface. These two animated and strengthened each other so that he never fell prey to sentiment (an excess of emotion or emotion for its own sake) or to a puritanical credo (ideology turning in on itself).

He tells his story as the spontaneous activist, a man responding to the dark space in our nation's heart where caste pride becomes a deadly tool. But you should not allow yourself to be fooled by that. First, in each of the accounts of his response to a caste atrocity, you will see an understanding of the Other, of how a caste-proud Hindu thinks. Then you will see a dramatic and fitting response carved out of available material. Next come all the actual nuts and bolts of putting such a response into action: the pamphlet to be written, printed and distributed; the people to be motivated, loaded up and taken to the temple; the food to be collected; and the risks that must be run. These things do not happen easily in rural Maharashtra; they are not magicked out of the red mud of Marathwada. They must be made to happen and that can take hours, days of hard administrative work.

For the people around him, he was often the only source of confidence, pride, dignity and hope. There was a dialectical mechanism of energy that ran between him and his people through the same modalities of hope and empowerment. But his definition of 'his people' was an inclusive one. He worked hard to erase the age-old war between the Mang and the Mahar. He did not see the Muslim or the Dalit Christian as the Other. 'His people' were defined simply as those who had been turned out of the fold for whatever reason. And when this injustice was brought to his attention, he would be there, with the law as his weapon, with an understanding of how the situation had arisen and a willingness to take a risk or two to break through. His work was not the outcome of textual interpretation extruded from cadre and camp, or a structured strategy created once and deployed again and again; each time, it was an organic emergence from his life-world.

His autobiography is a sociography of caste-ridden rural Marathwada. The villages where he lived and worked, and of which he speaks, mostly have a non-Brahmanical social composition but have inherited vicious caste hierarchical practices and therefore developed inhuman brutalities that parade as living structures, all rooted in Brahmanical ontology. Jija's life and activism can be seen as a series of responses to this situation.

He knew, perhaps, even in the moments of victory—when a village that objected to a single blue Ambedkarite flag became a sea of blue flags, when an upper-caste Hindu served tea to the Dalits in same teacups used in his own home by his own people—that the war was not won, the fight was not over. And this sense of what was not accomplished prompted him to fight all the more relentlessly. Therefore, this autobiography is not just a selection and synchronization of his selected memories but a series of lived struggles to overcome the horrors of caste.

In this autobiography, there are haunting memories of the household affairs and caste dynamics, food and hunger, barter and labour, caste humiliation and resistance against such humiliation, a strong desire for education, aspiration for self-respect and dignity, inspirations from Phule-Shahu-Ambedkar-Anna Bhau. At the same time, it is the story of a people's movement with its patterns of social mobilization and the emergence of NGOs and employment opportunities.

The incidents narrated in the autobiography are still part of public memory in Marathwada. They are the source of moral inspiration for hundreds of activists, some of whose names are mentioned here. Many of the intuitional initiatives which Jija led continue to run, though a few of them have hit roadblocks due to his absence.

I am glad to acknowledge Jerry Pinto for his translation and for making it available to an English readership. As I read the translated manuscript, it made me re-live the exact same experiences of reading it in my mother tongue, Marathi, with no loss of cultural sediment. I am thankful to Prashant Kunte who travelled with Jija for almost a year to record this autobiography in Marathi. Special thanks to Subhas Bhau Kulkarni and the publisher of *Jag Badal Ghaluni Ghaav*, Samakalin Prakashan. Last but not least, I am thankful to Ravi Singh, the publisher of Speaking Tiger, for his readiness to publish this book.

MILIND E. AWAD
New Delhi

Translator's Introduction

I am indebted to Dr Milind Awad of Jawaharlal Nehru University on many counts. In the first place, he sent me a digital copy of his father's remarkable book, *Jag Badal Ghaaluni Ghaav*, with the suggestion that I might like to translate it.

I began reading it far away from home and was almost immediately transfixed by it. Eknath Awad was obviously a rare human being indeed. For one, he seems totally honest. He is honest about his own tendencies to use violence to settle disputes, he is honest about the methods his activists use, he is honest about the casteism he sees among his own people and he never suggests that his monumental courage and his awakening to the consciousness of the injustices of the caste system was his alone. He points backwards to Mahatma Phule and Dr Babasaheb Ambedkar. If one is not familiar with caste politics in interior Maharashtra, this might seem a fairly ordinary thing. Here is a Dalit who drew inspiration from Dalit leaders and thinkers. But in so doing, one would be making the same mistake of monolithising the Dalit. We know now there is no Christian; there are only Roman Catholics and Protestants and Baptists and Lutherans…the term Christian is a rubric under which the outsider subsumes those who are perceived to share a faith. We know there is no Muslim; there are Sunnis and Shi'as and Bohris and Khojas and Memons… the term Muslim is a rubric. You can say this about Hindus as well and this can be said about Dalits too. Mahars claim Dr Ambedkar; Mangs claim Annabhau Sathe. Eknath Awad was the kind of man who thought this was wrong. He felt there was something in Dr Ambedkar's teachings, something big, something powerful, something that could be used by the Mahar and the Mang and the Vanjari and the Laman and by anyone else who had suffered oppression from an accident of birth.

When I was reading *Jag Badal Ghaaluni Ghaav*, I was often moved to tears. There are many images that will stay with me: Dalits being served food where the children shit and covering the excreta with mud before sitting down to eat; a young man electrocuted to fill a well with water; Rajamati refusing to give up her seat in the jeep to the village sarpanch; the old woman watching her home burn down but still celebrating the change in the name of Marathwada University to Dr Babasaheb Ambedkar Marathwada University; and then the image of a crop coming up over waste land, land going to the landless.

What is also truly magnificent—heroic even—is that Eknath Awad did not move to the city. He completed his Masters degree, he completed a Masters in Social Work as well as an LLB degree; that's a lot of learning for anyone. But when he found a job in Dahisar, Mumbai, he could not be content. He wanted to go back to Marathwada, one of India's many hotbeds of caste injustice. There were battles to be fought there, and he could not find peace in the city.

I am also indebted to Dr Milind Awad for helping with some of the more arcane formulations in the book, help offered without condescension for my ignorance.

My only regret is that Eknath Awad passed away in 2015. It is a commonplace to say of such men that their books speak for them in the silence after their departure. This is however true of Eknath Awad; here he is: uncut, saying the unsayable, rejoicing in his motorcycle, reinventing satyagraha, and turning temples, village squares, whatever space he could find into theatrical venues in which he stages his revolution.

Indeed, he took the words of Annabhau Sathe (which give this book its title) seriously.

He struck just that kind of blow.

It still resounds. In this book.

JERRY PINTO
Mumbai

1

My journey continues.

In front of me, a shepherd walks down the road, driving his goats before him. The sun dips towards the horizon. The air is suffused with golden light. The goats tarry, investigating the shrubs and plants along the way. The bells on their necks clank and jingle. At the head of this herd of twenty to twenty-five goats walks a boy, not more than six or seven years of age, in a grimy school uniform shirt. A fully grown man with a staff over his shoulders brings up the rear. I can hear the shepherd's call: Hurrr hurrr. I watch as they walk on. The shepherd's full-sleeved banian is torn at the back. Thin strands of thread hold the edges together over his shoulders. The torn banian has turned into a huge circle. It is a circle as large as the Earth, a zero, a planet-sized void that the shepherd carries on his back. I too once drove goats to pasture, in clothes as ragged as his.

*

I walk this road. The village of Sangam is along the way. Someone hails me. On a red placard, letters in white: *Maanavi Haq Abhiyaan* (Campaign for Human Rights). We have a branch in this village. The man who greets me with 'Jai Bhim' is Mahadev Saundarmal, a Dalit farmer. What was he earlier? He was a manual labourer with a large family. Every year he would have to move in search of work. In the year 1972, Mahadev received 2 acres of land from the government. But he had no bullocks to till it with and no plough. And so the land lay fallow. Mahadev was frustrated and starving. Around that time we had set up a grain bank project in order to help

Dalit families. The moneylender would loan the poor seed but later they would exploit Dalit labour by seizing the crop as interest on the loan. Our grain bank was meant to break this vicious cycle of exploitation. That year, the question of how to fill his family's stomachs was finally answered. Now what was he doing?

'What are you doing these days, Mahadev?'

'Jija, this year, we harvested twenty quintals of cotton from the pastureland. Three sacks of jowaar. One quintal of tur daal, two paaylis* of moog, six paaylis of til…now we have no worries.'

We started a bank for landless women labourers. Mahadev's wife is a shareholder in this bank.

She says: 'Jija, it is because of you that our fields have harvests to show. We have put the boy in school. We get to live in a decent house. This one** can behave like a Patil…What did those stone gods ever do for us, Jija? But you helped us as if we were your children.' I reply: 'Now, Aai, no need for all this undeserved praise. Tell me, did you take a loan from the bank? And what did you do with the money?'

She says: 'Jija, why would I lie to you? I took loans three times. All three have been paid off. I supply milk daily to a hotel in Dindrud. That brings in about three or four thousand a month…'

Wah! My heart swells with pride. There was a time when the Dalits of this village were not allowed to use common water sources. I encouraged Mahadev to protest non-violently, to perform satyagraha to get their rights. He went to the water source and began to fill a vessel with water. I had warned the village that it was his right to do so. The law was my cudgel

---

*A paayli is a pre-Metric measure. It generally represents about four kilos.

**By which she means her husband.

and my stick. The village did not fight this openly but they did stop using water from that source to pour over their deities. 'Those Mahars and Mangs have defiled the well,' they said. We snapped our fingers under the noses of the village by giving the Dalits economic assistance to dig their own wells on the common pastures. We taught them organic farming. Now they had no need for chemical fertilizers such as urea. Now many Dalit families such as Mahadev's could achieve a decent living from even a small piece of land. Over the last twenty-five to thirty years, I have crossed paths with about fifty thousand Dalit families. We came together to struggle and the sutra for our struggle was:

Jag badal ghaluni ghaav...
saangun gele mala Bhimrao.

Over me, Bhimrao left a banner unfurled,
Strike such a blow as will change the world.

*

Today? Where am I today?

I have travelled to different countries. But this globe-trotting was always with a clear purpose. I remember a United Nations conference in Durban, South Africa. It was the year 2001 and a World Conference against Racism had been organized. Representatives of the Indian government were present. In order to represent the nation's Dalits, twenty-five representatives of non-governmental organizations and Dalit political parties were also present.

Our government lost a historic opportunity at this conference. The least they could have done was to apologize for the thousands of years that Dalits had suffered injustice and atrocities at the hands of the upper castes. Instead, they informed Kofi Annan, then the Secretary-General of the United Nations that since a Dalit had written the Indian

Constitution, all casteism ended in India. We began to call out, 'Shame, shame.' We had worn our throats out shouting that caste was alive and well in India.

The ribbons we had tied across our foreheads read: Cast away caste. We played a dhol and walked in a march, shouting: 'Down, down, casteism; up, up humanism.' These slogans rocked the auditorium of that international conference.

*

I played this role again at the International Human Rights Conference at Geneva. Wherever I got the opportunity, I would speak out, breaking the silence that surrounds the sufferings of the Dalits of India. And I continue to do this, up to the time of writing.

My journey continues; I see no end to it. I still see that shepherd with the void of his torn banian in my mind's eye. I have calmed myself a little by telling you one of our success stories here. But this I know: the struggle has to continue. Our fight has not ended.

I was born to a Potraj*. This is my story…

*

The Mangs are untouchables. I was born a Mang. My father's name was Dagdu. He was a Potraj. He spent his day begging; when evening came, he drank and threw himself on the ground to sleep. That was my father's entire life. He would go to a house in the village, play the halgi** and sing to its rhythm: '*Aai maajhi Lakshmi… Aali utat-basat… Aali*

---

*A Potraj is a religious mendicant who is devoted to a goddess such as Laxmi or Mari-Aai. He is 'allowed' to beg and when given alms takes the karma of the donor's sins upon himself and then expiates them by cracking a huge whip around himself.

**A folk instrument, percussion, drum, played with two sticks.

utat-basat... Na vaada bhaktaacha pusat ga' ('Lakshmi is my
mother. Here she comes, here she comes, asking the way to
her devotees' homes'). The brass bells tied to his ankles would
jingle and jangle. He would jerk his neck around and swing
his hair about. Then the woman of the house would come
to the door. The grain in the thresher or some bhakri would
fall into his bag. He would bless the woman: 'May Lakhpati
Lakshmi bless you, may the one turn into the many, may five
turn into fifty, may your vines grow fruitful, may your cattle
and your animals give you wealth.'

Being a Potraj, my father did not have to do Mangki, the
work traditionally assigned to the Mangs and which had to
be done without pay and only in exchange for some share
in village produce. This was done by other members of the
family. On the occasion of the Pola* festival, it was our duty
to make bundles of reeds and rushes. Those bundles had to
be placed at the doors of the Patil's home. The farmers would
rub the heads of the cows with butter. The reed bundles
would be waved around the cows' heads as the feathers of a
peacock are. Then the yoke would gently be placed on their
neck. The Mangs were also required to make torans of mango
leaves. They made torans for every door of every upper-caste
home. They would also make a toran for the temple entrance
which would be shredded by the horns of the Patil's bullock.
Then the procession of the cattle would begin. On the day
of Bhau-beej, the Mangs would go to perform aarti for the
Patil...there were many such traditions. They had to make
brooms out of sisal, they had to weave ropes out of cactus.
But my father did not do any of this. He begged as a Potraj.

It *was* beggary. You can call it alms, you can call it charity
but what he got was bits of stale bhakri. Seventeen kinds of

---

*Traditionally, a day when the cattle are honoured by being painted
and decorated and taken in procession through the village.

grain. He would leave in the morning, in his abraheen, the costume of a Potraj. At his waist, several blouse pieces called khann of different colours; ghungroos on his feet with cloth bandages to keep the anklets in place; a huge whip across his shoulders; around his neck, the images of many goddesses in silver-plated splendour. Under one arm he carried the halgi, under the other his begging bag. On his forehead, bright blazons of haldi-koonkoo. This was the traditional costume of the Potraj. On bare feet, he would traverse the distances between four villages.

A Potraj was held to be Mari-Aai's* messenger and thus asked for alms in Her name. If anyone was ill, he would offer a remedy. 'Bai, on so-and-so day you went to the fields. When you crossed the border, such-and-such spirit got hold of you. Do this, do that, and these things will pass away,' he would say to one of them and he would get a rupee or eight annas for his pains. Sometimes a little jowar or other grains. On these hand-outs, my parents managed their lives.

If a Potraj had a healthy son, he ought to become a Potraj, or that was the Mang belief. Accordingly, my father would say, 'My son will become a Potraj too.' That did not sit well with my mother. She would fight him on this matter. Her name was Bhaagubai. I called her 'Bai'. Bai would say to my father, 'My son will become a big Mang. He will certainly not become a Potraj.' My elder sister, Kalabai, and my mother both wanted me to become a good Mang, a successful one. That meant I had two options in front of me: I could become a Potraj or I could acquire a skill that would befit a Mang. These were the limits of my family's ambitions for me.

Dukdegaon is my village. The real name of this village is

---

*Mari-Aai is a folk-goddess, whose special charge is fevers and poxes of various kinds.

Dukregaon (the village of pigs). But the Muslims in the village think of the pig as a bad omen and so they would not use such a name. They began to say Dukdegaon and the name changed over time. Dukdegaon is in the Majalgaon tehsil of Beed district. In those days, once you reached the board announcing the village of Kuppa, you had to walk another 4 or 5 kilometres into the interior to get to us. To the East ran the Kundalika River; to the West, the Kordi and they met near our village. Thanks to these rivers, whatever you planted would grow—even human beings, as the saying goes—for the land was rich and fertile. But the largesse of the land did the village much harm. All you had to do was plant the seed; the next job would be to gather in the harvest; that was how much the land had spoiled us. The result: idle men. It has been said that an idle mind is the devil's workshop. This was exactly what happened. Every day saw a new fight break out in the village.

There were about three hundred to three hundred and fifty people. Most of the homes were of the people of the Vanjari caste.* The next largest group was us: the Mangs. There were two Maratha households and one Chambhaar. Three or four Muslim households. There was not a single Mahar family in the village. That meant we got to do both the Maharki (the tasks traditionally allotted to the Mahar community) and the Mangki (the tasks traditionally allotted to the Mangs). The caste system was as strong as the land was fertile. The Mangs' routine was set as if in stone. The law had made the practice of untouchability illegal, but did the law have any say in the village? In the eyes of Majalgaon, we were still untouchables, we were the rejects of the system and we were still required

---

*The Vanjaris are a trading community. The Gazetteer of Bombay 1885 lists them as a subsect of the Kunbis.

to do such tasks as had been our lot and to do them without expecting any recompense at all.

I was either born in 1950 or 1951. I don't know the exact date. But when I was admitted to school, the schoolmaster plucked a date from his head and wrote down 19 January 1956 and that stuck. My elder sister's name was Kalabai. After her, there was an elder brother but he died within fifteen days of his birth. Aai would say, 'He had boils,' by which she meant he had pustules over his body. I suspect it was a visitation of the Devi, smallpox. After he died, for a long time, my parents did not have any children. Aai would say that I had been born only after she had made several vows. She believed that my elder brother had died because she had eaten the flesh of a dead animal when she was pregnant. When she found she was pregnant with me, she decided she would not eat carrion flesh. In reality, we were so poor that there was nothing to eat in the house, not carrion flesh and not much else either. Her health suffered from this deprivation. My starved mother found no milk flowing in her breasts. And so, in order that I might sleep without crying, my sister would feed me opium.

But even on the most inhospitable ground, some weeds will take root and fight to live.

*

When I was about four or five years old, my father began to think: my son can now help me.' He began preparations to consecrate me to Mari-Aai. If I were to become a Potraj, Baba figured, we could visit more houses and get more alms. But my mother and my sister offered strong and constant opposition to this plan.

And so Baba was not allowed to abandon me to Mari-Aai.

My mother and my sister wanted me to become a Mang with a skill. This meant that I should not beg. Instead, I should work for the Patil and serve him, I should weave rope...that was what being a skilled Mang meant to them. In accordance with this, I would get up in the morning and go with them to clean the cowdung from the Patil's house. As the only son of the family, I learned how a Mang was supposed to behave by observing my mother and father. How to talk to the Patil, how to talk to his son, how to keep one's head bowed, all this was what I learned. We were entitled to half the village's Mangki so Aai felt I should be well looked after. Taking out the cowdung, making it into cowpats, threshing the grain, sweeping up the chaff, washing the jowar for the old, washing the cattle on the festival of Pola, making rush bundles on Pola, playing the halgi with the sheda (sticks) for the gods...these were the jobs of the Mangs. I learned all this well. I was doing much of this work already. In about five years, Aai thought, my father would not have to bother about anything. She would explain this proudly to friends and family. Aai suffered from epileptic fits. When she had had a fit, she could not do any work. Then I would have to take over all the housework.

This was good training. I can still do all that I learned as a child. I can make rush bundles, I can weave rope, I can make a charpoy, I can still all do this easily. I was an expert in soaking sisal and spinning ropes from it. My wife Gaya and I can create the best charpoys out of rope, a tradition called roomali baaj. Gaya never went to school; but working by my side, she built a new life for herself. Later, she learned the alphabet from our children. Gaya and I were married at an age when we were heedless children.

One day, our relative from Pimparkhed, Jijabhau Shinde and his mother were on their way to Nithrud when there was a violent storm. The river was also swollen. So they stayed over with us. At that time, my father had bought some goats.

My job was to graze them and follow them around. In the evening, I came home with the goats. I must have been about seven or eight. Aai said, in her usual proud fashion, 'My son is already doing Mangki. And, we're entitled to half the village's Mangki. After all, he's the only son. His wife will be a lucky woman.' That was all it took. The families sat down to sort things out. It was like trading horseflesh. In those days, a girl had to be given hunda or gifts. My father gave her eleven nine-yard saris, four paaylis of wheat, two paaylis of jowar, two paaylis of daal and thirty-five rupees in cash and some ornaments such as bangles. He could ill afford this expense; to cover it, he had to sell the goats. Thus the goats which had been some help were taken away and we were thrown back on the bhakri my father would get from begging.

Each evening, we would all wait eagerly for his return. If he had grain in his bag, we would have to sort out the twelve kinds. Then this would have to be ground and bhakri made out of it. If he had been given bhakri, we would separate the good pieces first. The ones that were covered with fungus would be wiped down with a rough cloth and those would be eaten too. This was how we lived. All day, we struggled to get something to eat. On the days that we failed, there was nothing for it but to sleep hungry.

*

This is the time after 1956. Dr Ambedkar had just achieved mahaparinirvana. I don't think my parents knew much more than the basics: that there had been a great leader called Ambedkar and that under his guidance, the Mahars had stopped Maharki. My father would go to the villages of Kuppa, Chinchala, Tigaon, Pusara and Lamantanda and the areas around them. When he got there, he would tell other people: 'Aara, those Mahars have stopped doing Maharki.

What fights are going on! Everything's a mess.' That was how the information that the Mahars had stopped doing Maharki passed from village to village. I would see my family and relatives discussing this matter with serious and grave faces. At that time, because of Ambedkar, the Mahars had begun to move to the cities and to seek education while the Mangs of Dukdegaon were still ekeing out their lives on stale bhakri thrown their way. No one had the guts to take on the village. My father's was, at base, a weak nature. There was no question of him challenging the village or anyone in it. But my relatives were ruffians. My uncles on both sides were the kind who would take on four or five and come back for more. At that age, I couldn't understand why they were so meek when confronted with the upper castes. A couple of incidents from that time are stamped indelibly in my memory.

The Mang section of the village had a cactus hedge in front of it. One of my cousins, Kerubai, and my mother were hanging the washing to dry on the cactus. Seeing these Mang women putting out their clothes to dry, a Patil felt that they had violated the laws regarding purity and pollution.

'Hey you Mangnis, I'll shove a heated crowbar up your holes...' he started shouting filthy abuse at them. When I think of those words, even today, they have the power to sting. Kerubai had four sons, all strong, all muscular; none of them said a word. All of them listened to his vitriol with their heads bent. We, the little ones, were also around. But when the adults were saying nothing, how could the son of a Potraj find the courage to speak?

Another incident of the same kind: my elder cousin, Dashrath Awad, was thrashed in front of the Maruti Temple with the entire village for audience. Why? Because he had cut some wild grass. No one had sown it, it had sprouted of its own accord and it was therefore technically available to anyone. But that was not the way the Patil saw it. It was his grass, his fodder, by a law of his own invention. He went into a rage that made no sense to me. Why should he be so angry if a poor man were to cut that grass so as to put a couple of mouthfuls of food into his hungry children's stomachs?

'Dashrath has sold some fodder,' was on every tongue. That was all it took. Spewing curses, the Patil came to the Mang settlement, where a meal was cooking with the money Dashrath had made selling the grass. The Patil dragged Dashrath from his hut right up to the temple. And there, in front of everyone, he beat him. No one thought to say: 'His children are hungry; if he cut some fodder and sold it to feed them, what crime has he committed?' While the beating was going on, while the Patil was cursing Dashrath's mother and abusing his sister, not one of the elders of the village thought to say, 'Enough, now, Patilsaahib, let him go, that's enough.' After this, Dashrath Awad left the village. But the rest of us remained, stuck like leeches to the body of the village.

*

Around this time, a school opened its doors. The boys of the village began to attend it. My father had sold our goats to pay for my marriage but I would still go with the other boys to graze their goats. Some of them who were going to school would recite the alphabet and the times tables. I too would repeat this after them, though I didn't understand what was being said. I thought it was another game, one of the many we played in those days. And what was so great about that school? It was held in Anna Patil's cattle pen. During the rains when the cows and buffaloes were in the pen, it would be held in the Maruti temple. That was why we weren't fascinated by the school. Also there was no one who thought that the Mang boys should go to school.

But at that time there was a Vanjari Maalkari* called Gangaram Bade. He was the only one who would touch the Mangs. He also had some affection for us. He was a good man. One day, he called one of our relatives, Chudaji Awad, and my father to see him. 'Your sons wander around aimlessly. Why not put them into school?' My father and Chudaji both had the same answer: 'Patil, do the children of Mangs ever study?' Thus they answered a question with a question. If you put a boy in school, you lost a pair of working hands for no good reason at all. And his stomach would not be filled unless he begged too. This is what they probably thought. The general belief was that education was not for us. But Gangaram Bade managed to persuade them. And so it was that my cousins, Baliram, Satva, Shesherao and I were admitted to school.

When the school was held in the animal pen, the Mangs were made to sit separately from the rest of the class. When it was held in the temple, the high-caste boys and the teacher would sit in the temple courtyard and we would sit on the path that ran alongside the temple. If the teacher ever remembered our existence, it would be to assign us some lesson or the other. We had to write out our lessons on our slates. If we had to show him what we had written, we would have to throw the slates to him from outside the temple. If we missed, the teacher would throw his cane at us, again from a suitable distance. Accustomed to abuse, this long-distance caning was the one small advantage that we had.

From wandering around with the shepherd boys who were going to school, I already knew the thirty-six letters and their twelve vowel forms, as well as my one-quarter times tables

---

*A Maalkari (wearer of a maala, a garland) is said to be devoted to the service of Lord Vithala of Pandharpur. His maala is of tulsi beads. Generally, a Maalkari is a Warkari but in this case, he is a Vanjari.

and my one-half times tables. When my father took me to school, I must have been at least ten years old. The teacher put me into the second standard. This was not extraordinary. I knew my alphabet and my tables better than most of the children who had been in the school, and better sometimes than the children who sat closest to the teacher. But I didn't know why I was being treated like the stepchild of the family.

'But if it is because we eat the flesh of the cow, well then, the Muslims also eat it. The Muslim boys sit up there. The teacher doesn't think he is defiled by them. So why do we defile him?' I would think.

As boys we would all play together but if I were to go to someone's house, I would get water in a chipta, a small tin-can kept specially for our use. I would never get water in a tumbler. If we got something to eat, our share was placed in a separate basket. If by chance we were to so much as touch something made of brass or copper, it would be thrown into the embers of the fire to be cleansed of our polluting touch. When I came home, I would ask my father, 'Baba, you pray to Mari-Aai for everyone, so why do people treat us in this way? You pray, "Let those who are one remain united, let five turn into fifty, may this house prosper," but how come we don't even have jowar in our house?'

My relatives, Baliram, Satva, Shesherao, had all eaten the flesh of cattle with their bhakri and so could not be allowed into the temple. Boys were often paid in bhakri to look after cattle; and this often stood in the way of their education. Baliram was intelligent but his parents had promised him to a master to look after his cattle. He dropped out of school and I went on studying. And so there is a huge difference between my life and Baliram's. At that time, I did not have to worry about my food. My father went out begging and brought food home; so I could go to school. That was one advantage that I had. Perhaps it was this advantage that made my liking for education seem to others around me as if I were possessed by some evil spirit.

*

Usman is one of my childhood friends. We were together until the fourth standard in the school at Dukdegaon. When we talk about the old days, he can still bring those times to vivid life. We had a teacher whose name was Darade. Usman and I would tease one of our classmates mercilessly. Of course, we got into fights over this. But Darade Masthur would take the boy's side all the time. We had no idea why he was so partial to the boy. Then one day, Usman and I caught Darade Masthur with that boy's sister. We had him then. To make sure that he saw us, we coughed loudly. Masthur now knew we were aware of his secret. After class the next day, he asked both of us to stay back. He said, 'Don't tell anyone anything.' From that day on, he turned a blind eye to our mischief.

Another incident from my schooldays: one day, the teacher gave Usman and me a task. His wife had delivered. His mother-in-law wanted to send some sutavda for her daughter. Sutavda is a mixture of sweetmeats and savouries meant to be eaten by nursing mothers. On our way back with the bundle, we ate half of its contents. Mashtur's mum-in-law had also sent some oil. We went and found some shendur.* We smeared a stone with the oil and with the shendur. We put the stone on one of the borders of Ramkishen Bade's field. Then we went and delivered what was left of the goodies to Masthur's house and went home quietly. The next day, Mahadu went around saying that god had manifested in his fields. He offered naivedya** complete with halgi music. The two of us were

---

*Shendur is a pigment made from red lead.

**The offerings of food made to a deity.

watching all this to-do, and laughing up our sleeves. Usman and I, a Muslim and a Mang, had put together a deity that was being worshipped with great piety in the village.

My friends were what made school such fun.

And so the days passed. From time to time my father would think about making me a Potraj and consecrating me to Mari-Aai. But now I had absolutely no desire to leave school. My mother would also oppose my father vehemently. She too felt I should study; but our relatives thought otherwise. Since my father had always begged as a Potraj, he could not do the other traditional jobs of the Mang. Aai was also unwell. That meant we had no other means of sustenance and could only rely on what he brought home as alms. If I were to join him as a Potraj, a few more pieces of bhakri would fall into our bags, at least this was the general belief. And with my marriage, there was another mouth to feed. One day, we had gone to a relative's home. I had sat down to eat but I was dragged from my seat. 'This beggar should be helping his mother and father; instead he goes off to school,' he snarled. I felt the sting of his insult but there was nothing I could do about it. For I did want to study, I did want to go to school. I believe my mother too was forced to swallow this disrespect shown to me because of her desire that I study.

I have a patched-together picture of her in my mind. A short woman, her forehead smeared with koonkoo, a patched green nine-yard sari. She would take the jowar that my father brought home and sit at the grinding stone. In the darkness, she would compose ovis, songs women sing while they work. To the garr-garr of the grinding stone, she would sing in a crazy voice:

> *Limba-loni karite, tujhya shaalant yeoon*
> *Baal maajhya Eknatha, daav akshar lihoon.*

Limba-loni karite, tujhya shaalanchya vaatala
Baal maajhya Eknatha, vaagh janoo zaalitoon sutla
Shaalantlya pantojali, devoo keli khareek
Baal maazhya Eknatha, livhana baareek.

I will come to your school to cast out the evil eye
My son Eknatha, write some letters for me.
I will cast out the evil eye from the road to your school
My Eknatha is a tiger freed from a net
I will give your teacher dry dates
As you write fine letters upon your slate.

My desire to study and my mother's belief in me were both proved after the fourth standard examination results came out: I stood second in the area. Four or five other boys from our school also passed the exam; but I went one better, I stood second in the area. Aai must have overheard someone in the village exclaim, 'Aara, that Dagdu Mang's son passed the exam.' She was thrilled. She told my father to buy five coconuts and five kilos of jaggery. She took me with the coconuts and jaggery and we both stood in front of the Maruti temple. Since we were not allowed into the temple, she presented the jaggery and the coconuts to the god from outside the temple. And she folded her hands to pray: 'Marotiraayaa, may my son be brave!'

2

The school in our village did not go beyond the fourth standard so I had to go to a school in the village of Kuppa, about 4 or 5 kilometres from Dukdegaon. This school ran up to the seventh standard. I would go along with all the other boys. The extreme poverty we lived in meant that I did not have any bhakri to eat during the lunch break. The other boys would sit on the banks of the river to eat their bhakri and I would go and drink water from the river and sit there quietly, doing nothing. It was only in the evening that I would get something to eat. During this time I could not be regular at school. I don't think I managed a single unbroken week of attendance. My father was ageing and tired. He could not work too much but still he would go and beg. Aai was still prone to epileptic fits and was often unable to work. Gaya had to do the housework and if a summons came from the Patil's house at harvest time, I would have to go.

There was no timetable for this work that we had to do and no account was ever kept of it. The ears of jowar would have to be tied into bundles at the time of the harvest. When we had finished with one Patil's work, the next landlord would issue a summons and once again the work would begin. Walking behind the buffaloes as they ground the corn, we would become buffaloes ourselves. Then the grain had to be separated from the chaff. When that was done, we got the chaff and the landlords got the grain. Once in a while, an old man, sifting the grain would murmur, '*Kovaalichi vaaykar.*' This was a code for 'Throw some jowar among the chaff'. That meant when we were finished, we might have some grain, even if it meant that technically we were stealing it.

It was as if stealing had become a tradition with the Mangs. It was our complete helplessness that turned us into thieves. In 1871, the British passed the Criminal Tribes Act which labelled certain people as criminals by birth. Out of the fourteen so mentioned, we were number seven. This created an extraordinarily vicious circle. Our poverty forced us to steal, and once you were branded a thief, you could only live by stealing. That was our life. The need to steal meant we developed our own language, a code we could use without fear of being understood. We called the language Phaarshi.

There were about a hundred words. Some of them include:

Maratha: Daandaal
Mang: Aambuj
Mahar: Bhookar
Brahmin: Regaalya
Muslim: Jumaanya
Young man: Tulga
Young woman: Tulgi
Meat: Yelchya
Bhakri: Karpati
Rupees: Kharpya
Robbery: Khaavdi

This language has now been studied methodically and some scholars have even done their PhDs on it. But truth to tell, this was part of a terrible past. It should be buried. I only mention it because in that time, this code language was in use and that much needs to be recorded. Otherwise, undue importance should not be conferred upon it. To feed themselves, the Mangs would steal other people's ears of jowar, groundnuts and tur daal. If some footsteps were heard, of a Maratha who had been set to watch, the cry would go up: '*Daandaal pedla, nibal*' which meant, 'A Maratha has come, run.' Or once the tramp of the Maratha was heard, one might say, '*Daandaal tikla, vaapaalyaachi vaaykar.*' Or 'Throw a stone and hit him.'

To labour as much as cattle and be paid only in chaff meant that the Mang had to accept beggary as another way of earning his living. But it was not possible to quench the flames in one's belly with alms. How the Mangs of old had managed to steal and the fights that had ensued was one of the main sources of gossip in the Mang settlement. And so it was that even we found the idea of theft and of the Phaarshi code language fascinating. We had a gang at that time: Hari, Bali, Uttam, Namdev and I. We too tried out experiments in theft and in the use of Phaarshi. We had a lot of fun but we also began to get a reputation: they said of us, 'These Mang boys are real bastards.' When news of one of our exploits got out, one of us would say, '*Daandaala solkalaya, nibala,*' or 'The villagers know, run!'

Because of all these exploits and because of the work I had to do as a Mang, I failed the seventh standard.

In between, an incident occurred that left a deep impression on me.

It was the day of Shimga. The village was filled with the celebrations of Holi. It was a tradition to drink alcohol on that day. The Patil of the village, Sakharam Karpe, was completely drunk. My cousin, Vitthal, passed him on his way home. He did not notice the Patil perhaps, but the Patil was enraged that Vitthal could dare to walk past without doing the customary hayaaj or bowing, the Mang equivalent of the Mahar tradition of johaar (salutation). Vitthal was well aware of this tradition but he was on his way to his hut, lost in his own thoughts. He got to his house and set the meat to cook in a vessel. Right after him, the Patil walked in, abusing and cursing; he kicked the vessel off the fireplace and sent the meat flying. Vitthal was a strapping young man. The Patil's kicking of the food enraged him. He returned the abuse. The Patil went back to the village, and came back with a bunch of goons and lejim players to accompany them. That day, for the first time, the Mang settlement came together in a display of unity. 'Enough is enough. This must stop,' they said and it was the first time that this sentence had ever been spoken by Mangs in front of the village. The dispute ended there, but a spark must have ignited something inside my head. The incident gave me hope for a future of self-respect.

*

At around this time, I began to grow up. My body changed and developed. I was a wrestler, albeit junior, to be reckoned with in the village akhada. The boys wrestled before the men. My fights would be put on as early as possible for if the first fight was won by a pehelwan from the village, it was taken to be a good omen. I would not let myself be pinned. I used every stratagem I knew to keep my opponent down. Kabaddi was another favourite sport. Because my body was in good shape, I would drag three or four boys to the middle line and put them out of the game. Nor was I backwards in school work. I would take part in elocution competitions. The topics of those days were 'If I were the President' or 'If I were a teacher'. During my matric year, I gave a speech on, 'Was Shivaji greater or his mother?'; I chose to say Shivaji's mother was greater and presented my arguments with great panache. I won a prize for this speech. I had read that Abraham Lincoln would go into the woods and make speeches to the trees as preparation for public speaking. I, too, would do the same. On the way home from school, I would make speeches and the rocks, the stones and the trees would be my audience. I was drawn to the new but our Mangwada was afflicted by a near-total helplessness. I was not the kind of person who could join in their helplessness.

An incident happened when I was in the seventh standard. Whenever there was a marriage in the village, the Mangwada would be filled with happiness. This was because we would be given the remains of the feast, and could eat what was left on the used plantain-leaf dishes. At every wedding or religious festival celebrated at the Patils' homes, the Mangs would turn up to sit at the doors. The Patil, whoever he was, would curse us: 'Aara, let the guests eat their fill first. Then you pimps can take the leavings.' When the first serving was done, the Mangs would be fed. Their food would be given to them in the place where the little ones squatted to shit. The Mangs would kick dust over the shit and then sit down to eat at the same place. Once there was a sweet meal at a Vanjari home. As per tradition, we got the leavings and the scrapings from the used banana leaves. I too ate that food. The very next day, a nanny goat belonging to that man died at the edge of the river. The master of the house appeared at our door and demanded that I drag the corpse of the goat back to the village. I totally refused to do any such thing. Somehow, I had made up my mind that I was not going to do the traditional filthy jobs that were demanded of us. My refusal enraged the master of the house. 'How eagerly you swallowed the food last night. And now you refuse to do any work, you parasite!' The abuse only made me even more determined not to do such work. I sat tight, refusing to drag dead animals around. My father was out begging. Only the women were at home. The Vanjara grabbed my arm and dragged me to the elders of the village. There he began to abuse me again. Once again, he reminded me of the food I had eaten the night before. When I still refused to do this job, the old people began to take my side. 'Let it go, Patil. He's a boy. Is there only one Mang in the village? Tell someone else to do it.' The Patil got one of my cousins to do the job. This incident only encouraged me further. The incident at Shimga was also fresh in my mind. Perhaps I was slowly coming to the decision: 'This should not be borne.'

All this commotion meant that I failed the seventh standard at the school at Kuppa. My father thought: 'My son's body has filled out. He's failed at school. Now he can do the work of a Mang in the village.' Having failed, I had no other option but to do the work of a Mang for a year. My wife and I went to many a harvest. At that time, Communist Party workers would often come to our village. They would come to the places where we were labouring. They would organize meetings for us. 'The labourer is worthy of his wage,' they would say. I would feel drawn to those meetings, to their speeches.

At this time, Comrade Gangadharappa Burande was fighting the election on the Communist Party ticket. Their party had a meeting in our village. They asked if anyone would volunteer to be a polling agent on the day of the election. No one came forward. The village was dominated by the Congress. I stood up and offered my services. I must have been about fifteen years old at the time. In doing this, I was held to have challenged the political hierarchies of the village. Everyone was staring, wide-eyed at me. This was my first political action in the village.

Because my body had begun to mature so early, I began giving advice to people in the village. I remember another similar incident. To the West of the village was a haagandaari, an open-air space for defecation. My cousin heard that an animal had died there. At that time, there was such poverty that a dead animal too would be stripped and cooked and eaten. My cousin rushed off to get his share of the meat. My opinion was that we should not eat carrion flesh. And so I too went there. The animal was lying there, its legs splayed. Vittal and Satva were stripping the animal. Above us, vultures and kites were circling. I shouted, from a distance. 'Aara, leave that animal to the vultures. Because we eat carrion, the village treats us badly.' Seeing my mood, they said, 'And what are we supposed to eat instead? This is our food, our grain. If we leave this to the vultures, what are we to eat? Rocks? Dirt?' At this I went forward. Someone had left his shit in the haagandaari. I gathered some of the shit with my slippers and threw it on the corpse. My cousins were enraged at my behaviour but this forced them to abandon it.

And so while I was being drawn towards a new way of thinking, Baba was all for me doing Mangki. When he heard that I had failed the seventh standard, he said, 'Enough of school now.'

I insisted, 'Baba, I want to study further.'

My father said sadly, 'I'm getting tired now. If you keep on studying, how are we to eat and what?'

But I refused to give up my dream. Finally, Baba said, 'Okay, if you must study, go ahead. But if you're going to study, then study like that Mahar boy from Kuppa.' At that time one of the Mahar boys from Kuppa had become an engineer.

*

After my father gave me permission to study, I sat for the seventh standard examination and this time I passed. After this, I wanted to leave the school at Kuppa. I met the headmaster and asked for my school-leaving certificate. The headmaster said: 'We are starting the eighth standard class here too. Stay here.' I knew that if I stayed in Kuppa, the village work of the Mang would fall to my lot and so I refused. I had to leave the village. I took my certificate and went to Laul. Shri Gajanan Hostel was at Laul; it was meant for the Backward Classes and so was filled with Maratha and Vanjari boys. I got admission there but I had no money to pay the fees; the hostel cost fifteen rupees in those days. The headmaster of the school and the hostel at Laul was a man called Ratnakar Kulkarni. I met the headmaster and explained my problems. There was an administrator called Vaijnathanna. I told him my problems too. Perhaps he felt pity; perhaps my struggle impressed him. He gave me five rupees towards the hostel fee. My name was put down in the hostel. The headmaster agreed to allow me to pay the remaining ten rupees later.

Thanks to their compassion, I did get into the hostel but the ten rupees was still a burning question. I made new friends at the hostel: Uttam Dawre, Devrao Dage and Bhagwan Dawre. I had no thali in which to eat, nor did I have any bedding. They allowed me to use their vessels and shared their bedsheets with me. Thanks to my friends, some of my problems did get solved but the ten rupees was still an issue. I would lose my place in the hostel if I didn't find the money soon. After much thought, I hit upon a solution.

The hostel would bring grain for the mess by bullock cart. The bags of grain would be taken off the cart by a chaprasi; but he could no longer take the burden of this work. I was now in good shape. I owed the blood in my body to the rotting bhakri that my father had begged from the village. I talked to the peon and persuaded him to let me help. I began to carry the grain sacks on my back. The peon was happy to be helped in this way. I also began to chop their firewood. I was paid a little for doing this work and I used the money to pay the rest of the hostel fee.

The hostel was divided up along caste lines. The Marathas, Lamaans and Vanjaris were separate from the rest. They slept in a different row, they ate separately. The Mahars and the Mangs ate separately and slept separately. All the boys had white lice on their bodies but no one thought anything of this then; I had only torn clothes to cover my body. When my shorts tore at the back, my father would take them away. He had a Mahar friend, Sonawanebuwa, in Kuppa. Sonawanebuwa was a tailor. When Baba went to Kuppa to beg, he would get my shorts darned there. The Maratha boys would have chutneys, pickles and laddoos in their trunks. My father could give me none of this. So I stole from them to satisfy the desires of my tongue.

Since I had been put into school late, I was much larger than most of the other boys. I was pitch dark, with a filled-out body and a good height. My voice was deep and powerful. Because of this, I became a dada in the hostel. That a cremation ground was right next to the hostel frightened the boys. However, I felt no fear. When the statue of Ganpati was installed at the hostel, I was the only one to keep vigil through the night. No ghosts ever bothered me but I have to admit that as I kept Ganpati company, I consumed all the modak that were offered at this temporary shrine. Not a single boy had the strength to oppose me. The barber would come to shave the Maratha boys but he would not shave the Mahars and the Mangs. And so I did this job myself. I would take a blade in hand and soon I'd have a boy's head done and dusted... with blood! But they could not complain once I had them sitting in front of me. The upper-caste boys would get the washerman of the village to wash and iron their clothes for Independence Day and Republic Day. The washerman would not deign to wash or iron our clothes. And so we would put hot embers into a copper vessel and use this to iron our clothes. The water that was needed for the hostel would be brought there in waterskins. This would then be filled in huge vessels. Every day, four Maratha boys would serve the food and pour out water for everyone. Two carried the water and two served the food. We were not allowed, of course, to touch the water pots. But if a rat were to fall in and drown, then it was my duty to fish out its bloated corpse. No one else would do it. I would carry the flour on my head to the hostel. But once it entered the mess kitchen, it became pure and my touch would pollute it. We would have to bring our own flour and make our own bhakri which would then be served to us by the upper-caste boys.

There was a boy called Waghmare in the hostel, from the leatherworker or Charmakaar caste. This boy was not seated with the upper-caste boys. He probably did not feel anything about that but he did feel that if he sat with the Mahars and the Mangs, he would be polluted. He would have to sit with us to eat but he always saw himself as above us. This annoyed me. One day, puran poli was served in the hostel in honour of the Pola feast. My friend Dage, who was also a Mang, and I would always be seated next to Waghmare at meal times. As was his wont, Waghmare had put a brick between his place and ours. All the boys were looking forward to the puran polis but I could not get myself to sit down and eat. All I could think of was the brick that he had placed between us. And so I just got up and hit him. This caused an uproar. I kicked him. I hit him some more. The teacher came to see what the matter was. Waghmare complained about my behaviour. I told the teacher my side of the story. The teacher took my side. And so Dage and I plonked ourselves down on either side of Waghmare and we made sure our crossed legs touched his as we wolfed down the puran poli. I said to Waghmare, 'Go on then, eat. And if you vomit because we've made you impure, we'll stuff that back down your throat too.'

Waghmare didn't puke; he ate his puran poli quietly.

*

Before I joined the hostel, the Mahar students had opposed this practice of different castes eating their meals separately.

My friend, Dongardive from Chinchala village, was one of them. Chinchala was quite close to Dukdegaon and since I often visited, I got to know Dongardive. I, too, felt we had to do something about this way of sitting for a meal. This was in the 1970s when untouchability was practised quite openly. No one spoke up against it. One day the president of the social development cell of the zilla parishad had come to the hostel for a meeting. Baburao Mhaske had been elected on a Republican Party of India ticket but owed his post to the support of the Congress. When we told him about this practice, he said, 'Aara, what does it matter whether you sit close or far apart? What is important is that you should study hard and become an important person in the future. Don't waste time complaining. Your studies are more important.' That put an end to our attempt at changing things but it did leave me with the feeling that one must fight injustice. An education in servility seemed of no value to me.

Dongardive would face a similar crisis. His father was the Kotwal of Chinchala. The post was similar to that of a chapraasi to the talati, the village accountant. The talati of the area was a Brahmin by the name of Pande. Both of them were transferred to the village of Hivargavhan. When Pande decided to have a Satyanarayan Pooja at his home, he told Dongardive Sr to go to the village and chop firewood. Since this was not one of the jobs of a kotwal, Dongardive Sr refused to do it. Pande took offence and began to send false reports of Dongardive Sr's absenteeism and about jobs left undone to the tahsildar.

Dongardive Sr was suspended. We heard about this and were outraged. We decided that we should do something to help our friend's father. At that time there was a leader called R.C. Salve in Beed. We went to meet him. He interceded in the matter and Dongardive Sr was reinstated. But I remained angry at Pande's behaviour. Dongardive Sr's act of refusing to do work that was not required of him seemed important to me. I believed we should all have this attitude of self-respect. But I could not figure out a way to humble that Pande.

But then something happened and we got a chance to do precisely that. Chinchala, Kuppa and Dukdegaon were close to each other. We did not have a flour mill in Dukdegaon and had to take the grain to Chinchala to get it ground. Apart from the work at the hostel, Gaya and I would also take on physical labour. I would load the carts with the grain. Now a little more money was coming into the house. Up to this time, Aai had never seen a whole rupee in her life. Now it was actually possible for us to buy our own jowari. One day Vitthal Tupe and I went to Chinchala to buy jowari and have it ground there. Pande the talati had a provisions store there. I went to his store because he sold the grain a little cheaper; Vitthal Tupe bought the same weight in grain from the flour-mill owner himself. When we met with the grain tied up in our cloths, the flour-mill owner said to me: 'So you bought your jowari from Pande? Now watch how much flour Vitthal gets and how much you get. Pande sells his grain cheap because he cheats you on the measures.'

I measured the grain and Pande's was found wanting. The anger in my head at how this man had troubled my friend's father exploded. I marched off to Pande's shop. I scattered the jowari in front of his shop and began to abuse him. No one stopped me for everyone in the village knew that he was cheating on the weights and measures. Pande said, 'Enough, baba, don't abuse like that. Take your money back.' I took my money but only after I had I abused him some more. I got the satisfaction of having humbled Pande in front of everyone.

Now that I think about it, I wonder, how did I do it? My father was a beggar. I myself was a manual labourer, barely managing with what I earned at the hostel. And there I was, throwing good jowari on the floor! Abusing the talati? I could only have done this because of the example that Dongardive's father had presented to me, an example of self-respect, coupled with my own growing hatred of injustice. At around this time, I had written a poem that I still remember:

> How can you say this country has given you nothing?
> When your mother was pregnant with you, wasn't she given
>   a quilt of twelve rags to rock you in?
> So that her womb should swell, wasn't she given
>   the scraps from twelve houses?
> And still you say the country has given you nothing!
> As if that was not enough, as soon as you came forth,
> from the womb, you were given the wind and the rain
>   and the sun as companions.
> When you came of age, your mothers and sisters were
>   raped in front of you.
> To spare you the pain of seeing this, your eyes were
>   plucked out.
> To spare you the indignity of the life of the blind, your
>   hut was burned.
> And yet you say that your country has given you nothing?
> Now repeat: 'India is my country. All Indians are my
>   brothers and sisters. I love my country…'

Twenty-five years had passed since we became independent but my village was still practising untouchability. The Mahars had learned self-respect, they gave tit for tat, but the Mangs were still slaves. No one saw the Mang as a human being. Till today, you see temples erected to Mangirbaba. This was to commemorate the Mangs who had been sacrificed. At one time, if you were building a fort or digging a tank, it was the tradition to sacrifice a Mang. The eldest son of a Mang family would be chosen. His face would be covered with shendoor. He would then be taken out in a procession with music and dancing. Many village forts have a Mang buried under them; the Mangirbaba temple would be built over his grave. The Mangs had accepted this injustice as their destiny or as a social practice to which fate had assigned them. Only the remains of the Mang caste panchayat were left. I have only the faintest recollection of how when this caste panchayat had punished someone, a pair of slippers would hang upside down from the Dakalvaar's stick.

Who were the Dakalvaars you might ask. The Mangs were a caste of beggars. Therefore they were not allowed to grow their own crops. They could only beg from those who had the good fortune of being born into castes that allowed them to farm the land. Our caste system is such that the Mangs too had a caste that would beg from them. This was the Dakalvaar caste. The Dakalvaar were a nomadic community. They would go from village to village singing songs of how the Mangs had been kings at one time. They would beg from the Mangs who had to give them food they had begged from others. The Dakalvaars would drink water only from a Mang household.

But I was talking about the caste panchayats. When they had announced that someone was to be cast out from his caste, a pair of his slippers would be hung upside down from the Dakalvaar's stick. As he went from village to village, he would announce who had been punished thus. I have only the faintest recollection of this practice. Given a chance, I would let my anger rage. My parents were rather upset at this.

*

At around this time, the gram panchayat elections were held. The three villages of Dukdegaon, Chinchala and Kuppa had a common gram panchayat. One seat was reserved for our village.

Sakharam Karpe, the village patil, offered himself for election. This was the very man who had brought a complement of lejim players at the time of the Shimga festival to beat up my cousin for not having performed the usual hayaaj, the custom of bowing. When I heard that he was standing and had a good chance of being elected, I began to fume. Actually, I was a poor boy who earned his food by occasional bouts of manual labour. Who knows how I developed this desire to fight injustice even at that age. I began to work in my own fashion.

There was an old Muslim called Abirbhai Sheikh in the village who had Communist leanings. I gathered together a bunch of boys from the Mangwada who thought like me. We got Abirbhai on our side. The Mangs and the Muslims were minorities in the village but if they got together they could be decisive. We also put up a Vanjari candidate; his name was Dnyanoba Mauli. Both his legs were crippled. We would take him around the village saying he was a Communist. There was now a new spirit alive in the village. During this time, Gaya and I were both working at the harvest in various fields. There were others from the Mang community as well. Some people came into the village with weapons and threatened us: Vote for the Patil or else. After this incident, the Mang vote coalesced against him.

I still remember the day of the election. Gaya and I were off to vote. The landlords stood in our way. One of them screamed at Gaya: 'Listen girl, you'd better vote for the Patil.' I replied then and there: 'No chance. We are going to vote for the opposition.' No one had ever said this aloud before. The landlords were used to coming to the Mang settlement and announcing who everyone was supposed to vote for. They felt assured that those who lived on their stale food would obey orders, no questions asked.

When I voted and came out, the village leader was all hot and bothered. 'This Mang boy is acting too big for his boots. We have to set him right,' he was saying. 'Let's see how he comes out even to take a shit. Boycott him completely.' But then the Police Patil showed some sagacity. He told the leader: 'If you boycott him, I will let him come to my fields to shit so don't even think about it.'

The idea of the caste boycott was dropped right there.

The counting began. Dnyanoba Mauli was on the point of being elected. Then someone from the village committed an act of treachery. Someone concealed a ballot paper or may even have eaten it. Dnyanoba lost by one vote. But I was not going to stop fighting.

There were two factions in the village one was Parbhu Bade's; the other was Police Patil Aasruba Patil's. During the village election, Aasruba Patil had taken my side. Parbhu Bade wanted to keep the village under his heel by the power of his usury. Nor was Aasruba Patil any less. He had a gun on his shoulder all the time. He would always walk around in high style, with two of his goons in front of him, and two behind. I had nothing to do with either of these factions. But I had upset one of them by interfering in the election. I was now eager to take on the other faction as well.

Aasruba Patil had a ration shop in the village. Earlier the ration shop was run by a Vanjari, Gangaram Bade. Bade was a good man. He got us Mang boys into school. He would also extend the Mangs some credit. But when he died, the ration shop went to Aasruba Patil who would go to Majalgaon to fetch the grain meant for the Public Distribution Service and would sell most of it there. We would get very little of it. And certainly no credit either. The other farmers would have their own grainstocks but we were dependent on the rationing system for our grain.

The Mangs were upset by this but no one dared a single squeak of protest. I was about twenty years old at the time. I decided to challenge this and met Parbhu Bade. I had gone to see him armed with a written complaint against Aasruba Patil. This was just what Parbhu Bade wanted. He signed the complaint immediately. And he got seven or eight other people to add their signatures to it. He also gave me the money to register the complaint. I posted the complaint to the tahsildar. This was around the time of the Emergency and so complaints such as these were taken seriously and dealt with immediately. It was Indira Gandhi's way of showing how much control she had over the administration. Cases were filed against officers and investigations began even when the complainant was an ordinary person.

Investigators came to the village. The tahsildar sat on the paaraa* of the Maruti temple. Around him were the elders and the landlords of the village. The village folk were on the ground, beneath. Aasruba Patil was furious. He was glaring at everyone. The name on the complaint was mine. I was sent for. I went to the temple. Not just to the temple but right up to the paaraa where the tahsildar was sitting. At that time, it was forbidden for Mangs to go so close to the temple. But I paid those traditions no heed.

'You're Eknath Awad?' asked the tahsildar.

'Yes.'

'Did you complain that you do not get your rations?'

Aasruba was staring daggers at me.

Fearlessly, I said: 'No, I don't get any at all. Come to my home and see what I have and what I don't.'

---

*This is a concrete platform built around the base of a tree, generally a neem, outside the temple. It is used as an informal meeting space for the village.

The tahsildar turned to the people: 'What is this? Is he telling the truth? Do you not get your rations?'

There was a Lamaan seated there who was Aasruba Patil's puppet. He immediately replied: 'No, no, we get all our rations.'

Rage flamed from my bare feet to my head. I broke a branch off the neem tree at the platform and said to the Lamaan, 'Am I lying? Then take this branch in your hand and say that you get your rations!'

The Lamaans never lie if they have a neem branch in their hands. This threat frightened him. 'No, no, I won't take that branch.'

As all this was going on, one of the old men of the village shouted, 'How can you say he's lying? He's telling the truth. We don't get our rations. The boy is telling the truth.'

That did it. The tahsildar was forced to register a case against Aasruba Patil. He was taken to the police station. He stayed there for two days and then came back. He said to me, 'Eknatha, that wasn't a good thing to do.'

I said, 'What did I do, Patil? The whole thing was cooked up by Parbhu Bade. Where do I have the money to register a case? Parbhu Bade gave me the money and so I filed the complaint.'

Aasruba had no reply to that. He now saw this as his enemies' ploy. By sowing this seed of dissension, I intensified the fight between these two factions. I didn't care what happened to them; I had gained my own ends. The Mangs began to get their rations.

*

Since I was now known to have taken on both factions in my village, word about me began to spread to villages around. I began to get the support of the Mahars of these villages as a young Mang who was making some headway. I began to take part in other protests against injustice.

At that time, there was an organization called the Dalit Yuvak Aghadi, the Dalit Youth Front, which was doing good work. They had started the 'Ek Gaon, Ek Panvata' (One village, one common water-source) movement. The organization also had some Vanjari boys in it. At that time, there was revolution in the air. Ten kilometres from Dukdegaon was a village called Khalwat Limgaon. An incident that happened there became famous all over Maharashtra.

The Dalits and the upper castes had different water sources. There was an upper-caste person called Aambure Patil in the village. He had had his buffaloes shaved into the water source of the Dalits. Two Mahar youths, Madhav More and Shyamrao Tangde, were in contact with the Ek Gaon, Ek Panvata movement. These two young men decided that they would draw water from the upper-caste water source. This caused violence to erupt in the village. The Mahars were ostracized. This issue was on everyone's lips. One group of Vanjari boys who were working with the Dalit Yuvak Aghadi came to see me. The Vanjaris of our village treated us as untouchables. And yet, here were some young Vanjari men at my door, asking for my help. We had nothing to offer them, not even tea. I served them water in copper vessels and then went with them to Khalwat Limgaon. It was night when we reached the Dalit settlement there. We went about announcing, 'We want to conduct a meeting.' I went to the Mang settlement in the village. Unlike the Mahars, they had not made any claim for a common water-source.

I knew a couple of Mangs there, Lakshman and Dadarao. I went to their houses and invited them to the meeting. 'This isn't just a Mahar struggle; it is our struggle too,' I said but what I heard in reply, I have not forgotten unto this day,

'Here he is, Dagdu's son coming from Dukdegaon to tell us what to do. Don't you have any work to do, fucker? Don't drag us into that fight.'

I returned having failed at my attempt. But in Khalwat Limgaon, the boys were now divided into two groups: one for the Dalits and the other for Aambure Patil. To incite the other group, one would say, 'Mahars are getting above themselves'. The other group would reply, 'You're being unjust to the Dalits.' But the truth did come out at this meeting. We made notes about everything and then sent one or two of the boys to the Majalgaon Police Station to make a statement. And so a case against Aambure Patil was filed under the Protection of Civil Rights (PCR) Act. Aambure Patil went to jail for seven years. We succeeded in teaching the village and the upper castes that it would not be possible to keep practising untouchability in the old way.

*

And in due course, my matriculation examination came around. I passed the examination. Another incident from those days. It was afternoon and Baba had come back with the bhakri he had begged. I was not at home. Aasruba Patil was the village policeman. He came to our door, with his rifle proudly displayed on his shoulder. The people of the village called my father Lala. Aasruba Patil was drunk. He said to my father, 'Hey Lala, good for you, your son passed his matric. Now watch how I set him up for the job of a kotwal.'

Baba was very pleased. 'We will be highly obliged,' he said.

If his son were a kotwal, he was thinking, he would no longer have to go out and beg. At least, that's what he told me when I got home that day. I was very happy that I had passed. But Baba was completely uninterested in my results. All I said to him was, 'Look, Baba, I passed and the son of the Patil? He failed.' And as we were talking thus, the Patil appeared in the doorway again. I turned to him and said, 'Patil, your son failed the exam. Why don't you make him a kotwal? I passed.' The majority of the kotwals were Mahars-Mangs or Muslims. My words stung the Patil. He began to abuse me roundly. I refused to be silent and returned the insults with interest. He raised his hand on me. Finally, he went away, still cursing and swearing.

My body was filled with rage. I began to throw things about and break them. I broke the pots and pans. My parents and wife looked on in shock. They did not know why I was doing this. I warned them. 'You are not to clean up the hut at all.' Thanks to the Khalwat Limgaon episode I had become aware of the Protection of Civil Rights (PCR) Act. I had it in my mind to teach the Patil a lesson. So I went to the police station and said, 'The Police Patil came to my house and abused me and then destroyed everything.' If I had only said that he had come and abused me, no one would have registered a complaint for in those times, abusing the Mahar and the Mang, calling them names was commonplace. I brought the police back to the village. I showed them the broken pots and pans. There was then a foujdar by the name of Dangat. He took the Police Patil to the station. That a Mahar or a Mang should be able to complain about the Police Patil and that the Patil should then be taken to the police station for it was unheard of. Though no case was filed against the Police Patil under PCR, my status as a rebel and a fighter got a new fillip. But my joy at passing the matric was halved.

That was my childhood.

Can one call it a childhood? Hunger consumed it and made me an adult before my time. One does not have to explain politics and sociology to Dalit youths. This is because of the world in which they live. This is what happened to me as well.

In my illiterate family, I was the first to matriculate but there was no one to appreciate my achievement. After matriculation, one did the Pre-University Course (PUC). I chose to do my PUC at Majalgaon. At this time, I began to feel I should study and become a Collector. To achieve this, the only route was education. Now education and the social struggle would be the prime forces that would shape my personality.

3

The first step of every struggle takes courage. My own struggle began the moment I was born a Mang. As soon as I could recognize the world for what it was, I saw how it was filled with suffering. Up to the month of Ashadh*, there would be no food in the Mang homes. Begging was the only way to fill the belly. The wives and mothers of the Mangs would be in the homes of the upper castes, smearing the courtyards with cowdung. Some would be treated as the personal property of the men of these households; anyone, at any time, could take advantage of a Mang woman. Some would gather firewood from the jungle and sell it. Some would steal ears of jowar from the fields to fill their bellies. They would tear up their old rags and cover their children with them; they made no demands for themselves. When a Mang girl came of age, her life became difficult. There were always three or four young women who would sell their bodies to feed themselves and their families. It was the kind of poverty that ate into one's soul.

The men were bonded labourers. To earn a bhakri or two, they would play the halgi or other instruments at the time of a marriage in the village. Their complete helplessness made them accept this beggary. And then they would drink themselves into a stupor.

The Mang was supposed to wash the cattle of the Patil, he had to paint their horns; but once he was done, touching those animals meant they were polluted. The Mang could go into the village pond to dredge out the sediment, but once that job was done, he could not drink the water of the lake

---

*Ashadh is the fourth month of the lunar calendar and falls around June–July. It generally heralds the coming of the rains.

without polluting it. Until the jowar was harvested, it was Mang labour that brought the crop to readiness, but as soon as it was threshed, a Mang's hands would pollute it. It was a life constricted and confined. Even a cornered cat will go for your throat, but in this case, both the Dalit and the upper caste had accepted this injustice as part of the way of things. I wanted to say something, to fight with someone, but I could also see that it would be of little use. I was a dhobi in the land of the naked.

I saw their pain, I lived it; but I refused to rot in it. Gautam Buddha expounded the Four Noble Truths. There is suffering in this life. But there are reasons why we suffer and there are ways to end suffering. These are said to be the basic principles of Buddhist philosophy. At that time, there was no way for me to understand these Buddhist principles. But I feel that in some way, I had already understood these truths. But most of all, I saw education as a way out of this life.

All we had at home was what Gaya and I earned through manual labour and what Baba brought home by begging. Had I done Mangki, we could have managed a little better. But I did not want to abandon my education. Since I was studying like a Mahar, my relatives had begun to refer to me as *Maharcha aulad*, 'Son of a Mahar'. But however much they tried to provoke me, I refused to respond. In my head I would say, 'I have passed my matric. Now whatever happens, I do not have to be a Potraj. Whatever I do, I won't have to beg.'

'Education is the milk of the tigress. Once you have drunk it, you cannot but roar,' said Dr Babasaheb Ambedkar. Tiger milk was running through my veins now. The tiger inside me was asking: 'Can I devour all the suffering the caste system has wrought?'

*

After matric, I had no money to study further although I wanted to. So I collected what I could by doing manual labour. I got admission in a new college that had started in Majalgaon, 21 kilometres away from Dukdegaon. There was nothing for it but to walk the distance. However I could not do this every day. The college did provide a scholarship and I hoped to get one. But there was a problem with my scholarship. A caste certificate had to be issued by the Gram Panchayat. The sarpanch was delaying the matter. This was the result of my having taken an active part in village politics. I made two or three fruitless trips there. Finally, I had to use the strongest weapon I had. I warned him, 'If you don't give me the caste certificate, I will file a Protection of Civil Rights case against you.' We have a saying: 'Hold the nose shut and the mouth opens of its own accord'; when I brandished the weapon of the case, the certificate was issued immediately. I had found a powerful weapon against the caste system's cruelty and injustices.

I rented a room in Majalgaon. The village's name says it all; 'Majal' means wealthy. The farmers were rich and powerful and were diligent in their observance of caste rules. A Dalit was not even allowed to stand at their doors, never mind renting a room from one of them. Only the Muslims would rent rooms to the lower castes and it was in a Muslim home that I found a room to rent.

I had brought some jowari from home and I would make bhakri and go to college.

The same Waghmare who I had beaten up in the hostel at Laul was looking for a room in Majalgaon. He came to me now.

'Let me stay with you,' he said.

'So you'll stay in the same room as a Mang?' I asked. 'Or will you put up a wall so you can stay pure?'

He said, 'Enough, my friend! Let it go. Forget what happened.'

So I too, buried the hatchet and let him stay in my room. Later, Waghmare invited me to his home to have a meal. His father was dead. He told his mother, 'Aai, this is my closest friend. Serve us in one thali.'

And so his mother did.

*

I earned money by manual labour. This meant I could not go to college regularly. It was important to figure out a way to earn my bread in Majalgaon. Majalgaon had the Vinayakrao Patil Hostel for Maratha youths. I could not be admitted as I was not a Maratha but I did make enquiries as to whether they would allow me to mess there. Our zilla parishad member was a man called Pardikar. I met him with Waghmare and explained my problems. He gave us both recommendation letters to the hostel and that solved the question of two meals a day.

But I still could not attend college regularly. Aai was not well; she was getting weaker and weaker. I would go to the village once every fortnight or so. On one of my visits, Aai looked ill. I had to return the next day to Majalgaon. We had eaten and were about to go to sleep but Aai's mind was troubled. I asked her, 'Bai, what are you thinking about?'

'Eknatha, the city is a dangerous place. So many riots happen there. Be careful, my son. You were born after so many prayers, so many promises. You're the son of my prayers and wishes.' Her eyes were wet with tears. Even when the moon rose, she could not sleep. She kept staring at the lamp that stood on top of the grain basket. I did not sleep either. Dawn broke. I picked up my box and was ready to leave. Our neighbour Gangamai came limping up, stick in hand. She asked, 'Off again, Eknath?' Aai said, 'Yes, yes, my son has left.' She began to cry. I did not look back as I walked away.

*

Around this time, we had our first child. Gaya had spent some of her pregnancy at her mother's home.

There was nothing extraordinary about a first child. If goats and cows could have children, why couldn't human beings? That was how we looked upon it and how it was looked upon by others as well. We lived as animals lived. Our incessant frenzied hunger let us think of nothing else. Gaya continued to work right up to the time she was due. My family bore the burden of my education. My mother and her sister decided that my daughter's name would be Daivshala. I thought nothing of this name. But when the girl was to go to school, I put down her name as Shaalan. I deleted the 'daiva' (destiny) from her name.

By the time my daughter was born, I had completely stopped doing Mangki. This did not sit well with the village. It was difficult to find work to do. It was also becoming increasingly difficult to manage a family that comprised an ailing mother, an ageing father and a wife on whose hip there was a baby. I got a scholarship of thirty rupees from the college. I went to college only to collect that money. I had no other association with the college. The Pre-University Course (PUC) examinations came and I failed in English though I did well in all the other subjects. I was allowed to keep term and the next year I managed to pass the English examination. I got a final scholarship of five hundred rupees. The first thing I did with this money was to buy three nanny goats.

*

But I could not keep the goats I had bought with such high hopes. I did not have money for admission to the Bachelor of Arts degree so I had to sell the animals again. I took admission in the Balbhim College in Beed. Dongardive, my friend from Chinchala, was also studying in Beed. He had a room there. I began to stay with him. Every month, I would send half of the scholarship money home. I ate a hybrid bhakri every day: jowari and besan.

Even if I had studied, I would not have got an ordinary office job. At that time, however much a Dalit studied, no one would hire him. There was no one to encourage or empathize with a promising and educated Dalit. Thus my ambition was limited to getting a government job. But it was important to finish my education in order to achieve that aim. And to do that, I needed money. I sometimes found manual labour in the village and sometimes I didn't. I would weave ropes and sell those. But that didn't bring in enough.

There was an endless shortage of money. Sometimes, a storm would burst in my head. I would think: enough of this education. But then I would realize that if I gave up on studying, I might have to fall back on Mangki; and that would mean returning to a state of helplessness.

My sister was at Ghagharwada. I went and told her my situation. She was illiterate. Her husband was also unlettered. But she said, 'Do not stop your education. I'll pawn my pots and pans but don't lose heart.' I felt a little better. My sister put together such money as she could. I went to her village and began to work there too. I would cross six hills to fetch firewood, tying it into bundles and carrying them back on my head to sell in the market at Dharur. One bundle fetched about eight annas, at the most twelve, but even that much seemed like a huge support.

With the help of this money, I could begin to attend college a little more regularly. I would sit on the front bench in class. My reading had increased. Because of that I kept up a steady barrage of questions aimed at the teachers. I had read the entire Parliamentary speeches of Dr Babasaheb Ambedkar and Barrister Nath Pai*. I was totally obsessed with reading speeches and biographies. I had read the biographies of Karl Marx, Lenin, Hitler and Abraham Lincoln. I had read a collection of writings about the Russian Revolution in my first year of the BA. All of this was in my head and all of this provoked more and more questions. But I did not accept the teachers' answers; I would debate with them. One day, I asked one of the teachers, 'Did socialism arise out of communism or did communism arise out of socialism?' At the end of the period, he called me aside. 'I am new here,' he said. 'Please help me. I haven't done much reading in that area. Could you please ask fewer questions?' Around this time, there was an agitation to increase the scholarship amounts. The thirty rupees we received every month at that time was nothing in the face of the rising prices. I had to manage for myself and send money back to the family as well. Many Dalits were facing the same situation. And so it was the Dalit students who took the lead in this agitation. We undertook a College Bandh. This was how other student bodies in other colleges had protested. This caused a division between us and the upper-caste students. When we closed the Majalgaon College, things came to the brink of physical violence. The Principal intervened and healed the breach for a while at least. Whatever else, we did manage to increase the scholarship to seventy rupees a month. Now I began to send thirty-five rupees home every month.

---

*Barrister Nath Bapu Pai (1922-1971) was a member of the Praja Socialist Party and a Member of Parliament from Rajapur on the Konkan coast.

This was also the time I got involved with the Dalit Panthers, a militant Dalit youth movement. The youth of Beed who studied at the Milind College in Aurangabad had to sit for their examinations in Beed. I would go there to get their class notes. Since I could not attend class regularly, these notes were my only support. In those days, leaders from Mumbai such as Namdeo Dhasal and Raja Dhale would make fiery speeches to the youth. They would abuse the Hindu gods and goddesses. 'I begin my speech by spitting phlegm on the thirty-three crore gods,' the Panther youth would say at the beginning of their speeches. Their speeches about caste atrocities would be filled with a visceral concern for injustice. The boys who were studying in Aurangabad would bring these thoughts back with them. One of these boys was Atmaram Salve, a shahir. He was the zonal head of the Marathwada division. Before this, I had heard him at an Ambedkar Jayanti Programme, reciting his poetry, fierce songs of protest inspired by Ambedkarite philosophy. He would also help non-Mahar students in the movement. His contribution to establishing the Dalit Panther movement in Aurangabad was invaluable. His songs would make your blood race.

> *Pantherchya tu shoor jawaana*
> *Dhaav rahni, ghe bedya*
> *Naahi tar, bhar haati baangdya*

> You are fearless panthers.
> Fly to the battlefield, break your chains,
> Or else put on bangles as women do.

This was also the time of the struggle to rename the Marathwada University after Dr Babasaheb Ambedkar.* Salve would sing in a powerful voice:

---

*Henceforth, this will be referred to as 'The Renaming Movement'.

Vidyapeetala naav de Bhimaacha
Nasta paat vaahateel raktaacha.

Name the university after Bhimrao,
Or rivers of blood will flow.

Atmaram Salve had completed his MA in English from Milind
College. With a Masters' degree in English, anyone would
have given him a job. But he was completely absorbed in the
movement to change the university's name. He had inspired all
of Marathwada with his songs. He pawned 20 acres of his own
irrigated land to help the workers in the Panthers movement.
But he did not live to see the change in name happen.

*

The Renaming Movement was now slipping into oblivion.
Hundreds of barely literate men and women had shed their
blood for it.

During Babasaheb's lifetime, the Dalit movement had
seen such episodes as the Mahad Chavdar Tank satyagraha,
the fight for entry into the Kalaram Temple, and other such
momentous events. Of the ones he had left behind for the
Dalits to fight, the most important one was the struggle to
rename Marathwada University after Babasaheb Ambedkar.

The demand to change the name of the university was
first made in 1974. In 1978, when Sharad Pawar's Progressive
Democratic Front government was in power, he brought
resolutions in both houses of the legislature to effect the change
in names. The resolutions were passed by both houses and
the news was announced on the radio. Marathwada began
to burn. The whole of society seemed to be divided between
those who supported the change and those who opposed it.
The name was finally officially changed in 1994. The struggle
lasted for nearly twenty years. These two decades gave my life

a certain shape, as they did the lives of many Dalit youths who were involved in the struggle. My future personal and social confrontations were all shaped in some way by my participation in the Renaming Movement.

Before having the resolution passed, the Progressive Demoratic Front government should have made some attempt to understand the background to the struggle. The Janata Party government was at the Centre. At that time, the students of Milind College were under the aegis of the Marathwada University. Whenever there was a meeting of the university board, fifty to sixty students would march for the change of name. They would make speeches in front of the board. At one of these morchas, a speech went: 'When a university can be named after Patrice Lumumba, why cannot a university in Marathwada be named after Dr Ambedkar?' What do we learn from this? At the beginning, there was no real strong opposition to the change in name. Then the Dalit Panthers had a meeting in Mumbai. At this meeting, it was decided that the protests should be accelerated. At that time, I was studying in Beed. The Panthers had a strong network among the students. Thus a decision made in Mumbai was not limited to Mumbai. There were no mobile phones as there are today, but the students made up for this with their enthusiasm and commitment. Thus injustice anywhere echoed up and down the state. For the Dalits, this was the first or second generation that had reached college. The Emergency, Jayaprakash Narayan's call for Total Revolution, Vinoba Bhave's Bhoodaan (The Gift of Land) Movement, the rise of the Naxalites...all this was in the air. I too was active in the Panthers Movement. No sensitive and thinking youth could possibly be neutral in this charged environment.

And so, almost without my willing it, I became a supporter of the Renaming Movement.

The issue had divided the socialist leadership. The old freedom fighter Govindbhai Shroff and the editor of the daily newspaper *Marathwada*, Anantrao Bhalerao were against the change, while leaders like S.M. Joshi were for it. It was not as if the socialists who were against the change of name were an evil bunch. They had some sympathy for the Dalit cause but were not in favour of the Dalits aggressively demanding their rights. As human beings, they were on the side of the Dalits but they did not think organizations like the Dalit Panthers were helping the cause. This was the confusion in the thinking of the socialists. They were not very comfortable with the idea of the Dalits taking things into their own hands, working up the courage to fight their own battles and challenging the status quo.

There was another stream in the anti-Renaming faction. After India gained Independence, there were still some princely states that had remained untouched by the new dispensation. Marathwada had been part of the Nizam's territory and so a different battle had to be fought here to gain independence. One argument that was also put forward was that Dr Ambedkar had never fought for the independence of Marathwada, and had always been on the side of the Nizam and thus his name could not be used for the Marathwada University. But this held no water. In truth, Babasaheb had always been opposed to the idea of an independent Hyderabad. There were also a number of Brahmins who had benefited from the Nizam's support. Why are none of them seen as traitors to the cause of Independence? But those who opposed the change of name had put together a number of weak arguments like this one. It was also in the interests of the state government to keep this issue burning. With all these concerns around, the problem of caste could be ignored. The casteists therefore had their way. The Dalits who celebrated the birthdays of their leaders, refused to do Maharki, wore fine clothes and walked about in style were identified and killed. The upper-caste students were also infused with this enthusiasm. Their groups presented the Vice-Chancellor with a memorandum asking him not to change the name of the University.

In truth, up to this point in time twelve universities had had their names changed. The Kurukshetra University had had its name changed to B.N. Chakravarty University. Kurukshetra is held to be the ground on which the war of the Mahabharata was fought; the change in the name did not offend anyone's religious sensibilities. But here, changing the name to the author of the Indian Constitution seemed to create problems for Marathwada's feudal mentality. The Dalit Panthers decided to celebrate the fiftieth anniversary of the Mahad Chavdar Tank agitation.

The then chief minister, Vasantdada Patil, attended the celebration. The Panthers presented him with a list of ten demands, the change of name being one of them. The Chief Minister agreed in principle. Up to that point, the change in name had been on paper. But the PDF government then took over. This was Sharad Pawar's purogami (Progressive) government. It was their moral duty to propose the name change. They did make the proposal and the next day riots erupted in the villages. The homes of Dalits were burned. If a morcha supporting the Renaming went out on one day, a morcha against it would follow on the next day. This led to a chain of morchas, one after the other. The Shiv Sena was against the Renaming. Everyone, students, teachers, lawyers, doctors, right down to the villagers, were taking sides.

It was put about that the riots that broke out after the announcement of the change in name had come about spontaneously but this was a lie. The Mahars were the target of systematic arson. In most villages, the Mahars and the

Mangs live side by side, but the homes of the Mahars would be burned and the same people who tried to burn those homes would also wet down the houses of the Mangs to protect them from burning. If these were spontaneous riots, how did they know exactly which houses were the Mahars' and which were not? Actually, the upper castes did not want the rebellious Mahars around but they were fine with the Mangki-performing, field-minding, cow-carcass-dragging, bowing-and-scraping Mangs. These riots caused many Neo-Buddhists to leave their homes and live in exile. Rejecting this divisiveness, many Mang youths threw themselves into the Renaming Movement.

Pochiram Kamble was one of the most active Mangs in the movement and he was murdered with no remorse. He was from Tembhurni village, Nanded. He had a good life, two children, 4 acres of land and two buffaloes that had been given to him by the bank. He was always in the forefront of the celebrations of Ambedkar Jayanti, despite being a Mang. None of this pleased the upper castes of the village. The Dalits of this village were in good shape. They had built pakka houses for themselves. When the change of name was announced, the upper castes got the opportunity they were looking for to squeeze the Dalits. At around 7 a.m. a thousand or a thousand five hundred people got together and attacked the Dalits. They did not just set the houses alight, they made sure they were destroyed with fire bombs. The Dalits began to run helter-skelter.

Then a mob, a hundred or a hundred-and-fifty strong, began to chase Pochiram Kamble. He ran and ran until at last they caught him at the edge of the village. They stabbed him in the stomach. They told the half-dead Pochiram that if he stopped saying 'Jai Bhim' they would let him go.

Pochiram refused. They tied his hands and feet together.

They gathered firewood and they burned him alive. This was not enough to sate the demon of casteism in them. They came back to the village and performed pooja in the temple. In an act of ironic celebration, they distributed prasad in the village. This mayhem lasted twelve hours. However, not one newspaper printed an account of the murder of Pochiram. When the news was printed, lies were used to defame him; he was a rapist, they said, he was a thug, he was a criminal. The cement houses of the Dalits had been destroyed but the newspapers reported that four huts had been burned. The newspapers were, at this time, anti-Dalit. Pochiram had a son, Chander, a twenty-year-old. He was missing. He had watched his father's murder happen. His faith in the rule of law had been destroyed. Later, Chander would murder someone to avenge the death of his father.

In the village of Sugav, Nanded district, Janardhan Mevade was cut into pieces. It was reported that he was a thief and that was why the village had decided to use axes to cut him into pieces. It did not occur to any of the reporters to ask why he had not been handed over to the police if he were a thief. The newspapers were complicit in the sin of labelling a Dalit worker a thief and thus supporting the upper castes in their vigilante justice.

A hundred and eighty villages in Marathwada witnessed such violence. The riots raged for ten days. At eighteen places, there was police firing. More than a thousand Dalit homes were set on fire. At that time, I was studying in second year BA. As the news came in, I would grow restive; my mind would fill with anger. Then there would be meetings and morchas. I would come forward to make representations to the government. My mother would worry for me as I was upsetting many people in the village. The Patil was already my enemy, but even my caste members were spiteful in their opposition to me.

*

Because I did not uphold Mang traditions and because I socialized with the Mahars, the community wanted nothing to do with me. They did not invite me to religious ceremonies. In one sense, I was no longer a Mang. I had no caste left. I did not care. I was happy doing what I was doing, but Aai was worried about me.

She was getting weaker every day. One day, news came that she was ill. I went home. She had grown darker. Baba was also tired now.

Aai thought her time had come but I didn't think so. She would say to Baba, 'Save me. Save me for my son's sake.'

Baba would reply, 'What am I to do? What can I sell to take you to a doctor?'

We had only a few mud pots and bins left. Who would take them as security and give us money? Usury was rife in the village. Rates were as high as twenty-five per cent. If you did not pay the interest, the sahukar was likely to help himself to the family's girls and even beat them up if they resisted. I did not know what to do either.

I would say, 'Bai, just eat well. Nothing will happen to you.' But she would go on saying, 'Save me, save me.' I tried to explain things to Baba too. 'Now you must stop begging. Let us earn and eat with self-respect. I send you money from my scholarship, don't I? You're tired now. Stop begging.' Baba agreed and I left to go back to Beed.

Then a message came that Aai was ill again. When I got home, she was bed-ridden. I did not know what to do. I picked her up as she was and put her into an ST (State Transport) bus. I took her to my room at Beed. Baba came with me. How could I take her to a clinic? I took her to the government hospital. At that time, government clinics and hospitals were all obsessed with the family planning operations that they were supposed to perform. There was a sterilization camp going on at the government clinic. No doctors were to be found. So I took Aai to a private clinic. It wasn't much of a clinic; this doctor had set up shop in a small room. I don't even remember what kind of doctor he was. When I look back, I suspect that Aai had developed tuberculosis but at that time I couldn't understand what ailed her. All my hopes were pinned on the doctor. 'It will cost a hundred rupees to cure her,' said the doctor. I did not have that much money. 'I'll arrange the money,' I said and the doctor promptly gave her an injection.

But this seemed to cause her even more distress. I brought her back to my room. There she lost consciousness. Baba began to weep and wail. I, too, thought Aai had died. All night, I sat by her pillow. There was nothing I could do until morning came. I took her to the ST stand. How was I to take her corpse on to a bus? I carried her on my shoulders as if she were a bundle. I draped a cloth over her. I decided to suppress my tears or people might suspect I was carrying a corpse. Baba, too, was silent. We came to the village. When we reached the house, Aai revived a little. She had clung to life in order to be back among her things, to see her house, her vessels, one last time.

In a little while, she was gone.

All the women of the Mangwada gathered in front of the hut. My sister came from Ghagarwada. She and Gaya were weeping as they clung to Aai's body. The bier was built. My mother's frail, emaciated frame was draped with a new sari. The parting of her hair was filled with koonkoo. Baba had stuffed the edge of his dhotar into his mouth and was weeping. My Vaman Mama was trying to console him. 'Aara Dagdu, who is here forever? We are all going to die. Don't weep like a madman. Look at the boy,' he said, meaning me, for I was standing there, dry-eyed. They lifted her body to their shoulders. The final journey began for Aai. My sister was holding on to me and weeping. I did not have enough money to cremate Aai and so she was buried in the ground. Slowly the mud began to cover her up. The sound of weeping increased.

In my head, questions. Why do mothers die? No mother should die. No one's mother should die. She wanted me to study. I am studying. So why did she die? Reading Ambedkar's works had made me aware of how important it was to study. From my childhood, she had wanted me to become a successful Mang, not a Potraj. When I did grow up to be a successful Mang, when I had passed my exams, she went and stood in front of the Maruti temple and prayed for me: *Let my son learn and let him be brave.* What would that red stone in the temple understand of her dreams for me? But I had understood her ambitions and dreams for me. She would sit at the grinding stone and sing ovis. She would grind the jowar that had been begged from twelve villages but this did not limit the size of her dreams. One of her ovis was:

Dahaachi panchaaiit mazhya ekalyaana keli
Baal maazha Eknathana sabha saavleelaa nheli.

My son alone can take on a panchayat of ten
Now he will bring us to rest in the shade.

The second line meant I would ensure that the proper decision was taken. She wanted me to bring justice to the people; she wanted me to help the poor and raise the downtrodden. This was her dream as she ground the jowar of our poverty; how did she keep her dreams so big?

Disordered thoughts passed through my head. If I had just had a little money, I might have been able to save her. But Aai is dead now; what can bring her back? She can only live if I continue to study. The English paper is day after tomorrow. I should leave now…

I left for Beed soon after. I had to sit for the examination; I had to pass. I could not look back. The Aai who had taken my side and wept for me was gone. I sat for the examination. And I passed.

4

So there I was, grimly determined to get a college education, and simultaneously fighting against the economic privations visited upon my family because of our caste. Each time the fees had to be paid, I had to find some new way to do it. When I say 'college', you should know that the usual rosy picture of this time in one's life had not a whit to do with my experience of it. For me it was not about romantic relationships with young women, spending time with them or dressing up in the latest fashions. My economic conditions made me a misfit. I had only one set of clothes to wear. I would wash them in the night and put them on the next morning. I did manual labour. My face was burnt by the sun, my hands toughened and covered with callouses. The barber wouldn't cut our hair or shave us. And so my beard and moustache grew apace. How could I play the college dandy? Through all the years of my education, I only saw a single film. Waghmare took me for *Amar Akbar Anthony*. That was the only time I remember having fun. My family had never been educated. And so thinking and talking about books; discussions on issues and shining in debate: this was what mattered to me. I was always taking part in heated debates and public-speaking competitions. Students from different castes and creeds were all descending into the battlefield to make their points of view known to the others. There was an excitement in the air.

I did not feel this excitement about going to the cinema or going on picnics. It's another thing that I didn't have the money for that kind of thing. But I was truly excited by the struggle. Going on picnics, playing antakshari, as the only ways to enjoy oneself seemed frivolous. Someone might reply: 'Life for the poor is always a struggle. Does that mean they're always having a great time?' That's not what I mean. Deprivation has no joys at all. If you must swallow insults and disrespect all your life, it does not make for a life of happiness. But when a human being begins to fight the circumstances of life, when she takes up arms against injustice, then life offers another kind of exhilaration. In my experience, the struggle itself would create an outlet, a drain for my rage and anger. This became something of a habit with me.

At that time, my mind was so full of enthusiasm, that if any untoward event happened, I would jump in immediately, taking no thought for the possible consequences. Let what happens, happen, I would say to myself and set to work. I'll give you a couple of instances of this from my Bachelor of Arts years. The exams were over. I was returning to the village. The usual jam-packed ST bus. The usual near-stampede, the usual chaos. Dongardive and I were sitting in the bus. The conductor shouted at the passengers: 'Hey, shut up. Why are you behaving like Mahars and Mangs?' He said this and I looked at Dongardive. He was looking at me too. In an instant, we were on our feet. I grabbed the conductor by the neck. I let him have a solid slap across his face. Fireflies must have danced before his eyes. He was terrified: 'What happened? What happened? Why are you hitting me?' Dongardive said, 'I'm a Mahar, he's a Mang. You saw us and you said that.' The conductor was petrified, 'Aavo...no, no, I had nothing like that in my mind. It's just a way of saying things. I am a Mahar myself.' I slammed him down on his seat and said: 'Say it once more and see what happens.'

Another big fight. There was a jatra at the village of Pusra. I had always liked wrestling so I went there to see the wrestling matches. Wrestling means chaos. Baliram Aasbe, a pehelwan from the neighbouring village of Chinchala, was fighting too.

A rivalry existed between Chinchala and Vadgaon. Baliram defeated the Vadgaon challenger three times but they kept asking for rematches. They just would not admit to defeat. I went forward. I said: 'That's enough. Baliram has pinned your pehelwan.' As soon as I said this, someone grabbed my neck and began to insult me. I flared up. I picked up some stones that were lying there and pelted the crowd. I began to throw stones at the Vadgaon supporters. Back and forth it went, stones flying and them claiming the victory for Vadgaon. The pehelwan from Chinchala joined in the stone-throwing. The atmosphere grew heated as it seemed that the jatra was going to be spoiled. Finally the sarpanch of Pusra brought about a compromise. Baliram was announced as the winner and only then did the riot end. I insisted he be given the prize money for three victories.

Another similar incident. I was home for the holidays. But I had to go to the college to collect the final scholarship money. I went to Dongardive's home at Chinchala. Both of us left together for Beed. We were waiting for the bus at the ST stand. It was a time of drought and so tankers would bring water in. One such tanker was standing there. An old woman approached the tanker with her pot. The man giving out the water was disrespectful. For no reason at all, he threw away the woman's pot. It fell on to a stone nearby, clattering and clanging and smashing. The old woman sat down abruptly. She could only stare at the broken pot, her eyes full of horror. Where was she to get the money for a new one?

I asked Dongardive: 'Shall we teach this tanker fellow a lesson or two, right now?' He said, 'Not now, wait.' The ST bus arrived and we left.

Some time later, the same tanker fellow came back to the village. The truck was surrounded by the usual crowd. While he was filling pots with the huge pipe, he would deliberately spill some water on the young women and the girls too. Babita, from the Mangwadi, was among the crowd. Because of the drought, everyone's clothes were worse for the wear. He was getting an eyeful of the exposed bodies from his perch on the tanker. Trying to keep her body concealed, Babita too was standing in the crowd; she has been waiting a while but the tanker man was not filling her pot. I saw all this. I grabbed him and pulled him down into the crowd. I gave him a thorough pummelling. 'Deliberately wetting the girls and women?' I asked as I threw him to the ground. 'If you do this again, I'll just kill you.' In my head, I was still angry at him for having broken the old woman's water pot. These fights happened again and again. And the rage that burned through me would be given an airing.

There was an incident that took place at Dongardive's wedding too. Since the Mahars were no longer doing their customary work, the upper castes had decided to squeeze them as hard as possible. No Brahmin would come to marry a Mahar but they would come to perform Mang weddings. They would recite a couple of shlokas of the Mangalaashtaka and take their dakshina as well as offerings of rice and wheat and hurry off. It was the Gosavis who would marry the Mahars. The marriage procession would start off with the Mangs in attendance. The marriage procession of a Mang would even go past the Maruti temple. But the Mahars did not have permission to take out a marriage procession. Dongardive asked me, 'So what do you think about a baaraat after the wedding?' His relatives and friends were aghast at this proposal. They did not want to enrage the village for no reason. I said: 'Great idea. Let's have a procession.' I went to meet Foujdar Dangat and told him Dongardive's plans. He said, 'Aara, of course a new bridegroom must have a procession. I'll see who tries to oppose this.'

That was all I needed to encourage me to further efforts. I went to Dukdegaon and got all the halgi players together. I organized lezim dancers, brought in lantern bearers. Dongardive's marriage procession came out in high style. The newly married man even went into the temple. I strongly suspect that this was the first marriage procession of a Mahar in the entire district. Not a squeak or a squawk came out of anyone's mouths. Or rivers of blood would have flowed.

*

We did the same kind of things in our studies as well. One year, I did not get the scholarship. The college had neglected to send some necessary paperwork on to the social welfare department and so the scholarship was not sanctioned. It would be difficult without the money to live in Beed and pay for everything. So Dongardive and I thought about it and decided, 'Let's study from home. We can eat whatever our parents are eating.' We divided up the books. Every morning I would go out to work. Then by afternoon, I would finish and start off to Chinchala and Dongardive would start towards Dukdegaon. We would meet each other halfway, under a neem tree and sit and read our text books. There were no guides as there are these days. One had to read several books and answer examinations out of them. We would read until the sun had reached the horizon and then we would discuss what we had read. That tree was our college. Though we did not attend lectures that year, we scored better marks than in the years that we had.

That year, I had contrived the college fees in a completely different way. I was taking part in the political life of the village. I was trying to maintain good relations with both the factions. I needed someone's support. Everyone in the village, even the Muslims were tired of the ill-treatment meted out to them by the Patils, the usurious moneylenders and the landlords. I saw these downtrodden and oppressed people as my natural allies. In order to bring them to my side, I planned a jatra for Nanabubu. Nanabubu has a dargah in our village. I made a grand announcement of the jatra. I invited wrestlers. There was a giant wheel and balloon-and-whistle-sellers came. It was a good turnout with lots of noise. There was always a game or two going on at a jatra. I had decided it would be the three-card trick. The person running the game would have three cards, only one of which would be the one on which you could bet. He would move the cards expertly and you were supposed to place your money on the right card. If you got it right, you got double your money. A young man named Chand was the one who ran these card games. Everyone called him Chandya. This was an illegal set-up and it had to be made right with the gram panchayat and the police.

I was the head of this jatra. Chandya gave me the usual amount: three hundred rupees. I gave a hundred and fifty to the gram panchayat and the rest I gave to Foujdar Dangat. This was his 'right' by tradition. Foujdar Dangat knew me well. When I went to give him the money, he told me I could keep the money for myself. And out of this money, I paid my fees.

*

Sometimes I would tire of this constant striving and contriving and wonder if I should just take a job. Driven by this thought, I once went to a police recruitment drive. The selection process includes a running race. I stood first in that race. We had to come back on the second day. I knew I would qualify when they measured our chests and heights. There would be other tests on the second day but I felt my selection was a sure thing. I came back to my room. In those days, all of us had taken rooms in which we stayed together. Seeing me return from the police recruitment drive, the other boys began to mock me: 'Look, it's our brave leader. He's going to abandon the revolution and join the police. He'll be whacking us with his lathi when we go out on a morcha.' They all laughed loudly. I joined in the laughter. Then I said, 'Forget it. Who told you that nonsense?' The idea of joining the police died right there.

All the boys would put their names down at the Employment Exchange. There were few educated young people. This meant that call letters would arrive even for those who were still studying in college. Many young men would go off to full-time jobs. I had also put my name down at the Employment Office. I got a call from the Parli Thermal Power Plant. At that time, the boys would hear that So-and-So or Such-and-Such had sent out call letters. I heard that a call letter had reached my home in the village. I went back to the village. Gaya only knew that the postman had left a letter with my name on it. No one at home knew what the letter said, nor did I tell them, for I was in two minds about this employment opportunity. If I told Baba that I had a chance to work, he would say: 'Now enough of this studying. Grab this chance.' I didn't want that pressure because I wasn't sure whether I should continue to study or start working. The letter said that the job was as a 'Boiler Supervisor'.

Parli had a coal-based power plant. It was probably a job at the furnace, I thought, and set off for Parli. I reached Telgaon via Naganwadi. Here I had to catch a bus to Parli.

But then I met some college friends who were also part of the struggle. I told them about the call. One of them said, 'What will you do, working at the furnace? Go home.' Perhaps I was just waiting for someone to say this to me. If I had taken a job, I would never have finished my education. And for some reason, I could not see myself as a boiler supervisor.

and then you can arrest him.' He agreed. He came with his policemen to listen to the programme. Atmaram presented a stirring set of poems. As usual, he included a demand for the change of Marathwada University's name in his songs and poems. Foujdar Kadam too was shaking his head, listening in deep appreciation. He said, 'Wah, what a powerful poet he is.' This compliment notwithstanding he was standing by to arrest Atmaram.

But we were ready for him. Halfway through the programme we announced, 'Atmaram Salve has developed a cough. Since he cannot continue, another poet will take over.' Another activist took over and began singing and while this was happening we had spirited Atmaram away. Three or four boys concealed him. When Foujdar Kadam arrived to arrest him, he had vanished. When they asked us where he was, we threw up our hands in pretend surprise.

The foujdar was very angry. He said, 'You are concealing a wanted person.' We had an altercation with him. He tried his best but he had to return empty-handed.

Two or three days later, I was studying in the hostel. Someone came there in the afternoon, asking for me. I introduced myself. He said, 'I am Dr Mujumule, the President of the Dalit Yuvak Aghadi.' I was very happy to meet this young man. I was delighted that the head of an organization working in the same area had himself come to meet me; we could now have a discussion on the issues we faced; or so I felt. But Dr Mujumule had an entirely different intention in meeting me. 'You have started a Dalit Panther cell here,' he said. I said that we had. In a rather affected style he announced, 'You ought to know that the Dalit Yuvak Aghadi is already working in this area. As long as we are here, no one else can establish a presence in our area.'

'Is that a threat, Doctor sahib?' I asked

'Take it as one,' he replied.

My voice rose. 'You came here, looking for me on your own two feet. Now that you are here, sit down, have a cup of tea if you like. But if you threaten to close down the Panthers, you may never be able to use your own feet again.'

At this time, I was supporting ten or twelve poor boys who were in the hostel. Hearing my voice raised in anger, this group of boys came running. Dr Mujumule got the message.

Under the aegis of the Dalit Panthers of Ambajogai, we began to make representations for the change of name. It was a sensitive time. If we were arrested, it would mean an interruption in our studies. But I wanted an education and I wanted a revolution as well. So I was determined that we should continue to make our demands known but we should also stay out of jail. How to do this was the subject of furious discussion. We had decided to make our demands known in front of the Deputy Collector's office. Next to it was a timber mill. And so, Bansode, Rode and some other main student leaders and I went and spent the night, hidden in the timber mill. The other boys were to gather in different places. Then the police arrested our guide, Professor Bhatkar. They hoped, I suppose, that if they arrested the advisor, the protests would end of their own accord as the students would take fright. But the next morning, as we had decided, seven or eight of us arrived at the Deputy Collector's office and behind us a hundred or more students turned up from different locations. We started our protest. We shook the Deputy Collector's office with our speeches and our slogans. The police arrived to disperse us. They did arrest us but at seven or eight in the evening, they let us go again.

*

During the Renaming Movement, many had to leave their villages and live elsewhere. They lived in hutments in Mumbai, they collected rags and sorted rubbish to make a living but they never gave up the desire to see the university bear Babasaheb's name. The upper castes of my village were enraged. I took part in protests and morchas of the Renaming Movement. Since I was one of the leaders, my name would appear in the newspapers. None of this pleased the upper castes of my village. There was going to be a reaction. The upper castes had killed the Renaming Movement worker, Pochiram Kamble. The casteists were proud that they had killed this man. They wanted to keep the Dalits of every village under their heels. I might have had this happen to me but I was saved by my cousin Vitthal.

One day, Vitthal was on his way to the toilet. He saw the Patils of the village gathered on the Maruti temple paaraa. In the middle, they had placed a basket full of ears of jowar. Each of them had an ear of jowar in his hand and they were proclaiming, 'The Mangs are getting out of hand. Eknath is in the Renaming Movement. This time we will not let him escape. If he comes to the village, we'll break his arms and legs.' They were swearing an oath to kill me on the grain. But Vitthal said, without fear, 'Who are you threatening? Let's see who so much as touches a Mang.' Seeing Vitthal behave this way, they dispersed hurriedly. But Vitthal sent me a message, 'Don't come to the village; they're going to get you.' When I got the message, I went to Telgaon and met Foujdar Dangat. As soon as he saw me, he said, 'Eknath, what news?' I said, 'In two or three days, the villagers are going to break my arms and legs. Otherwise, I'm fine.' Then I explained the truth of the matter to the foujdar. That very day, Foujdar Dangat took three or four constables and went to the village. He called everyone to the paaraa and warned them: 'If Eknath is attacked in any way, I will arrest the entire village.' The village was shocked. No one said a word and the threat to the Mang settlement lifted.

When I got to the village, some good news awaited me. Gaya had given birth to our second child. This time too, she had been working right up to the time of delivery. Aai was dead, Baba had stopped begging, and so there was nothing for it but for Gaya to work. Our first child was two years old. Gaya's parents and sister had gone to the Konkan to earn their living so none of them was on hand to help. In the settlement, only my cousin's wife, Kalabai, was there to support her. On the day she delivered, Gaya had been working in someone's field all day. At around five, her labour began and at around ten or ten-thirty that night, the child was born. I returned home on the second or third day after that and that was when I found out about my son.

The nurse came from the government clinic to record the birth and the baby's name. Gaya had a name in mind. 'Yuvraj. Write his name as Yuvraj.' I said, 'Yuvraj? That's like having not a grain in the house and calling yourself royalty. Milind is his name.' That was the name we decided upon. There was no naming ceremony, no celebrations. At that time I had a great respect for Milind College, which had been set up by Dr Ambedkar. It was, then, a centre for the Dalit movement. Ten thousand young Dalits from Marathwada were studying in the college at the time. They would come with their bedding rolls to the college. The form cost one rupee. As soon as you filled out the form, you got a scholarship of thirty-five rupees. This single college brought thousands of backward Dalit families on to the road to a life of self-respect. The atmosphere there brought the winds of change blowing in our direction. That was why I wanted to name my son Milind.

I was also reading Buddhist literature at the time. The

Tripitaka—literally 'three baskets'—is held to be one of the central texts of Buddhism. Besides this, there is also the *Milindapanha*, or *The Questions of Milinda* (King Menander of Bactria) that were answered by the sage Nagasena. It is said to have been written around four hundred or five hundred years after Gautam Buddha. It is a discussion of the Dhamma, the questions that Milinda has and the answers offered by Nagasena. Was that why Dr Ambedkar had named the college Milinda, so that young Dalits might come there and work out philosophical questions about their lives? I cannot say. But I was reading the *Milindapanha* at this time and it was also perhaps in this context that I named my son Milind.

*

I was born to Mang parents and so I got stuck with their caste. Some people are proud of their caste status. I was not one of them. I had all but abandoned my caste; 'all but' means it still existed on paper. But it was because of this paper that I got a scholarship from the college. Beyond that, I had no pride in my caste.

On the contrary, in the movement, young men from different castes would get together to discuss ways to break the caste system. This process had two parts. We young men would come together and talk about the specificities of our caste situation and bond over the pain we had endured. There, I represented the Mangs in an attempt to forge some unity among us. On the other hand, I wanted to wash away the vestiges of caste from my behaviour, from my life. My relations had cast me out already. Now I wanted to remove the marks of caste from my home as well. My father bore the marks of his low caste on his head in the form of the clump of hair. The clump of hair a Potraj wore was supposed to signify the ornaments of Mari-Aai. When my father begged for a living as a Potraj, he would often be called to a village. This was because Mari-Aai would possess him. When the goddess descended into him, he would begin to spin. His face would be smeared with turmeric and koonkoo and shendur. Whoever had a question would put a lime into Baba's hands. He would rip this with his teeth, shouting Ha-ha-haa. Then a baby chicken would be put into his hands. Baba would take that live chicken's head between his teeth and with a single jerk of his head, he would decapitate it. A fountain of blood would spurt from it. Baba's mouth would fill with blood. I wanted him to stop doing all this. I wanted to rid our home of this Potraj business once and for all.

Once, I was home for the holidays. I had to get some money together and go back to college. That was how it was with me in those days. One day, Gaya and I had woven some ropes. We had to take them to the bazaar at Kuppa to sell them. When I got to the market, a crowd would gather around me, for they recognized me as an activist and a worker in the movement. That meant I could not sit in the market to sell the ropes. Baba and Gaya would sit to sell the ropes. Once they were sold, we would return home with the money. That was how we spent those days. I sent Gaya ahead and told her to cook some meat.

Baba was walking in front of me in the market. From where I was, I could see his clump of hair. It began to bother me. I said: 'Baba, cut your hair.' Baba was startled. 'What now?' he asked. I knew that he was not going to agree easily to cut this hair, which he had maintained for so many years as a sign of Mari-Aai's blessings. So I said again. 'Baba, we are managing somehow with the work that we do. You don't even go to beg any more. Then why keep your hair like that?'

Baba stopped to stare at me. When I was in the fifth standard, I had thrown a tantrum demanding that Baba get me a compass box. Then, Baba had taken a loan of ten rupees. Each week he had agreed to pay a rupee in interest and only then could my poor father buy me a compass box. Now I was throwing another tantrum. And Baba was looking at me in the same way.

Baba had a ready tongue with abuse. He would curse me, both in anger and out of love. Baba took his hair in his hand and said, 'Cut my hair? Go on then, motherfucker, you cut it.'

Since he had agreed I took him immediately to Eknath Warik, a barber who sat with his implements in the bazaar. People would sit with their heads bowed in front of him. When he was shaving you, he would rub the foam off the edge of the blade on to the base of his thumb. That meant his hands were always flecked with hair and foam. I sat Baba down in front of Eknath and said, 'Cut off that clump.' He was stunned. He said, 'Aarra, his hair is Mari-Aai's tree. *This* you want me to cut? Nothing will happen to you but the sin will be mine.'

I said, 'Aaho, I'll cut the clumps of hair. Will you do the roots? If anything happens, I take it upon myself. I promise nothing will happen to you.'

Warik agreed. Baba sat down. I took one strand of his hair in my hand and shouted, 'Hey Mai Mari Aai, if anyone is to shit or to vomit, let it be me. If I am cutting a tree that belongs to you, then let the punishment be mine.'

And so saying, I plied the scissors. Warik took care of the rest of the hair. Baba's head was shaved bald. For all his life he had walked around with the weight of that hair. Perhaps he felt lighter now. One of my aunts, Lakshmibai, had come to the market that day. I sent her and Baba ahead. I was walking behind them. I had to prepare mentally for what was coming.

As I expected, Lakshmibai was enlightening Baba about what had just happened. On the way, there was a farm by the name of Savaashi. That was where I heard what she was saying, 'What have you done, cutting down the trees of Mari-Aai that grew on your head. You have spawned a devil.' Listening to Lakshmibai brought Mari-Aai down into Baba's body. He began to tremble and shake even as he walked along. I set them on the road to home and went to my cousin Hari's liquor still. I got a good bottle of *pehli dhaar*, the first distillation. When I got home, Baba was still spinning. I took a cup with a broken handle, filled it with alcohol and said to Baba: 'Come on, Mari-Aai, come on. This is the first distillation.' Baba scoffed it in a single gulp. I filled the cup a second time. By this time Mari-Aai seemed to be missing in action. Baba put the cup to his lips a second time. He said, 'What possession! These beliefs ruined my life. Mari-Aai even broke my teeth. For the sake of my stomach, I would dance for her, but the cursed one never gave me one good day in return.' Baba smiled. His front teeth were missing. Killing all those baby chickens had ruined his teeth. That night Baba abused Mari-Aai to his heart's content. In the devhaarya, the shrine at home, we had some tin images. He said: 'Throw that stuff out of the house.' That was what I wanted. I wrapped the images in a cloth and put them into the river. The last remnants of Baba's Potraj days floated away. Every sign of being a Mang had been erased from the house.

5

To an observer, the state of a man who rejects caste must seem like that of an ant. Imagine an ant that has found a scrap of food and is carrying it back to its anthill with much effort. Now some vicious little boy catches the ant in a pair of pincers. An antlion has carved out a slope in the sand at the side of the road and now waits, hidden at the bottom of the slope, for its prey. The boy drops the ant right into the middle of this path. The ant tries its best to work its way up the slope. But its struggles make the sand come down faster and faster. It is engulfed. Then the antlion comes along slowly and kills the ant. Only once in a while does an ant escape and make its way into the world.

Even if one rejects caste, does caste reject one? Its traditions, its rituals and customs are all around us. The roots of these strangulating traditions lie in poverty. The misery of India's people forces them back into the clutches of caste. The young who study, who come into contact with new ways of thinking, who incorporate this knowledge and these theories into their lives, find that the same old systems are in place around them, the same relationships are maintained. These circumstances play the role of the vicious little boy with his pincers.

We all need an identity and a sense of belonging to a community; hence we maintain a network of relationships. Relationships are all well and good, but why anyone should take pride in caste was a question that puzzled me. I could understand the upper castes taking pride in their caste. Of course, this pride hurt them too but at least they could squeeze some advantage out of the lower castes. But I found it difficult to understand when Mangs, Mahars and Pardhis* took pride in their caste and made much of it. That means whenever something related to caste is mentioned, I find an anger rising in me. I have often made fun of the traditions and rituals of caste. It is the butt of my jokes and this has probably upset some of my caste brothers. I can think of plenty of occasions on which I have had fights with both my caste brothers and those of other castes over the subject. These attitudes began to take root in my college days.

We now had two children. Our family was growing, a creeper climbing up its trellis. We lived on Gaya's physical labour and my scholarship money. Her pregnancies had weakened Gaya. Milind was always crying. Gaya had no milk. We had no money to get her additional food to eat. Milind would fall ill often. One day, Gaya's maternal aunt Lakshubai came to visit. She said, 'Have you performed a Satvaai pooja for him?' In rural areas, there is a tradition that one must perform a Satvaai pooja in the first five years of a child's life. I did not allow any such thing to happen in the house. Lakshubai and Gaya got the Satvaai done on the quiet. Lakshubai took Gaya and Milind to the Satvaai rock of Veshivar. Poor naïve Lakshubai and Gaya felt that some deity had put a curse on Milind.

Veshivar was one of the many asura deities of the Untouchables, always to be found on the border of the village. He was a deity believed to be easy to anger and so people had to propitiate him often. If anyone fell ill, it was held to be the demon god's anger, so went the superstition.

In front of the rock of Satvaai, five stones had to be placed and smeared with turmeric and koonkoo. An old

---

*With the Mangs, the Pardhis were also included in the list of criminal tribes created by the British.

woman would place a thali in front of the Satvaai stone and hold a coin on top of this thali. Then the old woman would name all the gods she knew in her head: Mari-Aai, Jaakhaai, Satvaai, Avghadbuva, Mhasoba, Yedoba…and so on. If the coin rolled, it meant that none of the gods thus named had been at work. If the coin got stuck to the plate, then the god who was named at that moment was to blame. When you had done this once or twice, the sweat of one's hands would cause the coin to stick to the plate and the mischief-making god would be named. Then one would have to perform pooja and fast to propitiate the god. Lakshubai felt this was the problem. Even though Gaya was uneducated, she knew that she was not lactating properly and her son was crying out of hunger and falling ill because of it. But she was helpless too.

I heard about this. I lost my temper. There was no point getting angry at Gaya. Actually, I was angry at myself. In a rage, I went to that Satvaai stone. I said, 'If you really exist, come and get me. What has my son done to you? Why trouble him?' It was night. No one was around. I uprooted the rock of Satvaai and threw it in the river. And since then there has been no Satvaai in Dukdegaon.

After cutting off Baba's dreadlocks, I wanted to cut off those of other Potraj too. Every Mang household had a Potraj. Mahars had also had this tradition but they had already begun to stop begging long ago. Vitthal Potraj in Bhogalwadi was the Potraj guru of the area. He was quite old but still shrewd. He knew many of their songs. His son accompanied him on the halgi. After I had got my father's hair cut, he began to incite people against me: 'He must be the son of a Mahar. He's doing what the Mahars do.' We would have regular fights about this. One day, he came to the village to beg. I did not want him to be begging or doing Potrajki. I said: 'Listen, Kaka, you're not to beg here. If you want, I'll give you jowar too, but you're not to beg.' The old man abused me roundly. I bore the abuse quietly. But this began a tradition. If he came to the village and I was there, we would begin to fight. I took a lot of his bad words and I must say there were times when I answered him in kind too but I did not let him beg in my village. Finally in 1983, at a public function, I myself cut off his hair.

Cutting the hair of Potraj had become my number one occupation.

Dukdegaon itself had ten or twelve Mang families and a Potraj in each. I remember an incident that happened around this time. In the summer, some of the people of the Mang settlement would get together for a chat in the shade of a neem tree. Bhaguji was one of them. He still had his dreadlocks. I said to him: 'Friend, let's cut your hair today.' He replied, 'Don't say whatever comes into your head. What do you mean, cut my hair?' I said, 'Come over here, let's arrange some sweets and feed everyone.' No one was doing anything in particular. We gathered four- and eight-anna coins from here and there to make a sweet dish. If you heat some jaggery with jowar, that's the poor man's sheera. Everyone thought this a great idea. And in the spirit of things, Bhaguji let his hair be cut. But in a couple of years, he had grown it back. So be it. But during that time I had motivated at least ten or twelve of them to have their hair cut.

My father had been a Potraj; now he was a human being again. I wanted everyone else to enjoy this status. Later, I would mount a campaign against the whole system of Potrajki. More of that later.

At that point in time, I did not know what direction my life was going to take. But one day I suddenly found a way forward.

I had just given the first year MA examination. I was still

at the hostel. One of our seniors, R.S. Khandagle, had come to the hostel. I hadn't met him in a long time. We greeted each other with 'Jai Bhim'. I asked, 'What are you doing now?' He said he was studying at Ahmednagar. 'What are you studying?' I asked. He said, 'MSW.' I had never heard of such a degree before. 'What is this MSW?' I asked. 'Master in Social Welfare,' he said. 'Once you do this course, you can become a social worker. You get good jobs as well.'

Arre wah! My eyes lit up. A social worker would be able to work for the betterment of society and he would have the right to do so. And with the panache of a sahib too. I asked Khandagle, 'What does one have to do to get in?' Khandagle said, 'Nothing special. You have to apply. Then you get called. There's a written test too. And an interview. You're already a leader, you give speeches. I don't think there'll be a problem in you getting in.'

That was it. I had been given wings. I was going to become a social welfare officer. I would forward files of problematic cases from our community. I would solve problems, left, right and centre. My shoes would click-click-click as I walked into the office. I would issue suspension orders against corrupt officers. One signature of mine and Dalits would have the projects and industries they needed to get out of poverty...I was already building castles in the air. I had taken the address of the college from Khandagle. Powered by those dreams, I sent in an application. I was called for an interview. By then the results of the first year of MA were out; I had got a first class. But now I wanted to do an MSW. I borrowed some money from a friend and went to Ahmednagar.

*

CSRD. Centre for Studies in Rural Development. Baap re! Such a big English name. What a posh building! All the college buildings I had studied in before looked decrepit in comparison. My heart sank. As it is I was hungry and now my stomach plummeted into my shoes at the atmosphere of privilege here. But I took the form anyway and met R.S. Khandagle. With him, there were some seniors. One of them said, 'How will he manage here? Look at the state of his clothes. He'll never make it.' I had already noticed that all the students there came from rich families. Their fathers were leaders, legislators, landowners, Block Development Officers…

Looking at them, I have to say I was a little overawed. I had also heard that there were no scholarships here. While I was waiting to submit my form, some of the other students in the line looked at my state and said, 'Don't even try for this course. Go back to your village. Find something to do there.' This advice acted as a challenge. I was even more determined now to do the course. I gave the interview and sat for the written examination. Then I returned to the village. A few days later, I got a letter informing me that I had been selected.

Now how was I going to get the money to go to Ahmednagar again?

At the door, an old neem tree rustled. I looked at the tree and thought: this neem tree will help in this time of need. It had given my hut a lovely deep shade for many years. Now it would help me in my studies. I decided that I would have to get the money by selling this old tree. I told my cousin what I was thinking for he had half the rights to the tree too. At that time, it was our only property. Together there were four of us cousins. Vitthal and I got together one day and cut down the tree.

Hausabai, the Patil's mother-in-law, was then the sarpanch. I was her opponent in village politics. Hausabai sent a peon of the gram panchayat to my hut. 'This tree is the property of the gram panchayat. Whom did you ask before you cut it down?

The sarpanch has called you to the office. Or she's going to register a case against you.' I said, 'Aara, go on with you. Do what you want. I had a tree growing at my doorstep; I cut it down. Go the police, go to the Commissioner, go wherever you want. I'm not afraid.' The peon was turned right back. The sarpanch did not do anything either. This was another attempt to frighten me.

In a week, we had reduced the tree to timber. We went to the bazaar in Kuppa and sold the logs. I got two hundred rupees and my cousin got two hundred. With that money, I went to Ahmednagar and took admission. The fees were three hundred rupees. Once again, the question of money. I came back to the village, worried. I could not think of any way out. Once again I went to my sister. And once again, I experienced how large-hearted my brother-in-law was; he had a heart as large as a winnow. I told him, 'Daji, I want to do this course but I have a problem with the fees.' He said, 'Why are you worried? Let's see what we can put together.' He began to search in the millet sacks. He had saved money for a rainy day in the form of two-rupee notes and hidden them there. He gathered them all and put together two hundred rupees. Looking at those soiled, crumpled notes, I wanted to weep. They did not cover all my needs but that day those notes were too vast to fit in my pocket. I needed another two hundred rupees. Fifty rupees were left from the money the logs fetched. My cousin gathered two hundred rupees, borrowing from here and there. And that is how I got together the money to do my MSW in Ahmednagar.

The other worry was that I would no longer get a scholarship. This was a question as large as the sky for me. And since I had taken admission late, it was going to be difficult to find a room in the government hostel. Since the only person I knew there was Khandagle, I went to talk to him. He took me to meet his friends. He told them, 'He is a Mang lad and he's very good.' His friends were Dilip Rupavate and Ashok Kalokhe. Rupavate was a Mahar and Kalokhe was a Mang. They said, 'Let's do something for him.' There was a boarding house about a mile away from the MSW college. At that time, there was a Mang by the name of Baburao Bharaskar who was the Minister of Social Welfare. He had set up this boarding house for students from the fifth to the tenth standard. Khandagle, Rupavate and Kalokhe took me to that boarding house. The administrator was M.V. Devchakke; the manager's name was Vaidya. My new friends told them, 'This is a Mang boy. He is in a difficult situation. He did not find a place in the college hostel. If he can at least eat at your hostel, it will be a blessing for him.' Devchakke and Vaidya were good men. They patted me on the back. They were quite proud to see a Mang boy taking such pains to get an education. 'Don't worry,' they said. They told a Maratha man called Patil about me. This fine person bought two stainless steel dabbas for me from the market. My food began to be set aside in these dabbas. The question of food was solved.

But what about the hostel? Up to that point I was still staying in the rooms of Khandagle and other friends in the college. But this could not go on for too long. I had to find some alternative. A Maratha boy called Sahebrao Gavhane lived in the garage where the vehicles of the college were kept. He was a chaprasi in the college. At the same time, he was also doing his MSW. His state and mine were about the same. He was the son of a labourer, as I was. He was married and so was I. He had to work and study at the same time, and that was what I had to do too. We became friends. I asked him to see if I could also be accommodated in the garage. He got permission from the principal. That was the next problem solved. The garage was now referred to as The Poor Boys' Hostel.

With these two basic problems resolved, I could actually start studying.

But it was not going to be possible to do this without a scholarship. I had to pay three hundred rupees as tuition. In order to be able to send a little money home, I needed a stipend of some kind. The Social Welfare Officer was a man called Shitole. I met him and said, 'Sahib, MSW students also need a scholarship.' He looked at my papers and said, 'MSW is a professional course. The rule is that you can get a scholarship up to the MA.' I said, 'Sahib, I agree that this is a professional course. But I haven't done a B.Ed or an M.Ed or an LLB. I've only appeared for the first year of MA (Regular).* How can someone like me get an education?' I don't know what he thought but he said: 'Awad, I see your point. But you will have to come again tomorrow.' At that time, Kakasaheb Rupavate was President of Social Welfare. I met him too. The next day I went to the Social Development Office. Shitole was waiting for me. He saw me and said, 'Arre, Awad, come, come. I took out the Government Resolution and looked at it and saw that you can apply for a scholarship even for the MSW.' I was delighted. 'Sir, please inform the college about this. Or give me a letter.' He said, 'Arre, I'll phone them right now.' And so he did. That was it. My problem was solved.

When I got back to the college, I told the other boys of all that I had done. There was a boy called Sarwal from the Bhangi community. He was a body builder. All the Dalit students

---

*B.Ed is a Bachelor of Education; M.Ed is Masters of Education. LLB or Bachelor of Laws is the degree with which one qualifies to be a lawyer. MA (Regular) means he took classes as opposed to reading for his degree by correspondence.

gathered around me. Sarwal lifted me up on his shoulders. He said, 'This is our leader. He has made the impossible happen.' All the boys were delighted. They paraded me on the verandah of the college, shouting, 'Leader, leader.'

At the beginning of the course, there was a debate in class. The tradition there was to shape the ideas of the students on the social issues of the day through the medium of discussion and debate. The topic of the debate was the Renaming Movement. This was a subject close to my heart. There must have been at least a hundred and fifty students in the first and second year of the MSW at the college but not one of them wanted to argue for the change in name. When they spoke among themselves, the Dalit boys were in favour of the change of name but they lacked the courage to say this in public. I stood up in class. In my usual style, I began to talk about how important it was to name the university after Babasaheb Ambedkar. My voice began to rise. The Dalit boys began to murmur and mutter. 'Marathwada pethlela, Marathwada pethlela' (Marathwada on fire). The upper-caste boys were also trying to get a word in. But I was not aware of any of this. All of them opposing the change in name and I should sit silent? That wasn't going to happen. Finally, everyone fell silent. Only my voice could be heard in the classroom. I spoke with conviction and passion. After this happened, the boys began to call me 'Pethlela Marathwada'.

Professor A.R. Munshi, Professor Simon, Professor Vasave were all very pleased with me. They praised me to the Director of the institute, Dr Halbe, who was also a Dalit. When he heard that I was the only person in the entire college who had defended the idea of the name change, he must have felt something about me. The next day, a peon came with a message that I was wanted in the Director's cabin. I had no idea that news of the debate had reached his ears. I was a little hesitant when I entered his cabin. Halbe praised me highly. He told me to go to the accountant. There I received a five-hundred-rupee advance on my stipend. I could have danced for joy. All that money at one time. I was the king of the world that day. I took the first bus out of the ST stand and went to the village. I went and returned all the money I had borrowed. I also took some sweets for the children. My MSW Express had shot out of the station and was on its way.

*

My speaking out for the change in name did not just affect the Dalit students; the upper-caste students also began to respect me. They began to see the point of the Dalit arguments. Uttam Pawar was one of the Maratha students. He came from a wealthy family. After the debate, he came up to me. He said, 'I want to stay with you.' I was surprised. How could a boy from a rich family live with me and Gavhane in a garage? But Pawar was as good as his word; he brought his stuff to our room. We pushed the two cots together and the three of us began to live together. We would do so for those two college years. Pawar did not let me spend for things like oil and soap during those years. He would account for all my necessities in the way a blood brother would have. During the Diwali vacations of my first year of the MSW, Uttam bought new clothes for himself. But he also bought me a shirt and a pair of trousers. This was the first time in my life that I had put on crisp new clothes.

Boys like Chhabu Bansode, Dilip Rupavate, B.K. Brahmane also helped me greatly. They were the ones who named me 'Pethlela Marathwada'. Whenever they were going out for tea, they always invited me. But when we were drinking tea, were I to put my hand into my pocket, they would say, 'Leave it, Marathwada, just keep burning. We'll pay for the tea.'

The college staff would also help. One of the staff members was a man named Kamble. He had a sweet-lime orchard of nearly five hundred trees. He gave me the job of digging a ditch around each tree. I would do such work on the weekends when the college was closed.

The professors also were fond of me. I was taking part in movements aimed at bringing about social change. The teachers at the college supported this. The rest of the students were of a different class altogether. They were there to find secure jobs and settle down. I was also there to improve my economic condition but my basic nature did not allow me to be comfortable with that. When I heard that a morcha was going out, I'd simply bunk class and run there. Field work and lectures were compulsory for everyone. I was the only one who was allowed to take off for morchas and protests. There was a Maratha lecturer called Pansare to whom the other boys complained. Pansare had a rough tongue. He said to the complainers, 'Aara, he's going on protest marches, working for society. What are you doing? Get away with you and mind your own business.' That certainly cooled them down.

To go into every village and every settlement to do social work, to collect in disciplined fashion all that was needed for this work whether it was equipment or information, to analyze the information statistically and then to present it graphically, these were the skills we were taught at the MSW course. The lectures were in English. I had never been afraid of English. I enjoyed social work, I knew the basic problems at the heart of social issues, and so things didn't go over my head. My own experiences were being taught here, only they were described with greater rigour and method. As part of the course, the students also had to undertake a research project. Most students chose subjects like the district's irrigation system or the administration of Shrirampur's workshops. I chose 'The

Social and Economic Conditions of the Mang Garudis' as my topic. Professor Pansare was my research guide. The Mang Garudis were a sub-caste of the Mangs. The Mangs were a caste of low status. I wanted to see how those who were even lower in status than my community lived.

How did this sub-caste come into existence? The British government declared the Mangs a criminal tribe. Every Mang is a thief, or so the law declared. This meant that the Mangs had to present themselves to the police thrice a day. Some Mangs began to hide their caste. They began to declare themselves as Mang Garudis to avoid these trips to the police station. But they were still poor and they still had to steal to fill their bellies. Eventually, the Mangs' condition slowly improved but the Mang Garudis continued to steal.

There was a settlement of Mang Garudis near Beed at Barshi Naka. For my project, I needed to interview the heads of twenty-five Mang Garudi families. I started visiting that settlement. The settlement also had its own chieftain. He had two wives who did all the work. The man contented himself with winding the turban of the headman over his head and striding about the village like a dandy. I met him and told him the subject of my study. He said, 'Aara, what study is this? We manage to get along. No one even does khaavdi now. What will you study about us?' Khaavdi is the word for robbery. He must have thought I would report this to the police. But I slowly gained his trust. How many people have land? How many have a livelihood? How do they marry? Do they give dowry? These were the questions that I asked as I walked around. It was very difficult to manage even those twenty-five interviews. Petty theft was a way of life with the Mang Garudis. The women stole, the men worked. But what was this theft really? When feeding cattle, to conceal a couple of heads of jowar for one's own use; to sell some cotton on the quiet; to pick a pocket or two. The children did go to school but no one had got to senior school. Scabies-infested boys were to be seen all over the settlement.

Few people had rainfed land. Buffaloes and dogs were their only wealth. There was a tradition of the boy paying a bride price for the girl at the time of marriage in the form of a radio, a watch or grain. The girl's father would get all these gifts. Alcohol was in common use. Their condition was the same as that of the Mangs; and yet they would not maintain any relations with Mangs. They were my people—and yet they held themselves to be different. This was a truth about Indian society that I learned during this exercise.

6

I was nearing the end of the MSW course and the question, 'What next?' began to bother me. I wanted to study a great deal. I had a year of the MA to complete as well. I wanted a nice long line of degrees after my name just as Dr Ambedkar had. I thought I should study the law but I also knew that it was important for me to get a job. Baba had had a stroke that had left him paralyzed. Gaya had given birth to Rekha, our third and last child. The eldest girl was in school. One of the walls of the house had been ruined by the rain. I was torn between concern for my family and the desire to further my career.

When I went home, Gaya would say, 'All your friends have stopped studying, how long are you going to continue?' She was right. Of all my acquaintances, I was the only idiot who was still studying. Gaya had to deal with an ill father-in-law and three little children on her own. She was the real head of the family. At that time, the daughters of the poor were never safe. Only Gaya can tell you how she managed to survive without me. It was all the same to her whether she had my support or not. It was difficult to explain things to her. 'I do not want to live the way my parents lived. Wait and watch, our children will never have to live like beggars.' This much I would say to her each time. She could not even weep in front of me. I would arrive like a guest and then go away again. That was probably why she avoided crying or bewailing her fate in front of me. She simply said yes, yes, to whatever I said.

At one time, little Milind's leg was covered with scabies. He would weep as if the skies had burst. Gaya had no money to take him to the doctor. She would sit and weep with him.

It was in tears and in deprivation that my three children grew up. Gaya was both father and mother to them; and Phule and Ambedkar became my mother and father. The words from their books would fill me with restlessness. So deeply was I immersed in conversation with them that I could not hear the cries of my family.

But had I paid attention to their pain then, I would not have been able to reach where I have today. It is only by thinking that a man develops sensitivity; but in one sense, because of my thinking, I turned hard-hearted with my family.

At the end of the MSW, the stipend would also end. I began to worry about getting a job. My experience has taught me that however worried you are, it is important to appear fearless. The universe has something lined up somewhere. You have to pay attention to what's going on; then you will find the correct path. Life had such a path ready for me.

*

Two of my college friends, Mirikar and Bhange, had gone to work with Vidhayak Sansad in Thane District for their Block Placement exercise. This organization worked to organize the Adivasis and to fight with them for their rights. Vivek and Vidyullata Pandit had only just founded the organization and begun work. They were organizing sports for the children, running libraries for them and so on. But in reality they wanted to work on the issue of bonded labour. Their main intention was to bring the Adivasis together and unite them and make them aware of their rights. As part of their Block Placement activities, Mirikar and Bhange had organized children's running races and the like but when Vivek Pandit suggested the issue of bonded labour to them, they said it was not their focus. They also suggested my name as the right person to be part of a movement, to get people organized and aware of their rights.

The students who had completed their Block Placements came together to share their experiences. Mirikar and Bhange explained what Vidhayak Sansad sought to do and said that I would fit in well there. The teachers were also seized of the idea. Professor Munshi and Professor Halbe talked to Vivek Pandit about me. It was agreed that I would go to Dahisar to meet him. My friends loaned me some money. I was going to get the kind of work I wanted to do and I was going to be paid for it. I wanted to go back to the village to see my children but I knew that if I did, I would get stuck there. So I left for Dahisar from college.

I had only come to Mumbai once, around the time of my matric. I was a construction worker in Bhiwandi. I only knew that area, between Kalyan and Bhiwandi. But I had friends, Uttam Dawre and Bhagwan Dawre, who lived in the Damunagar slums in Kandivali. I stayed with them for a day. The next day, Uttam came with me. He had been my friend since the time we were in school together.

Vivek and Vidyullata Pandit were staying at the Sane Guruji Colony, Malad in a small room. They were a very young couple, about my age. At that time, they were both working with the Community Aid & Sponsorship Programme (CASP). It was easy to tell from their clothes and their conversation that they were socialists. They had also been part of the Rashtra Seva Dal.* Both of them were fair-skinned Brahmins. They used words like 'revolution' and 'ideology' easily and fluently. I was dark in colour, I spoke with the Marathwada accent. They had a picture of Gandhiji up on a wall. I owed much of my intellectual development to the Dalit Panthers. I had a deep suspicion of the whole sentimental society, about Brahmins

---

*The Rashtra Seva Dal was founded in 1941 by various socialist leaders like S.M. Joshi and N.G. Goray and litterateurs such as Sane Guruji.

too. Gandhiji's behaviour towards Dr Ambedkar at the Round Table Conference, and the Poona Pact were things I held against him.* But I still liked this couple for what they said resonated with me. I could feel the concern with which they addressed issues. They were talking about the slavery of the Adivasis, about the issues they faced. They called me Eknath-bhau (Brother Eknath) and I responded with Vivek-bhau (Brother Vivek) and Vidyut-tai (Elder sister Vidyut).

They had started social work in Dahisar, near Virar. They had met as members of the Rashtra Seva Dal. They had decided that after they got married, they would work in the villages.

At that time, Dahisar was a village. Vivek-bhau's maternal uncle was the pujari of the village temple. Vivek-bhau had spent much time there as a child. That was why they had chosen the area for their field of work. They were running the Jayaprabha Baalwadi, named in the memory of Jayaprakash Narayan's wife, Prabhavati. At first they had thought that the high drop-out rate among Adivasis was the most important problem and so they had started this venture. Then they found out that every Adivasi was in debt and this debt kept them in slavery. It was not difficult to break the bonds of this slavery. In that area, the Adivasis worked for the Brahmins and the Agris as bonded labour. This couple began to fight for the rights of the bonded labourers and so had incurred the animosity of the land-owning class. Their relatives had disowned them. This area had a bonded-labour system that was specific to it.

In order to pay off their loans, the Adivasis had to work

---

*After the 'Depressed Classes' were given a separate electorate in the Poona Pact of 1932, Gandhiji went on an indefinite fast to make sure this did not happen. In Chapter 13, Awad explains his beliefs about how this affected the lives of the Dalits.

day and night in the fields of their masters. And how much were these loans? Some owed five hundred rupees, some owed a thousand. The largest sum owed was three thousand rupees. Most of this money had been borrowed for weddings. People who borrowed money to marry and ended up slaves were called lagingadi. The Adivasi boys were made to look after the buffaloes. They got one meal a day and two sets of clothes a year for this. When the boys were old enough to plough, their masters would fix their marriages. The wedding basta (box) would be filled by the master. They would also spend on the food. And then in order to pay off the money so spent, both husband and wife would have to labour for him. Some of the masters even demanded use of the woman. Each year, the men would get two banians, and two loincloths. Each month they would get twenty kilos of rice. The workers were illiterate. They had no idea of how to keep accounts. This meant that they never paid off the wedding debt. And so any children they had would also end up working for the master. There were many Adivasis who were paying off their parents' wedding debts.

Thirty years had passed since India had gained independence but the Adivasis were still in bonded labour. A bonded labourer is one who is coerced either by force of economic and social circumstances to become someone else's servant. In 1979, the Indian government had passed a law making bonded labour illegal. It was decided that the focus of my work should be to try and free the Adivasi from bonded labour, with the help of this law.

It was not easy. The Adivasi had grown used to the idea of slavery. They did not seem to realize that they were being treated unjustly. Whenever Vivek-bhau and Vidyut-tai had tried to bring up the subject of their status as bonded labour, they had been met with resistance and the Adivasis had begun to keep them at a distance. It was decided that my responsibility would be to make the Adivasis aware of their rights.

There was an international aid agency called Oxfam which had a fellowship programme. I was to get six hundred rupees each month in order to fight bonded labour. I would work from their office, gather information on the systems of bonded labour in the areas around. I was to begin by starting balwadis (crèches) and then slowly expand operations into building awareness and making the Adivasis question the validity and logic of the system. I would have to conceal my real reason for being there, at least at the beginning.

All this seemed like a challenge to me. The caste system was a form of slavery. According to me, the Adivasis had to stop doing this forced labour in the same way that the Mahars had stopped doing Maharki.

I had stopped my own family from doing Mangki. Babasaheb's philosophy had ignited a spark within us. Phule-Ambedkar thought had not yet reached the Adivasis. Working with people whose condition was worse than the one from which I had arisen appealed to me. Vivek-bhau gave me an advance of two hundred rupees. I took that and left.

Uttam was with me. We went to the station. From the footpath there, we bought a white sadra and a pair of black trousers. When I left college, I did not have very much luggage: just some books and the clothes on my body. I bought some other necessities and was now ready to take on whatever work I had to.

The office of the Vidhayak Sansad was in Dahisar Khardi. It wasn't so much an office as a shed. There, the organization was breeding foreign pigs. Some books had been got together and a small library had been created. Shanvarbhau, an Adivasi, was the caretaker of the office. Now I too took up residence here with him. I had no sheets and no mattress with me.

The organization however had a tarpaulin and that became my bedding. There was fodder for the pigs. I would spread some of that on the ground and cover it with the tarpaulin and upon this mattress I would lie and read books from the library. The snorting of pigs kept me company all night. In my head worries about my family would coexist with the question of bonded labour. I sent a postcard home: 'I am at Dahisar. I have a job; but don't expect money from me just yet.' Once I dropped the card in the post-box, I was free to think about bonded labour.

Two of the workers of the Rashtra Seva Dal, Gautam and Prabha, would come there. Then Gautam stopped coming but Prabha continued. She would run the balwadi and teach the children songs and their numbers and letters. We would go—sometimes all three of us, sometimes Prabha and Gautam, or sometimes I alone—into the fields around us. We would introduce ourselves to people and try to get to know them. We would try and talk to the Adivasis but to no avail. If we started talking about slavery or bonded labour, people would put us off.

Right next to the office was a settlement. There were some Neo-Buddhist families there. I always mentioned Ambedkar and Phule in all that I said. This probably made them feel I was one of them. These families had not been of any help to Vivek-bhau; but they softened a little towards me.

There were also some Mangs in that area. There are no Mangs in the Konkan coast. There were Mangelas, who had begun to catch and dry fish to sell in the markets. Therefore they had a new identity, that of the Mangela, in place of the old basic identity of the Mang. I also increased my interactions with these people. The Mangs would not drink water from the homes of Mahars; nor would the Mahars eat at the homes of Adivasis. I began to talk to them about Babasaheb's ideas about caste and they began to mix with each other a little more. I believed that this relationship would be useful to me when I dealt with the touchier problem of bonded labour. I did not tell anyone my own caste. I was just a man who brought people together for some important conversations.

The Mahars were skilled bamboo basket-makers and so a programme was started to get them making these baskets and so earn a living. But it was still difficult to get a foot in the door with the Adivasis. The Konkana, the Warli and the Kathkari are by nature not very communicative. Those among them who are in bonded labour are even more withdrawn.

Vivek-bhau and Vidyut-tai would come every weekend. Vidyut-tai expected quick results and she kept asking me for reports. My nature would not allow me to be bossed around by anyone and so we began to have arguments. Then Vivek-bhau told her, 'Don't supervise his work. Leave that department to me.' Vivek-bhau and I would take long walks and talk about these things. His relatives too had bonded labourers working for them. He would call these relatives, 'badmaash'.

*

Around this time, Vivek-bhau dispatched me to Narayangaon, near Junnar. I loaded up a pair of Saanen* goats. We called the nanny-goat the poor man's cow. It was because of the goat that the Adivasi's economic condition has improved marginally. It was decided that we should try and breed the male goat with a nanny goat from local stock, a goat with a good milk supply to improve the local gene pool. But the male goat just would not. He was never ready to breed. Perhaps the sea air did not agree with him. One day he had a stroke.

The whole project ended there. I was in charge of the

---

*This breed originates in the Saanen Valley of Switzerland.

operation. I had to weigh these goats, give them injections and the like. All this took a lot of my time.

There were also twenty piglets of the Landrace and Yorkshire breeds. One sow could give birth to twenty piglets. All night long, the sows would be giving birth under the office. They had to be attended to as well. There was no independent shed for the birthing. Since all the pigs were in one place, there would be fights among them. They would bite each other. These wounds would soon get infected and we had to sit and remove the maggots. I spent the first three months doing these chores.

One day, I took a thousand rupees from Vivek-bhau and came to the village. I explained my job to Baba and to Gaya. But Baba was in no position to understand what I was saying. He was now very weak. He had crossed the border where he understood the difference between happiness and sorrow. Gaya had sent our eldest daughter to live with my in-laws. She was now going to school there. She was managing with Milind and Rekha at home. I do not remember whether I managed to reassure her or not but when I returned to Dahisar, I knew what was going on at home. I also returned all the money we had borrowed. This took a huge burden off my shoulders.

*

I began to work now with even greater discretion. Even Vivek-bhau's name was enough to raise opposition in the area. The Agris and Vaitis are people of a difficult disposition. Their tongues are rough, their behaviour matches their speech. They were our enemies. I had to conceal my identity even further. I had my white shirt and black trousers; now I added a belt to this. I had already figured out who was the thorn in the bouquet. There was an Agri sarpanch called Dattu Patil. He had a tea stall at Vaitarna Railway Station. I had the feeling that it might be possible to make some headway with the community through this man.

So one day, I tucked my shirt into my trousers and smarted up as much as I could and went there. He did not know me. I stood where I was sure he could see me, reading the newspapers. As expected, he greeted me. I merely smiled back. He said, 'So sahib, how come you're in these parts?' Raising my paper even higher in front of my face, I said: 'I'm here as a field officer. We're going to set up some balwadis in this area.' He immediately poured me a cup of tea. 'Come on, have some tea,' he said.

Now I had him. I told him we would need some educated young women to run the crèches. He suggested his daughter's name. I agreed immediately. I said, 'We are going to start seven or eight of these. If you know any other educated girls, let me know.' This was exactly the kind of suggestion he wanted. 'I'll be back tomorrow,' I said and left. The next day, Dattu Patil even showed me some places where the crèches could be run. I reported all this to Vivek-bhau. He gave me the green signal. This was an attempt to get some support at the local level.

I even got Dattu Patil to inaugurate a couple of the balwadis. Seven or eight bright young girls were hired for the balwadis. We organized a training camp for these girls and some Adivasi girls as well. Vivek-bhau and Vidyut-tai came down and spoke on topics like why the poor with all their skills remain poor and why the rich remain rich, what independence really means and other subjects. The young women who had come to work in the balwadis began to take part in these discussions with enthusiasm. They began to discuss how a rich man had tied up a lagingadi Adivasi's buffalo to his own door post. They began to see that what was happening around them was wrong and unjust. They began to enjoy singing the songs about human rights that we taught them. Whatever else, we had been outsiders who had come to their area. When these young women began to see our point of view, I knew that we had begun establishing our base in the area. This was our entry point into their lives.

Around that time, we organized a flag-hoisting ceremony on 26 January. We invited the Patil of the village too. At this meeting Vivek-bhau sang a song. '*Karzaapoti maalkaancha zulum sahan karu naka*' (Do not endure the crimes of your masters because of your debt). This enraged the Patils. They began to feel even more strongly that we were instigating the Adivasis. As a result, Vivek-bhau and Vidyut-tai were attacked.

One day, on their way from Vaitarna Station, a bunch of young men surrounded them. Vishaya Bhave, a social worker, was also with them. All three of them began to be beaten up. Someone sent word to me through one of the balwadi women. I ran there. The balwadi women also came with me. There were five or ten boys who were beating Vivek-bhau and Vidyut-tai, warning them to leave the village. There was a crowd of idle onlookers too. I waded into the fray.

At the time, Vidyut-tai was pregnant with her first child. So I first pushed her into a ditch. Then I turned to protect Vivek-bhau and Vishaya-tai. I placed my body in between theirs and the boys. When they tried to attack me, the women of the balwadi came forward. They said, 'This is the sahib of our balwadis. You are not to lay a hand on him. Your fight is with Vivek-bhau. Get away from him.' These women were their relatives and so they obeyed. The women bandaged Vivek-bhau and Vidyut-tai. But after this incident Vivek-bhau was made the subject of a boycott. He had been staying at his uncle's house; his uncle now put Vivek-bhau's stuff outside the door.

Even if we did have a local base, the Adivasis still kept their distance. So I tried another trick. I was now famous as the sahib of the balwadis. I thought I might use this to make

some headway. I began to intensify my friendship with the
Patils. There was a Brahmin called Bachchu Patil. I started
going to his house frequently. He had eight or ten bonded
labourers working for him. Since I was often at the master's
house, I grew to know them as well. I made contact with them
and quietly I would tell them, 'You are being made slaves;
this is unjust.' They would listen but not respond. I did not
have enough information about their situation. None of them
dared make so much as a squeak of protest.

Then it was the time of Gauri–Ganpati. The Adivasis
were supposed to go and dance at the festival. Bachchu Patil's
bonded slaves had also gone there. I was sitting with the Patils,
drinking tea. Just to provoke him, I said to the Patil, 'So Patil,
you have to wash your own buffalo today? It seems you've
fed it yourself too. None of the servants seem to be around.'
He replied, 'They must have all gone to dance. The bastards
sleep with their mothers. Let them come back. See how I
geld them.' I said to the Patil, 'They won't learn unless you
geld them.' After I'd thrown oil into the flames, I left. In an
hour or so Balya Chendya Kirkira, one of the Patil's bonded
labourers, arrived. When they dance for Gauri–Ganpati, the
Adivasis drink. Balya was also drunk. He was a strong and
powerfully built young man. I knew him well. As soon as
he saw Balya, the Patil decided to show him who was boss.

'Where had you gone?' he demanded.

'To dance,' Balya said.

The Patil slapped Balya across the face. This I was told by the
other workers. I had expected something like this to happen.

I left the village and went and waited at a tea stall. I expected
Balya to find out that I had been talking to the Patil and for
him to get angry and come to talk to me. In anticipation of
the argument, I lit a cigarette. And just then Balya arrived. He
began to abuse me. He said, 'Motherfucker, I got a beating

because of you.' I said, 'I've been saying it again and again. You are slaves. But you want to lick the Patil's feet. If you have the courage, stop working for him.' Balya calmed down a little and said, 'I owe him money.' I said, 'Come with me. I'll free you from his clutches. Or else sit there and play with his shit. Send your wife to warm his bed.' He got angry again and told me to shut up. I knew then that he had finally realized what slavery meant and that he was a slave.

He said, 'Come on, I'll go with you right now.'

I said diplomatically, 'No use just one of you coming. Bring four or five people with you and only then will we be able to get you out of this.' I was promising him freedom from bondage with only my self-assurance to back it up.

In half an hour, he had got together eight or ten other labourers. They were all drunk. Balya had incited them all. I told them: 'Come tomorrow morning. Let this intoxication fade. Don't tell anybody what we plan to do. Tomorrow you will be free from this slavery. You have my word on this.' They were all excited at this reassurance and went home happy.

At that time, two workers of the Rashtra Seva Dal, Pramod and Prabhakar, were at the Vikhroli branch office. I told them what had happened. One of them left to meet Vivek-bhau that very night. The next morning, Vivek-bhau and four other workers arrived. We left on foot, taking the byroads. We walked about 10 or 12 kilometres. Then we caught the train for Vasai. Vivek-bhau had organized some reporters to come down from Mumbai. I took the reporters and the workers and we went to the office of the tahsil. Even we had no clear idea what we were supposed to do to free bonded labourers. Vivek-bhau and I presented the case of these labourers. We wrote applications in their names to the tahsildar. We took their thumb impressions on the applications. We went to the tahsildar. The tahsildar wasn't sure about the rules either.

At that time, Indira Gandhi had just launched her Twenty-Point Programme.* Vivek-bhau showed the tahsildar this document. The tahsildar did not know how he was supposed to go about this.

He accepted the application that we had made and we immediately turned to Balya and the other labourers and announced: 'You are free!'

But they could not believe they were actually *free*. For generations all they had known was debt incurred by marriage, debt that kept them in bondage. It was vital for them to believe that a single application could set them free. This was our experiment. It had become second nature to the Adivasi to do as the master asked, to behave as the master desired. It was impossible for an Adivasi to refuse to do any job demanded of him. The system of bonded labour had roots that ran deep. What we needed to do was to get them to believe that this was only a form of slavery, that it was a system that could be destroyed. It was also important for them to know that there were people as powerful as their masters. And to this end we devised a little trick.

Dr Tamhane, the executive director of the Animal Husbandry department, would sometimes visit Dahisar. Vivek-bhau knew him well. He would come to have a look

---

*Indira Gandhi, then the prime minister, launched her Twenty-Point Programme in 1975. Point 6 was 'Special programmes for rural labour', and Point 11 was 'Justice for Scheduled Castes, Scheduled Tribes, Minorities and Other Backward Castes'. *The Indian Express* of 2 July 1975 quoting from the prime minister's radio broadcast says: 'The 20-point programme included steps to bring down prices of essential commodities, promote austerity in government spending, **crack down on bonded labour** [emphasis mine], liquidate rural indebtedness and make laws for a moratorium on recovery of debt from landless labourers, small farmers and artisans.'

at our goat- and pig-breeding programmes. His home was on the eleventh floor of a skyscraper in Malad. Vivek-bhau told me that since he was such an important officer, it had been decided that he would play the role of the person who was setting the bonded labourers free. As decided, I took four bonded labourers and went to Vivek-bhau's office. We entered the lift of the building in which Dr Tamhane lived. That was the first time those four bonded labourers had been inside a lift. It was also their first experience of being in such a tall building. When the lift reached the eleventh floor, Vivek-bhau showed them how high up we were. They were shocked. They began to feel we were going to meet a really prominent official.

Dr Tamhane was told the cases of the bonded labourers. He listened calmly to everything that was said. Then in the manner of a thespian, he said to them: 'Now you may go home. There is no need for you to go to do that kind of work any longer. Fear nothing.' All four bonded labourers were overwhelmed.

On their way to Malad, they had been subdued. On their way back, they were ecstatic. 'The boss has set us free,' they told all the others in the village.

There were only eight bonded labourers in the Dahisar area. There were more in other areas. We knew that as this idea spread, the atmosphere would heat up. For even if the Adivasis did not know that they were the victims of an unjust system, their masters certainly knew it. Our efforts were going to pose a threat to what they considered their rights. What they got in the village, the benefits of these economic crimes would vanish. So it was a given that there would be attacks on us. But we were not averse to this; on the contrary, we welcomed them for they proved as nothing else would that we were the defenders of the rights of the Adivasi.

And one day, what we hoped for happened. Vivek-bhau

was on his way to the office when three or four thugs set
upon him. I heard Vidyut-tai shouting, 'Eknath-bhau, come
quickly, see they're going to kill Vivek!' There were some
bamboos lying around the office which we had bought for
the basket-weaving enterprise. I picked one up and ran to
the spot. Vivek-bhau was already on the ground; I began
to whirl the bamboo around, laying into those goons. One
of them stabbed me in the ribs but when I began to bleed,
they fled. The wound was not deep but I lost a lot of blood.
Vivek-bhau was also hurt.

*

My life was going along fine or was it? I had finished studying
and got a job immediately. My major responsibility was to work
on an issue that was close to my heart. But in my heart I still
felt: I am an Ambedkarite. This work is happening under the
banner of socialism. How did I reach here? Where am I? Am
I in ideological agreement with the people I work with? The
job was one I liked but there was something about it that left
me uncomfortable. I could not put a finger on it. Something
felt incomplete. But in the hurly-burly of getting things done
every day, I was able to ignore it. In the meantime, two new
members joined our team: Sadashiv and Dashrath. Our work
grew concomitantly with the size of the team.

The eight or ten bonded labourers in Dahisar were not
sufficient for the movement so we decided to work on a new
demand: minimum pay for work. At that time, the minimum
wage was seven rupees a day but women got three rupees and
men got five. We began to agitate for agricultural labourers to
get the minimum wage. It was harvest season and the need for
labour was acute. We gave a call: 'Don't go to work unless you
get seven rupees a day.' We held meetings with the workers.
Mainly women came to these meetings. They were the ones
who were seized of the idea of minimum wages. None of the

workers went to the fields. It was an agricultural labourers' strike. The landlords brought labourers from neighbouring villages. We would go to those labourers and request them, 'If you have been paid for your work, take the money and go back. Don't break our strike.' We would say this in tones pregnant with warning. Some would yield, some would not. But after fourteen days, the village yielded and the minimum wage began to be paid to all labourers. This was one more success for us. We now had the agricultural workers on our side as well.

*

It was agreed that we would now conduct a survey of bonded labour in the neighbouring villages. We formed teams and began to scour the area. The work was growing into a mountain but my mind would often turn to the village. When I returned one day, I found that Baba was weakening rapidly. I made a temporary arrangement for him. I told my cousins to take care of him; Baba did not need much food. I returned to Dahisar with Gaya and the two younger ones—the eldest was with her grandparents—and threw myself into the issue of bonded labour.

While conducting the surveys, we would take the freed bonded labourers with us. We would stay with such relatives as we had in the area. There we would quietly bring the Adivasis together. We would ask them how long they had been working, how much they were paid, how many hours they had to work and other questions of this kind. We conducted detailed research in the area around Adne, Bhatane, Medhe, Bhinar, Deepivali, Majivali, Karanjon and Tilher.* We made a list of about three hundred bonded labourers.

---

*These are all villages that fall in Vasai tehsil of Thane district.

Then we decided to organize a camp for these three hundred. Even going to invite them for this camp was an arduous exercise. We would dress as the Adivasis did, in shorts and banian. We walked and walked and finally we managed to persuade them to come. The camp was full to capacity.

And then the usual, songs to be sung, speeches to be made and slogans raised.

Camp followed camp. This resulted in tension building up in the area. No one could be sure when the next attack would happen. Gaya would have to protect our two young children during the day. When I fell asleep, Gaya would be awake and keep watch. She would start up in fear at the stirring of a leaf. When she and the children were asleep, I kept watch. That was how those days passed.

At this time, there was a discussion about bonded labour with the Labour Commissioner. The then chief justice of the Supreme Court, P.N. Bhagwati,* advised us to bring the matter up before the court. Here, however there was a split among the Adivasis. Some took their masters' side and some took ours. At this time the tahsildar was a certain R.V. Bhuskute. He began to support us in our struggle. R.V. Bhuskute's father had been active in Senapati Bapat's movement.** This made him very different from the usual tahsildars. With Bhuskute-bhau's support we managed to arrange camps in village after

---

*Prafullachandra Natwarlal Bhagwati (1921–2017) has been described by many observers as the Father of Public Interest Litigation in India. Says livelaw.in in a tribute: 'He was a great defender of human rights and dignity in the apex court of the country. He was a judge par excellence.' http://www.livelaw.in/justice-p-n-bhagwati-tribute/ Accessed on 9 October 2017, at 09:56am.

**Senapati Bapat (1880–1967) was a major figure in the Independence Movement. Bhuskute's father may have taken part in his agitation against the erection of the Mulshi Dam and the forced eviction of farmers.

village. Bhuskute-bhau would often come to the camps himself. To see a tahsildar coming to meet the Adivasis and the bonded labourers shook the landowners and moneylenders. The bonded labourers would form a queue. Bhuskute-bhau would ask each one about his particulars. The hitherto silent Adivasis would begin to talk their hearts out. They could not believe they were being freed and their frail bodies could not contain their happiness.

According to the law, the responsibility of eradicating bonded labour rested with the tahsildar. And so Bhuskute-bhau would approve schemes of employment in villages where bonded labourers had been liberated. They would then be employed in these schemes. Sometimes the fields of the Adivasis would be taken by the moneylenders into their possession. The rightful owners could only watch as the paddy grew parrot-green in their fields. The breeze would ripple through the ripe heads and waft the aroma of rice to the rightful owners who could not touch the grain. They could only watch and burn. So we started a programme in an organized way to harvest this crop when it was ready. The social workers would be waiting on the dam. They would tell the Adivasis: 'Harvest the rice. It belongs to you.' The Adivasis were infused with a new zeal. The harvesting would begin and soon be in full swing. We would announce in stentorian tones: 'Patilbaba, Patilbaba, are we supposed to eat mud?' It was a wonderful sight.

There I would be in jeans held up by a belt, my shirt tucked in, in my hands a baton, on my lips a basic question: 'If the crop belongs to the moneylender, what is the Adivasi to eat?' This image—of me on one side, the social workers on the other and the Adivasis harvesting their rightful grain—can still move me to joy.

*

The work was going well but still a nameless discontent would raise its ugly head. I would think: if there is bonded labour here, there is bonded labour in Marathwada as well. They need someone to do this work there as well. Just as Vivek-bhau and Vidyut-tai had started an organization here, one was needed there. But I did not feel it was the right time to tell Vivek-bhau this. In order to understand how to set up an organization, I wrote down all my thoughts about and observations of the Vidhayak Sansad. I kept this carefully with me. In my head, I had already moved on. I had decided not to get trapped in the Adivasi question for the rest of my life.

Actually, the work at Vidhayak Sansad was suited to my personality. I was even earning some money. But I wanted to go back to Marathwada. I must have been at Dahisar for about two years by then. My house in the village was almost in ruins. My father was with my sister now. My eldest daughter was with my in-laws. Gaya and I were at Dahisar with two of our children. The family was scattered. I could not understand what to do.

I told Vivek-bhau of my dilemma. I had a year of the MA left. I told him I wanted to finish that. Pravin Mahajan was then the officer in charge of the fellowship programme at Oxfam. Vivek-bhau and Mahajan agreed that I should be placed in Ambajogai with Manavlok, a self-help group. Dr Dwarkadas Lohia was one of the socialist circle. Manavlok was his organization. I now had a job in Marathwada. Now I would also be able to finish my MA. I took my family and went to Ambajogai.

*

Twenty kilometres from Ambajogai is a village called Bhavtana. Manavlok ran a weekly clinic there. I began to live in this clinic.

The fellowship brought me six hundred rupees a month. I

took admission at the Yogeshwari College but I did not attend classes. I would read books and study at home. Every week a doctor would visit to examine the ill. I also had to supervise the organization's balwadis. But this service-oriented work did not suit me. My spirit was that of a revolutionary. So I began to look for that kind of work to do.

At the time I joined Manavlok, an important change took place in Gaya's life: she began to learn to read and write. When Gaya went to have her tubes tied, the nurse asked her to sign a form. I told some lies and signed the form on her behalf. I lied because I did not want others to know that my wife was illiterate. This must have left an impression on Gaya. When we were at Dahisar, she must have seen Vivek-bhau, Vidyut-tai and the other social workers, and also the young women of the Rashtra Seva Dal. These young women took active part in discussions and also spoke English. Perhaps she too felt she ought to be able to speak like them, behave as they did. Really, Gaya was no less intelligent than any of these young women. The lie I was forced to tell at the clinic must have hurt her. Perhaps she decided that this man should not have to lie again about her lack of education. She began to learn the alphabet with the women at the balwadi. In other words, my children and my wife learned to read and write at the same time. Now Gaya could sign her own name.

*

I was happy that Gaya was educating herself but my mind was not at ease. I could not be happy unless I was working for the Dalit cause and here I was, in a service-oriented job. In Bhavtana, I could see there were many Dalit issues but for the organization I was working with, those questions did not exist. But my restlessness gave me no peace. I saw my job as handling all kinds of issues that came up. I was friends with

many of the Dalits of the village. And so their issues began
to come to my ears.

Once there was a week-long reading of the *Dnyaneshwari*
in the village temple. The entire village participated but of
course the Dalits were not allowed inside the temple. And so
it was difficult for them to participate in it. I decided to start
collecting money from the Dalit basti too. A mandap was set up
in front of the temple and bhajan- and keertan-singers would
be invited. That year, for the first time, the contribution from
the Dalit settlement went to the village at the very beginning
of the programme. How could the village refuse? The village
began to collect money from the upper castes. The week-long
recitation began. The people began to gather at the temple.
I took some Dalit boys from the settlement and we sat with
the bhajan singers. We began to sing in deliberately loud
voices. Our presence began to bother the villagers. We said,
'We have contributed to the festival and so we must be part of
it.' This was the first time the Dalits had taken this position.
The village was not going to take this lying down. Within the
week, a fight broke out. Mutual accusations were exchanged.
The police intervened and so bloodshed was averted. Because
of this incident the conflict between the Dalits and the upper
castes came out into the open.

*

That issue had not been settled when I made another aggressive
move. There was a Mang farmer, Dattu Kharat, in the village.
The document certifying his ownership of his bullock had
been taken by the moneylender, as surety for a loan. Kharat
had finished paying off his debt but the moneylender refused
to return the certificate, saying he would only do so if Dattu
Kharat paid double the amount lent. The certificate was
important because Dattu wanted to sell the animal but no

buyer would take it without the paperwork. I told Dattu Kharat to go ahead and look for a buyer. 'Let's see what happens then. We'll see what the moneylender does.' Dattu Kharat was vastly encouraged. He found a buyer and brought him to me. I explained the matter to the buyer and he agreed to take the animal. We decided how this was to be done. We called some halgi players and took the animal in a procession, announcing that it had been sold by Dattu Kharat to its new owner. The moneylender could do nothing about it.

Dr Lohia heard about this. He thought I was going too far. His organization was service oriented and here I was creating an atmosphere conducive to social conflict. Perhaps he felt it would be difficult for the organization to operate in the village if I kept doing things my way.

Around this time, a Mahar boy from the village ran away with a Mahar girl. This girl had been abandoned by her husband. I knew the boy. The girl's father did Maharki, working at clearing the dung from a Brahmin jahagirdar's (landowner's) house. The jahagirdar went to the police and registered a case of abduction against the boy. When the boy heard about the jahagirdar's complaint, he came to see me. I talked to the girl too. She was over the age of consent. I went with both of them to the police station. She told the police that she had gone with the boy of her own will. Her father had not been willing to marry them. Finally, the girl went back to her father and the boy went to his home, a resolution brokered by the police.

The girl began to live with her father again but now the jahagirdar began to abuse her sexually. Every day, he would take her into the fields. The boy came to see me. 'Awad-sahib, okay, she's not with me. But the jahagirdar should not be using her like that. I can't stand it.'

I said, 'Find out where they go.'

'They go and sit under a mango tree.'

'Okay,' I said, 'take my cycle and go there. Hide the cycle carefully and then you must hide as well. When they come there, you give him a good beating. But be careful, he must not bleed. Just beat him on the soles of his feet.'

I also wrote out a complaint in which he claimed to be the victim of caste violence under the PCR. If the jahagirdar tried to complain against him, I told him, he should give this to the police; the jahagirdar would then be thrown behind bars for attacking a Dalit. They say in Hindi, '*Laaton ke bhoot, baaton se nahin maante.*' (Where words don't work, kicks will.) Since words had failed with the jahagirdar, one had to use other means.

The young man went to the mango tree, hid the bicycle and concealed himself. In due course, the jahagirdar came there with the girl. The boy remained hidden as long as they were talking. When the jahagirdar began to make his amorous advances, the boy leapt out of the tree. The girl ran for it. The jahagirdar couldn't get his clothes back on. And so the boy got a good chance to give him a fine beating. Then he hopped on to my cycle and raced back to me.

As expected the jahagirdar went to the police. The boy presented the complaint that I had written out for him. The jahagirdar saw the complaint and took fright. He withdrew his case and promised to have nothing further to do with the girl.

This matter also reached Dr Lohia's ears. The jahagirdar was a great help to Manavlok in the village. Dr Lohia got angry with me. He called me and said, 'You had better stop doing all this. This won't do with me.'

I said, 'Well, if this won't work for you, then the job won't work for me.' That was it. My job at Manavlok ended there. I took my family and went back to Dahisar to Vivek-bhau.

*

Once again, I began to work with Vidhayak Sansad. The bonded labour movement had made great advances. Three hundred bonded labourers had been freed. Vivek-bhau had started the Shramjeevi Sanghatna (Labourers' Union). Now they were getting involved in other Adivasi issues too. They were trying to secure the rights of the Adivasis to the forest land where generations of them had worked. In order to be able to continue doing this, they had to keep the forest officials happy. The officials had to be served meat and alcohol whenever they visited the village. The Sanghatna had decided that this system of bribes must stop. A talati had said that he would get an Adivasi right of access and had taken four hundred rupees, beer and the slaughter of a good laying hen. But giving such access was not in the power of the talati. This problem came to the Sanghatna. We went on a morcha to the talati's office. The gathered people occupied the talati's office. Finally, he had to ask for pardon. But the Adivasi was having none of that. He wanted his beer, he wanted his money and he wanted his hen. The talati gave him back the money and the beer but the Adivasi would not be appeased until the talati had bought him a bird that was as good as the one he had slaughtered for the talati's feast. We took the talati and the Adivasi to the market to find such a bird and then the matter was settled.

I plunged back into the world of protests and marches. At around the same time, the Renaming Movement caught fire again. A protest march was to make its way to Vidhan Bhavan. We were all arrested for this satyagraha. We spent two days in Mumbai's Arthur Road Jail.

*

Again the old unease. I was doing the kind of work that should have satisfied me. But were I to continue, I would not be able to create something that would reflect who I was. Sometimes I thought I should apply to the Indian Police Service.

On the other hand, I was also strongly drawn to the idea of staying in the movement for the rest of my life. My village home was in ruins. The children were being neglected too. I often felt I should return to my village. But what would I do there? What would become of my job? I did think of starting my own organization. I would often think of aggressively pursuing the rights of the Dalits. Different thoughts would bubble up in my head. But I could not tell how to turn these into reality.

By that time I had some ideas about Adivasi society. In any social movement or revolution, they join only as followers of some other group or leader. They have had no leader of their own. Right up to today, there are very few leaders among the Adivasis. It is a community that asks very few questions. They do not seem very eager to get out of their state of misery and deprivation. Each generation seems content to live as it always has; so does the next. No one seems in a hurry to change things.

Many people believe that the Adivasis live beautiful lives in their natural homes. Their lives are said to be as natural and free as animal lives are. As a soldier of Ambedkar's thought, I do not accept this romantic view at all. I do not think people should live lives of deprivation and poverty in the jungles and that we should be impressed by this. These people also believe that the Adivasi is the king of the jungle. This is a myth. They live extremely difficult lives in adverse circumstances. The lion, the elephant and other wild animals may be described as kings of the jungle but not a human being. There is no point making facile comparisons between the lives of human beings and the lives of animals.

As I was growing to understand the Adivasis, I could see

that there were some basic differences between their struggle and the struggle of the Dalits. The exact opposite of the Adivasi, the Dalit has many questions. The Adivasi struggle does not have a base in the villages; but if the Dalit wants a revolution he must first break the network of relations as it exists in the village. The Adivasi can bear much hardship; the Dalit can bear much struggle.

There is a geographically identifiable Adivasi belt. Therefore it is comparatively easier to work among them. There is no such Dalit belt. Dalits are everywhere. Therefore to work with them requires much more effort. The struggle must be much sharper, much more pointed. But that was my struggle. I did not want to be trapped in some small village issue. I began to look for a way out.

7

One day in Mumbai I met Chhabu Bansode, a friend from my MSW days. I told Chhabu about my work among the Adivasis, how difficult it was to manage with my salary what with my father's illness, my home's decrepit condition and all the rest of it. He told me that a vacancy for a Field Officer was going to open up in CASA; he said I should apply for it because the pay was also good. I took the address and when I got back to the Sanghatana office, posted off my application. This was only because I wanted the salary.

CASA stands for Churches Auxiliary for Social Action, a Christian organization as the name suggests. However the words 'Social Action' and the good salary were enough for me. By 'social action' I figured that they meant one was supposed to go into society and shake things up a bit. I had been an activist in Vidhayak Sansad; I had applied for the post of Social Worker. The work was about the same but I wanted to do something different and I wanted to change my frame of reference while remaining an activist. A letter arrived inviting me to their Mumbai office. I put all my papers together. This was the first and last time I ever was interviewed for a job.

The interview panel was a series of serious faces. Behind them a picture of Jesus Christ, looking warmly into the distance; above me the fan rumbling as it moved the air, and on the other side of an impressive desk, the interview panel. There were three of them: the director Major Michael, the chief officer of the Mumbai office T. K. Abraham and a young man, Shalvin, the project officer. My name, my village, my education, my family background, were all inquired into.

Then Major Michael asked: 'Do you know what untouchability is? Explain the caste system to us and the problem of untouchability.'

Through all my life, this was the question I had thought about most. Hardly had he finished asking the question when I began to answer.

'Yes sir, I know about the caste system and about untouchability very well for I am a victim of this system. The caste system is the basic identity of Hindu society. My father is a Hindu Mang and Hindu society forced him to be a beggar. This society wants us to do their duties without any complaints. The bonded labour system turns us into slaves. All religions promote hierarchy. And hierarchy is the second name of the caste system.'

I did not need to think; I could say all this off the top of my head. It was only when I was sitting outside on the bench that I began to wonder whether these men who were of a religious persuasion were likely to give me a job when I had spoken against religion in all forms. A little while later, I was asked to go back into the cabin. There I was told, 'We conducted the interview for the post of social worker but we would like to offer you the post of field officer. One thousand rupees per month is your remuneration.'

One thousand rupees a month and a post that exceeded my expectations! I was delighted but there was one problem. I did not want to live away from my village now. I explained my position, my problems, my father's illness, my scattered family and asked if it would be possible for me to work out of my village. The answer was: 'Okay, from now on Dukdegaon will be the regional office of CASA; and you will be in charge of the Dukdegaon office.' What more could I have asked for? It was as if a blind man had asked for one eye and had been given a pair.

I was appointed as the Field Officer in charge of Marathwada and western Maharashtra. I would report to Shalvin and he to T.K. Abraham. It was decided that my responsibilities would include selecting workers at the village level, starting new programmes in the villages, and implementing other programmes of the organization. I was in charge of six districts in Marathwada and six in western Maharashtra. I would have to tour them regularly as part of my work.

Working with Vidhayak Sansad and Shramjeevi Sanghatana had given me a certain perspective. I was determined to bring that into my work as much as possible.

*

By this time, certain ideas were clear in my mind. One of the foremost was that one should leave no stone unturned when engaging with the enemy. In other words, if the bull wouldn't charge at you, you had to swing your cape to make sure that he did. You had to incite the enemy, you had to provoke him, and only then would you get a suitable response. You got only as much as you risked. But when you enrage a powerful animal, you must also make sure your chest is as tough as a shield.

The other issue was that of the funding self-help organizations received from abroad. During that time, a lot of money would come in from foreign countries for the welfare of the poor. Funds poured in to feed the hungry, heal the sick, and provide shelter for the widow, the orphan and the differently-abled. These were no doubt important activities, but what of those who had arrived in the world, handicapped by their very birth? It is not possible to solve the problem of Untouchability by providing the Dalit with food and building a few cement houses for them. It is much more important to awaken their sense of self-respect. Why could this money that came in to be used for these superficial measures not be used for what was truly important to us? Dalit activists often had to sacrifice their self-respect in order to make a living. If activists were paid well, they would be able to build a better movement. I saw no point in charity, in service. If you make one hand-out, a thousand hands will be extended immediately.

Some people even want to demonstrate their sympathy for the poor by living as if poverty-stricken. This has never convinced me. Some activists who work among the poor dress as if they are poor, thus giving the poor lessons on how to remain poor. Actually, this is a pretence. Some people wear this veil without thinking too much about it and others do it deliberately. Those who prescribe 'simple living and high thinking' to someone like me who has dragged himself out of poverty are simply impertinent. Many activists still live in poverty. It is only because of the paucity of resources that they cannot improve their own lives or the lives of their fellowmen.

Thus when money comes in from foreign sources or from any source, the activist wants to use the money to its best effect but tries to make sure that the work is not affected nor is there any hypocrisy and excess. They would also want their work to have some lasting impact upon society. The problem is also that society is in constant flux. It is important to understand the fundamental processes underlying this constant change. An observation such as, 'The poor always remain poor' is of no help to anyone. I began to feel, without consciously thinking about it perhaps, that what was needed was a barrage, an incessant barrage of attempts to build the self-respect of the poor.

It was not possible for me to put these thoughts into action so long as I remained an employee of CASA. There was no room for issue-based work. All I could do was choose the activists and offer them some financial assistance. And so I decided to make the most of this opportunity.

*

After the interview I went home and told Gaya about the job. She began to pack our bags. The next day I told Vivek-bhau. We bade each other farewell. When I got home from Dahisar-Vasai, the house had all but fallen into ruin. Only a few asbestos sheets were left standing. I hired a daily labourer and with his help, I plunged into house repairs. We had to rebuild the back wall of the house entirely. In the front we put up a wall of cowdung mixed with mud. There were no bolts on the doors. We made a temporary shanty out of tur waste. The house came up again. Now I wanted to bring the entire family back to live under one roof. I brought my father home, my eldest daughter too. The thugs of the village were watching all this with a great deal of ironic attention. The Mangwadi however was infused with a new enthusiasm. Sayabai from the Mangwadi circled my temples with her hands and cracked her knuckles.* Satva was sitting and chatting with my father. The house was again filled with laughter. The family could at last settle down together.

Now I could get back to work.

*

I came to Mumbai. They told me I would have to spend the first fifteen days going around the districts to understand the work. I would travel with a programme officer, by the name of Varghese. He was a Communist. He would go to each district and have a meeting with the 'Paalaks', the men in

---

*Thus she acknowledges his new-found success and seeks to protect him from the evil eye.

charge of the affairs of the village. My responsibility, at this time, was to listen to what he was saying and to see what kind of programmes he suggested. During these meetings, Varghese would talk about the differences between the haves and the have-nots.

Since Jesus worked for the poor, they too must try and ensure that the poor got the benefits of the social welfare schemes devised for them by the government, he would say. After two days of travelling with him, I realized I would be able to do the kind of work I wanted here.

By the second or third day, I too began to speak at the meetings. Even if the people were Christians, they were basically Dalits and so we shared the same opinions and experiences. I also felt that Varghese and I had the same ideological framework. We finished this round of meetings and returned to Mumbai.

Varghese gave me a good report. I was rather pleased with this. I was told that I would have to appoint some social workers. They gave me the responsibility of expanding the scope of this work as well. To this end, they gave me ten thousand rupees in cash. This was the first time I had seen such a sum all at once. I took the money and came home. I showed Baba and Gaya the money. It was in bundles of crisp five-rupee notes. They were stunned: neither of them had ever seen so much money before. I had a cousin by the name of Hari. He was a bit of a terror but he was also quite naïve. When he saw these bundles of notes with me, he was filled with joy. He had to share this joy and so he took the bundles and went off to the village. He showed the notes to everyone he met and said, 'Look, our sahib's notes. It's my brother-in-law's money.' It was a happy moment in the home. Everyone was now sure that my luck was about to turn. I gave Hari some money. That day Baba and Gaya were very happy.

During this time, politics in the village had reached a new low. Aasruba Patil and Parbhu Bade and their factions were both competing in a game of one-upmanship. The Mangwada was being crushed in the middle of this game of personal agenda-driven politics. Parbhu Bade was involved in black magic. He was the third of seven brothers and built like a wrestler. In order to maintain his aura, he would go to the cremation grounds and pray and perform rituals. If a woman were possessed by a spirit, he would pretend to be able to exorcise it. The gullible would be fooled by this. Since he was an 'expert' in black magic, people would try not to cross him in any way. Aasruba Patil was the Police Patil of the village. His group also controlled the Gram Panchayat of the village. Both these factions had identified me as the enemy. When I returned, willy-nilly, the leadership of the Mangwadi was handed over to me. This meant that there were now three factions in the village.

*

My work with CASA began in orderly fashion. I went for a meeting at Mukhed in the Nanded Taluka. It was held at the Borali village's Hiranagar area. On a deserted plain, two hundred or so workers and farmers, men and women, had gathered. The organization's activist, a man called Rathod, was to conduct the meeting. Here, too, my role was that of a learner. Rathod's was the main role at the meeting; mine was subsidiary.

After Rathod began speaking, a young man, about twenty years of age, rose to his feet. He began to ask question after question, speaking a rural dialect with a rough accent. His dhotar was dirty, as was his sadra. He wanted to know what CASA's purpose was, who had established it, what it aimed to do. He said that he was a Dalit as were many of the people there. He said that they faced injustice and endured atrocities every day; he wanted to know what CASA was going to do to prevent this from happening. He did not give Rathod a chance to speak. Finally Rathod got annoyed: 'Why are you running on so much? Sit down,' he snapped and got the poor man to sit down. I did not think this was right. 'Let the fellow speak,' I told Rathod. 'What is he saying that is wrong?' I liked the young man's spirit. I let him speak freely. I thought it much more important to give someone like him a chance to speak than to lecture those gathered there. Because of this, the respect the people felt for me increased and I got hold of a good activist as well.

The rustic youth was Sakharam Waghmare. He calls himself Sakharam Barhalikar now. In all my life, I have never met such an extraordinary activist. His elder brother's name was Tukaram. He was a graduate. People called him Guruji and they called Sakharam: 'Yada Khata' or Crazy Section. This Mang boy's job was to look after the landowner's cattle.

But in the area in which he lived there was a group called the Progressive Friends' Circle (PFC) that worked to spread awareness about social inequality. They had written and staged plays with names like *Saavdhaan Janta Jaag Zhaali* (Beware, the people are waking up) and *Hi Jaat Maanavaachi* (This human caste). Sakharam saw these plays and was inspired by them. Odd and unlettered, he might be but that did not stop him from joining this well-educated group. He gave up his cattle-herding job and joined an adult-literacy class. He might now be able to read and write with ease, but at heart he remained a firebrand.

A well-educated social worker will know how to write a good application; she will be well-acquainted with the etiquette of speaking to government officers. Sakharam might well have learned to read and write in an adult-education class but at base, he was a ruffian; he had some set ideas. That kind of person has only his powerful physique to put into play. Thus Sakharam's policy was that wherever he saw any injustice, he would simply begin to beat up the perpetrators. And though I was educated, this was a policy we shared.

Sakharam was filled with rage at the injustices of the caste system; his way of fighting this was completely different. There was a poor barber in his village. He persuaded the barber to shave him too. 'If you can shave a buffalo, why can't you shave me? I won't tell anyone.' He got the barber to cut his hair in the middle of a field. But anyone could tell he'd had a haircut. So the rumours started: 'The barber's been cutting the hair of that Mang boy.' The rumours grew into discussions. And out of these discussions came the decision that a caste boycott would be pronounced against the barber. He went to Sakharam in tears. 'See what's happened to me because of you. Now what am I to do?' Sakharam calmed him down and sent him away.

Then he got to work. He kept an eye on those who were behind the boycott. The village would come to the area near the Mang settlement to urinate. Behind the Mang settlement was a temple to Mari-Aai. The village people would squat behind the temple to shit. Sakharam concealed himself in the bushes. The man who had proposed the boycott made his way there. As he squatted to shit, Sakharam began to beat him. 'Will you shit right in front of Mari-Aai?' And so saying, he gave him a good beating. Actually, Sakharam had no feelings for Mari-Aai. But the man who ran away, clutching his dhotar, knew very well why he had been beaten. After that, there was no more talk of a caste boycott.

One more of Sakharam's escapades. The son of a Police Patil raped a young woman. She was drenched in blood. The rapist took her and her parents to a clinic. An attempt was made to hush things up. When Sakharam heard about this, he arrived there. Sakharam asked: 'What happened?'

The Patil's rude son brushed him off. Sakharam persisted: 'Go on then, tell me properly.'

The boy said, 'What will you do if I don't? Bend me out of shape?'

Sakharam lost his temper. He was a burly man. If the boy had not been a Patil, would he have dared speak that way? Sakharam knocked the boy over. He got the yoke of a pair of bullocks and tied the young man to it. He beat him all the way to the police station. The police also beat him until he shat in his pants. But then some money must have exchanged hands for the woman's parents withdrew the case. It was all hushed up. The only justice the girl ever got was that Sakharam beat the shit out of the boy. Literally.

That was Sakharam.

When we started the struggle over the Dalit's rights to till the gaayraan*, Sakharam said at a meeting: 'Babasaheb said I was born a Hindu but I will not die a Hindu. I say: We were born landless but we will not die landless.' This naïve worker had discerned the intention behind Babasaheb's words. I began to meet many activists like Sakharam in my work with CASA.

But I was talking about my first camp with CASA. At that camp, I met a gang of workers from Nanded, all like Sakharam.

After the camp, Sakharam, his brother Tukaram and their friends all came to meet me. They said, 'We are from the Backward Classes. Will you come home for tea?' I agreed immediately. In the village of Barhali, there was a Neo-Buddhist family, the Gaikwads. Though they were poor, the

---

*Eknath Awad himself offers a definition of gaayraan land on Page 264 of this book: Gaayraan means the land reserved as pasture for cattle around the village in Marathwada.

father would encourage all the young men. The old man told me about the slavery in Barhali. There were zamindars of two kinds, the Deshpandes (who were Brahmins) and the Deshmukhs (Marathas). If one had to pass by their homes, one had to carry one's footwear in one's hands. If one encountered them, one had to bow. If the Patil were at his door, one had to salute him before passing or he would feel insulted. If anyone was forced to leave the village for some reason, they would pounce on his land. These were the injustices the young men were fighting. They would meet at Gaikwad's hut. Any visiting social worker or activist would be entertained there. One of the young men of the family was Subhash, an intelligent lad. Today, he is one of the chief activists in the Maanavi Haq Abhiyaan. We had a great discussion.

The next day these young men brought others to the camp. These boys had a theatre group that would sing Babasaheb's songs with great zest. I managed to organize many programmes using this group. We got them a harmonium and a dholki. This, and other groups, began to take Babasaheb's messages into the area around Barhali.

*

After Nanded, I was made solely responsible for setting up training camps in Kolhapur and Osmanabad. I had my own independent space in CASA. I had the reputation now of being a bold worker who could carve out his own identity. I threw myself into the work of organizing training camps. Talking about the injustices of casteism was my prime focus in the camps. At the training camps in the village of Vadingle, I recited my poem 'What Are You Saying This Country Has Given You Nothing?' The Chief Officer, T.K. Abraham, called me to see him. 'What happened in Kolhapur?' he asked.

'Nothing, sir,' I replied. 'The training went very well.'

He said: 'I received a letter from the Bishop of Kolhapur. He said you make inflammatory speeches, that you're a Naxalite. He has suggested that we rusticate you.'

This startled me. I spoke with fervour, people responded and this upset the bishop? Was it a crime to speak out against injustice and exploitation? Were they going to sack me? But T.K. Abraham had no intention of doing so. His opinion of me was still high. 'Don't worry,' he said. 'Go ahead. We are with you.'

Wah! I now had the strength of ten. I had been encouraged but I was also given the responsibility of ending a fight. CASA had a 'Food for Work' programme. It was aimed at the poor. They were given food grain in exchange for work. The rural poor, of course, meant the Mang and the Mahar. For generations, these two communities had been fighting. In villages where there were no Mahars, the Mangs would do the village's unpaid labour. The two communities had always been at each other's throats over baluta, the system by which certain communities were entitled to a share of the produce of the village in return for performing certain duties without payment. Even today, these two communities, equally oppressed, are still political enemies. The old policy of 'Divide and Rule' used so skilfully by the British was in force here. But the causes for the division were petty indeed.

One such cause erupted in the village of Chorakhali in Osmanabad. The Mangs felt that the Mahars were getting greater benefits in the Food for Work scheme. The Mahars felt that the Mangs were taking more of the grain. I was supposed to resolve this. I went to the village, with a leader of some years, in a jeep. We had a meeting and I listened patiently as both sides exchanged accusations.

Then I asked calmly, 'After having stolen all this grain, has anyone in the Mang community eaten so much that he has had diarrhoea? Has anyone in Mahar community eaten so much that he has put on so much as a finger's breadth of weight?'

No answer.

Then I said, 'When this work wasn't there, what were you doing? The work the Patils asked you to do, right? What did you get in exchange? One bhakri a day. Wearing a saffron robe and begging, the Gosavi would get raw grain and you would get stale bhakri. Was that charity sweet to taste or do you prefer the dignity of food you have earned? If you can work together with us, we will be happy to run this programme. But if you fight among yourselves, we will close it down in this village.' This announcement calmed both sides down. The fight ended.

What had kept the Mahar and the Mang apart? They had been fighting over the scraps thrown to them from the master's table. When the scraps were taken away, what was there to fight over? Both sides were hungry. Sometimes the elders would snatch the share of the younger ones and vice versa. It was better to share a small piece of bhakri, even if each got a tiny bit; this they knew and I knew but the senior leader who had come with me in the jeep did not know. He found my methods somewhat out of the way.

I then took the jeep I had brought with me to Dukdegaon. There was no road in the village then. But I told the driver to take the jeep on the mud road right up to my home. The driver was a man called Samuel Alhat. He was also a Dalit. Without a murmur of complaint, he drove the jeep over the rough and unpaved road right up to my door. I was the cynosure of all eyes in the village. Gaya and my children were delighted and surprised. The entire Mang settlement gathered around the jeep. Now they were sure I had become a big man.

After this incident, I was given charge of the Food for Work scheme. I chose many different villages. I also started the scheme in Dukdegaon. I brought five trucks of wheat into the village. But now where were we to store this grain? No one in the village had seen so much food all at once. I devised a simple solution to this problem.

We divided up the grain among all the Mang households in the village. If the grain did not fit in the houses, we used the temple as a storehouse. Due to this, the people began to support me. I had already been seen as a leader but now I began to behave like one. But with this, I became Parbhu Bade's Enemy Number One. He was said to carry a knife around with him. He had ghungroos tied to it. He would show this knife to people in the village and say, 'This knife with ghungroos is meant to finish off Eknath.' The village folk would look at this alarmed.

One day, Asruba Patil was standing on the paara. There were other people around, also chatting away. I was walking past them. As I went by, I said hello. Asruba Patil called me over. 'Eknathrao, you're doing some fine work. I do not approve of it however. You will always be my enemy.'

In short, my enemies were becoming aware of my increasing stature. But now they also knew that they would not be able to control me easily so they began to spread the rumour that I had converted to Christianity. In my opinion, finding one has an enemy is a good sign indeed. The more gossip the enemy spreads against one, it has been my experience, the more one is helped to grow. Because of the way they opposed me, my stature as a leader grew. The dogs bark but the caravan passes, it is said. And this is precisely the attitude I took to the rumours they spread about me.

The Vanjari Patils in the village had some issues over property. And so they too came over to my side against the powerful Parbhu Bade who had oppressed them. Bansi Tonde was a poor farmer in the village. Another Vanjari group had tried to expel him from the village and confiscate his land.

This Bansi Tonde's uncle had been instrumental in getting me admitted to the village school. I stood firmly behind Bansi, a Vanjari too. This made the poor Vanjaris into my followers. I began to store the grain brought in for the Food for Work programme in Vanjari houses as well. This community that had once seen me as an Untouchable now accepted the grain I had brought into the village.

While working with the Food for Work programme, and in the Dalit settlements, I formulated a special policy. I would announce that we were not offering charity. I would also remind them that it was the government's responsibility to provide them with work and with good grain. I did not want them to end up dependent on the organization for the grain would eventually run out. They would then go back to being hungry. They would look forward only to the time that CASA came back with new programmes and projects of work. I found a way out of this. In the Marathwada district, many Dalits had been accused of encroachment on the gaayraan for it was not registered in their names. With great courage, they had taken on the enmity of the village to till the land. But the land did not yield much. And so they were forced to go back to the Patils for work. In CASA's history, I was the first to work to improve the gaayraan land. The Dalits would work on their own land and CASA would give them grain for doing so. In the case of other landowners, their saat-baarah* was enough proof for the government to help with any improvement schemes on their land. Those who worked the gaayraan got no such benefits. Our Food for Work

---

*The saat-baarah is the name of the primary document for rural land-holding. It derives its name from the Hindi words for Seven-Twelve. There are two etymologies offered. The first is that the numbers refer to the numbers of the provisions of the law; the second is that the information that defines your landholding is collected by two forms: Form Seven and Form Twelve.

scheme began to be run as a support programme. This gave the Dalit a good opportunity to work and gain self-respect at the same time.

At this time, there was also a programme to help with the digging of borewells. I approved a number of borewells to be sunk in the gaayraan. Through the time I was at CASA, I approved more than three hundred borewells for the poor and the Dalit farmers. The work was on in full swing.

*

I had a good position in CASA. But soon T.K. Abraham moved out of being Chief Officer of the Mumbai office. Shalwin took over his place. Shalwin was a religious man. He was always quoting Christ. I had nothing against Christianity or Christ but I was also a committed Ambedkarite. I did not bring Christ into my camps and trainings. But if I excluded Christianity, it was because I excluded all other religions and gods as well. Despite this, I had some standing in CASA. Perhaps Shalwin was also envious of me. He began to oppose me. As my senior, he kept demanding that I submit reports. I began to have fights with him and at the same time, I had an argument with a colleague called Deshmukh.

Every month all the workers came to the office to share their experiences with each other. Each one would talk about the status of work in his district, the programmes that were planned for the coming month and such matters. We would analyze each other's styles of functioning and seek to learn from our mistakes. At one such meeting, I brought up something I had against Deshmukh's style of operation. Deshmukh was a Maratha from Beed. When I went with him to his village, I saw the Dalits bowing their heads in front of him. I described this at the meeting. 'A social worker should take no pride in caste. If the Dalits in his village bow before him, Deshmukh should himself offer them pride of place and seat them next to him. But he has not been able to deal with his pride in these matters.' Deshmukh was deeply offended. He replied, 'It is Eknath who is the casteist. He sees caste everywhere.'

I said, 'If by speaking out against your caste consciousness, I am labelled casteist, I accept the accusation.' At the end of the discussion, Deshmukh had tears in his eyes but I did not withdraw my words.

It was not as if I reserved my accusations of casteism for the upper castes alone; I also examined carefully the actions of my own caste brothers. BAMCEF,* a socialist organization, had organized a meeting of the Matangs in Aurangabad. I went there as an observer. A Mang professor mounted an attack there on the Mahar community. 'It is the Mahar who is responsible for the backwardness of the Mang community. The Mahars get all the benefits and there is nothing left over for the Mang. If Dr Ambedkar is a Mahar leader, we should take Annabhau Sathe as our leader. Lahuji Vastad Salve can be a symbol of our pride and we can progress…' and so on. After he had spoken, I spoke too and without restraint. 'You are dividing us up on caste lines. Should an educated person from our communities offer correct direction to the people or should he be leading them astray? Dr Ambedkar is the leader of us all. If anyone seeks to put Babasaheb into a caste box, such a person should be greeted with slippers.' This was greeted with a hearty round of applause. The BAMCEF people came to meet me. The next time, they asked me to preside over a session too.

*

*The All India Backward (SC, ST, OBC) And Minority Communities Employees Federation, known as BAMCEF, is an organization of employees from Scheduled Castes, Scheduled Tribes, Other Backward Classes and Minority Communities in India.

Thanks to the CASA job, my days of hunger had ended. I was beginning to be recognized in society as well. My salary had also been increased. I had settled down into my work. Had I continued in this fashion, I should have turned into a happy, middle-class, middle-path-taking, speech-making sock puppet. But I was not willing to accept this role. I began to take on more of the malpractices that plagued the Mangs. I began to start cutting the hair of the Potraj again with increased zeal.

The way I had begun the eradication of this tradition was a little different. Before me, there were two loyal Ambedkarites by the names of Madhav More and Shyamrao Tangde who had also been cutting the matted hair of the Potraj. They had an interesting way of going about it.

*

Madhav More and Shyamrao Tangde were both part of Baba Adhav's 'One village, one water source' movement.* They were activists of the Dalit Yuvak Aghadi (Dalit Youth Front). They were from the village of Khalvat Limgaon. When a Potraj came to the door to beg from them, they would welcome him in. 'Come in, brother, come in. Sit down.' They would seat him with great respect. Then they would call out to the inside of the house. 'Send some tea for our relative who has come to see us.' The Potraj would generally be tired after walking around several villages. He would be glad of the tea, and happy to be treated with such respect. He would relax and settle down. He had no idea what was in store for him. The boys of the village would now gather to watch the fun.

As they waited for the tea, the Potraj would be counselled. 'So brother, how many villages have you walked around today? You must be tired.'

---

*Pandurang Adhav, also known as Baba Adhav, began this movement in 1972, to ensure that Dalits have access to water in the villages.

A copper vessel full of water drunk, the Potraj would be in bliss. 'Oh yes. But what can one do? This is my destiny and I can only accept what comes with it.'

'Brother, what destiny are you talking about? You're hanging on to Mari-Aai. You beg from door to door in her name. And what abuse you get! Some say, "Hey Mangtya, get on with you." Others say, "Go away now." Right?'

The Potraj would agree. As soon as he agreed, he would be made to face a volley of ignominy: 'Aavo, no intelligent person would like to beg. Only an idiot would like to beg. Can you possibly be happy with some stale bhakri to chew? Can you even fill your children's stomachs?'

The Potraj would be agreeing with all this, nodding away, saying, 'Yes, yes.' They would ask: 'How does it feel to beg? Do your children like it that their father begs? This jungle you've grown on your head probably has lice. Does Mari-Aai come to kill your lice?'

Question after question. The Potraj would be completely stupefied. Then the two would pull out their infallible weapon: 'So why beg, brother? From today, you must give up begging. Come on, let's cut your hair. You look like a wise man. You won't object to a good haircut. And even if you did, what good would it do you? Look how many people have gathered here. They won't let you go until you've been shorn.'

And in whatever manner they could, Shyamrao and Madhavrao would motivate the Potraj to have his hair cut. Some of the more naïve ones would agree to have their hair cut. Some would simply surrender to get it over with.

Shyamrao and Madhavrao were Neo-Buddhists. Thus when they opposed the traditions of the Potraj, they were crossing caste lines and could face opposition. It could be said, 'These Neo-Buddhists are harassing the Mangs; they are hurting their religious sentiments.' Perhaps this was the reason why they chose to use persuasion and counselling in their process. But I had no such problem. As a Mang, it was my birthright to attack the traditions of my own people. And my personality did not allow me to take things easy and to go slow. And so I began my own Potraj-shaving programme with energy and vigour.

When I was done with my work for CASA, I would take a few young men and go to the bazaar at Kuppa. There would always be a Potraj or two there. If the boys saw a Potraj they would get hold of him and bring him to me. I would be waiting with my scissors. No barber would be willing to touch the hair of the Potraj. I would take hold of one of the dreadlocks and in the tone of one chanting a mantra, I would declaim: 'Hey Mari-Aai, I am about to fell one of your trees. If there is any ill to come of this, may it fall to my lot. This Potraj will no longer beg using your name. And let the sin of that also be visited upon me. Let all your rage be expended upon me-e-e-e, oh Mother.'

As soon as I had cut one of the dreadlocks, I would hand the Potraj over to the barber. I would even pay for the haircut. And so I went from Dharur, Ambedgaon, Vadvani, Majalgaon, Rajegaon and other weekly bazaars, getting the Potraj to cut their hair. Not all the Potraj were beggars. But even without following the tradition of begging, some Mangs would let their hair grow into dreadlocks. They would wrap their hair up in a turban or tuck it into a topi and come to the bazaar. When we saw a rather swollen head, we knew it was a Potraj. We would get hold of them and cut their hair forcibly. There came a time when as soon as I turned up in the market, the Potraj-es would take off, running. This would cause a storm of chasing and catching Potraj-es. By going to every bazaar, we managed to get at least twenty to twenty-five Potraj-es shorn. When no barber was present, we would cut the hair ourselves. But when you had to cut hair in such numbers, there would often be a bit of confusion. Then we would cut half the hair of one and then move on to the next. This meant the half-shorn would be pleading, 'Come now, finish the job. Why are you leaving this half-done?' One Potraj objected vociferously. There was a bit of a fight and one of the rather over-enthusiastic workers worked the scissors with such zeal that he stabbed the Potraj's head. The Potraj began to howl. His shirt was drenched in blood. We had to take him to the doctor and get his head stitched up.

This programme of shaving the heads of the Potraj-es was seen as rather unusual. No one until this time had taken on Mari-Aai so openly. And so on bazaar days, the name of Eknath Awad became a subject of discussion. I began to take on the proportions of a character in a folktale. People began to call me a 'Jaanbaaz Mang' and a 'Danger Maanoos'.*

---

*Jaanbaaz is Hindustani-Urdu for risk-taking; manoos is Marathi for man.

8

My leadership of the community now began to take shape. I had gathered a circle of workers around me. I was preoccupied, as farmers are during the month of Jyeshta. Now the first rains would come and then it would be time to plough, to turn over the ground and get it ready for the seed. It was time to get the firewood in; time to gather fodder for the animals, these preoccupations leave the farmer no free time. This was exactly what was happening to me. This was the time of the moulding of the activist in me.

I got Subhash Gaikwad of Barhali a job at CASA. In a short while, he was looking after Dukdegaon. Ashok Tangde, the nephew of Shyamrao Tangde, also came to live there. I began to organize programmes with names like Dalit Jagruti Melava (Dalit Awareness Meeting) and Haq Jagriti Shibir (Rights Awareness Camps). A Mang youth told Ashok Tangde about one of these programmes. After that, Ashok became one of the programme's steadfast workers. Other young men like Baban, Rama, Shesherao also became activists. Even Parbhu Bade's blood brother, Motiram Bade, began to work with me. I now had my own gang.

Our operations spread beyond Dukdegaon to Tigaon, Chinchala, Pusara, Devdi and Limbgaon. Our theatre group began to travel among these villages. With the harmonium on our heads and the dholki, we would walk from one village to the next. As we walked through the night with these instruments on our heads, people would see us and say, 'The tamasha people are here.' Our entourage would go straight to the Dalit settlement. Once we got there, we would sing Bhimgeet until the moon went down in the sky.

Aai Bhimaaicha re garbhaat vaadnaara
Bhim janamla Manuchi aulaad gaadnaara
Beeja-beejant aahe ankur aaj supt
Laakhon jeevanchaa chaara tya ankuraat gupt.
Jabda gulaamgiricha shouryaane phaadnaara
Bhim janamla Manuchi aulaad gaadnaara

In the stomach of Bhimai, a life unfurls,
Bhim took birth to bury Manu's sons.
In every seed, a seedling lies hidden,
And fodder for millions in that seedling are hidden.
He who came to tear the jaw of slavery:
Bhim took birth to bury Manu's sons.

We would sing these great songs. And then chatting and joking, we would walk back to Dukdegaon as the moon set.

*

As long as I was in the village we would have these camps and meetings. I had been given a cycle by CASA. This was around 1985–86. Our major mode of transport was the State Transport bus. Where the buses did not go, we walked. To have a cycle was tantamount to having a helicopter. My nephew Baban was eager to go about giving the news of the camps. He would go wherever I wanted him to deliver a message, one foot always on the pedal of the bicycle. Baban, Ashok and Subhash would all compete to take the cycle out. These boys would travel double seat for distances of 15 to 20 kilometres to give villages the news of the camps. At that time the word camp, 'shibir', was new to people. Some would say shabir, some would say shebir. The young ones would say with pride, 'We're off to Eknath's village to a camp.' There was a kind of thrill attached to the words: going to a camp.

Our camps were full of conversations. Someone would talk

about the fact that Dalits were not allowed into the temple in their village; another would talk about how the Dalits had the task of clearing away dead animals; others about the different ways in which caste played out in their villages. Some of the old people would also come to the camps. They would tell us about old times. 'Aara, what to tell you about those days! When Mahars from another village came into ours, people's hearts would beat faster. Seeing a Mahar, they would hawk and spit. "Here comes the M'harda bearing bad tidings," they would say. The Mahars would bring news of deaths; the Mangs would bring news of a birth. But when the Mahars stopped doing Maharki, the Mangs took over their work. Now the Mangs would bring the news of death too and so people began to spit at the sight of us too. See what we have come to.'

Someone else would say, 'Whatever his caste, a newly-wed boy would have to go to the paara. He would have to break a coconut in front of Maruti, fold his hands and say to the god, "Up to this time, I was celibate as You were, Marutiraya. Now I am going to be a householder." But the Mahars were not allowed to do this. Mahars were not allowed to go near the paara. Mangs were allowed to go up to the paara.'

In between, I would ask, 'But why can't Mangs enter the temple, have you ever asked? When the Mahars were not allowed darshan of the god, they simply abandoned the god. Now Ambedkar is the Mahar God. But the Mangs still go to the Maruti temple. So be it then. But why only up to the paara? Why can't we go right into the sanctum sanctorum?' As soon as I asked a question like this, angry discussions would break out and would continue for a while. And then I would give something very like a lecture on the subject. I would make them laugh, I would curse them roundly. I would motivate them to abandon the bad old ways.

Around ten or eleven boys from other villages would gather

in Dukdegaon. My supporters in the village would see to the arrangements. We would sing songs such as '*Naahi mhana re naahin mhanaa, gulaamgirila naahin mhanaa*' (Say no to slavery, say no) as often as was humanly possible. The word 'gulamgiri' would be replaced by the various practices that we wanted stopped and then the refrain of 'say no' would follow. Thus someone might say, '*Mayyat niropaala nahin mhana*' (Refuse to go with news of a death) and the refrain would follow. Or someone might say no to cleaning the floors with cow dung. And so it would go on, never tiring, never failing.

But there was also the question of feeding those who had come to the camps.

Instead of the usual bhakri with some vegetables, we had created our own unique way of feeding everyone. We combined the electric supply the government had provided and the common property that was the river and we used this to produce food. This is how. As soon as the sun was overhead, the camp would take a break. Two of us would set out for the river with a nice long bamboo to which a wire had been attached. One would check that there were no animals or human beings in the river. When he had given the all-clear, the other would link one end of the bamboo to the electric wires overhead and let the other dangle in the river. All it took was a few seconds of current for fish of a fresh, silvery hue to float up to the top. When there seemed to be enough a second signal would be given and the wire would be disconnected. Then the boys would jump into the river and collect the electrocuted fish. When a basketful had been collected, the boys would return to the camp. While the fish curry was being cooked, bhakri would be slapped on to the coals and discussions about social change would begin again. Lunch would be served around three p.m., spiced with much jokes and laughter. Then more discussions. In the evening, we would have a mehfil of Bhimgeet. The discussions, the fishing, the restlessness would make one feel like one could not sit around and do nothing.

*

Like the Potraj's begging, the 'kaaran' was another disgusting tradition that brought the Mang into disrepute; I began a struggle to eradicate it. The kaaran was a public feast of the flesh of a sacrificed bull.* Another word for it was 'kanduri' though kanduri was a little different from kaaran. Kanduri requires a goat; for a kaaran, a live animal has to be sacrificed. If a villager suspected that he was the victim of someone's evil eye, he might make a promise to Mari-Aai: 'Remove this burden from me and I will have a kaaran in your name.' After this promise had been made, a bull would be let loose in the village. It was free to go where it chose and when it waxed fat, it would be sacrificed. The Potraj too would advise people, 'Have a kaaran and this problem will end.' Behind such advice was only the desire to have a week-long supply of meat; alcohol would also be served at these feasts. Before the sacrifice, the animal would be taken in procession around the village. The Potraj would sing and play the halgi. Women would be possessed by the spirit of Mari-Aai. They would jerk their heads and dance in the procession. A paan of five leaves would be placed on the neck of the animal. The privilege of cutting the paan was given to the Police Patil. This was held to be a mark of respect, for a huge sword would be placed in his hands. He would then cut the paan in high style. Others would then step in to slaughter the animal. A large amount of meat would be made available. This would all go to the Dalit

---

*See the short story 'Sacrifice' in Baburao Bagul's collection of short stories, *When I Hid My Caste: Stories* (Speaking Tiger, 2018) translated by Jerry Pinto

homes. Every house would be roasting bhakri in readiness for this meal. Often there would be a public meal and alcohol would also be served. The names of Dhrupadai and Ambabai would be raised in loud slogans. This tradition—one that is used to demonstrate the lowliness of the Mang—is still in practice. I waged constant war against it. It is much more difficult to fight one's own caste brothers than it is to fight people of other castes. My fight against the kaaran seemed to me to be a symbol of my struggle with my caste.

In our area, the annual kaaran at the village of Pusara was the most celebrated. The Mangs and the Mahars of the village would perform the sacrifice together. The village Patils would give the Mahars and the Mangs the meat, alcohol and money. This, you might say, was their way of keeping the Dalit where they wanted them, under their heels. Ten to fifteen Potraj-es would come together for Pusara's kaaran. At one time, seven bulls were slaughtered. It was a huge festival. But to me this was a sign of slavery and I wanted to abolish it.

I printed a leaflet saying, 'The kaaran at Pusara will not be allowed to happen. Mahars and Mangs are not to participate in this' and had it distributed in the bazaar. My name was well known now for cutting the hair of the Potraj. But no one could quite believe that I would be able to stop a tradition in which the Patils were involved. 'The Patils won't let Eknath Awad interfere with their festivals,' so many Mangs and Mahars felt.

*

I registered a complaint against the kaaran at Pusara with the police. The police said, 'This is a religious festival. How can we stop a religious festival from taking place?' I said, 'If they want, let them serve a meal of ghee-poli*—I have no objection.

---

*A poli is the way Brahmins in Maharashtra refer to the chapatti.

But to kill an animal collectively is against the law protecting animals.' The police had to agree with my argument. The police then made this announcement in Pusara. The Patils of Pusara remained adamant. It was their tradition and my complaint was not going to stop it. This is precisely what I wanted. For it was my intention to show that I could stop such a tradition in its tracks.

The Mahars and Mangs were afraid that if I got my way, they would miss their meat feast and so they were cursing my name. I had a distant aunt on my mother's side in Pusara. On the day the kaaran was supposed to happen, I went with two or three policemen to the village. I had let my beard grow out a bit, picked up a Shabnam bag* and set off. When I got there, there was some trepidation in the village. The procession of the bulls had already set out. I went and sat in front of my aunt's hut. As my aunt roasted her bhakris, she was abusing me. 'This Eknath, poking his nose everywhere. Does he want to shovel mud on to our plates, this corpse? We should get his funeral pyre ready, the swine. Taking the food from the mouths of our children. His father was a Potraj. He's forgotten the debt his father owes everyone, rotting corpse that he is.' She had no idea I was sitting outside. But then she began to sense my presence and came out.

As soon as she saw me, she said, 'Nephew, when did you get here?'

I replied, 'Maami, I was here to hear your first cuss word.'

Maami was a little ashamed of herself. I said, 'Are your curses going to hurt me? I know the entire village will be delighted when I stop this kaaran.' Maami had no idea what to say to that.

---

*A sling bag said to be named after the film *Shabnam* (1949, Bibhuti Mitra) where both the protagonists, Dilip Kumar and Kamini Kaushal carried them.

In the village the procession of the buffaloes had ended. I went there with the police and the social workers.

The Police Patil said, 'Eknathrao, this is a religious matter. Do not interfere.'

I said, 'Okay, go ahead. Sacrifice the bull. But you too must take some of the meat home.'

The Police Patil was annoyed. 'Do we eat such meat? What rubbish you talk!'

I said, 'The Mahar and the Mang must eat this meat and you will eat chicken and mutton? How is that a religious tradition?'

The Police Patil fell silent.

Then I shouted: 'If anyone raises a hand on this animal, he will go to jail.'

No one came forward. The police took hold of the animal. The kaaran at Pusara had been stopped. I won the battle and since that day, there has not been a kaaran at Pusara. However, they do celebrate Ambedkar Jayanti and Annabhau Sathe Jayanti with great vigour. And I became famous as Eknath Awad, the man who could take on the Patils.

This stance of mine became famous. A friend of mine, More Guruji told me about a kaaran at the village of Kitti Adgaon. I registered a complaint with the police. A foujdar, two hawaldars and my friends Vijay Alzende and Gangaram Bhise came with me. By the time we reached, the animal had been sacrificed and its pieces were lying in various baskets. Stoves had been lit. Women who had been possessed by Mari-Aai were spinning round and round. The Potraj were playing their halgis. I looked at this and rage burst inside me. I went and stamped one of the baskets in which the meat had been placed. There was meat in four or five other vessels as well. I kicked one over and immediately the dogs who had been hovering around pounced on the pieces and ran off with them. The women began to curse and swear and threaten me. 'Lakshmibai will curse you. You will be ruined. That wonderful meat you threw into the mud. You rotting corpse, you should be eaten by vultures.' The women cursed me from the bottom of their hearts. I understood their anger for the hungry rarely get such food. But I could see this was not food given with respect. So I did not mind the abuse.

Vijay and Gangaram kicked over all the other vessels in front of the dogs. Seeing the police with us, the Mangs and Potraj-es tried to run off but I caught each one and whacked them good and proper. Then I pushed them into the police van and took them to the station. They were arrested under the Prevention of Cruelty to Animals act; I suspected that the Patils of the village would now come to get them out. They had heard of my doings in Pusara so they had already gone to their elected representative, Radhakrishna Patil.

He refused to help them and even so, this group came to the police station. There were four or five of them, wearing their phetas, their mouths red with paan, their clothes white. They greeted me and I reciprocated. One of them said, 'We have a request, let these Mangs go.' I asked, 'Why?'

Another one said: 'We gave them the money for this. We didn't want Lakshmibai to curse the village so we gave them the money. They're poor people.' This show of sympathy for the poverty of the Mangs enraged me. 'Get out of here, you pimps. You think you'll come here and get them out of jail and then you'll go back to the village and tell their wives, "Hey, didn't I get your husband out of jail? Now come with me," and you'll get to mount their wives, will you? If you don't get out of here quickly, motherfuckers, I'll tell the police to throw you into jail with them.' Seeing this avatar of me frightened the Patils. They could tell the police were also on my side. They hurried away. The Mangs who were sitting in the police station began to cry. They said, 'So what should we eat, tell us?' I said, 'Eat mud but don't take this meat that is soaked in your helplessness.'

For the next four years, I followed up the case of the Mangs from this village. There was a Potraj in this village, Aasrya Kamble. He had slipped away quietly on that day. I knew this and I was determined that this case should be a warning for all of them. I also knew that although his name did not figure in the case, he was frightened of me. I told the police to go to the village just to stir things up, for no real reason. As soon as he saw the police vehicle, Aasrya would make a run for it. We kept this up for a while. Then one day Aasrya Patil turned up at my home. He was going hoo-hoo-hoo. I thought he had come under the influence of Mari-Aai. I asked, 'So tell me, Mai, what can I do for you?' But it was Aasrya himself, terribly frightened. 'I'm so cold, Awad-sahib, I'm so cold,' he moaned. 'Cold?' I asked. 'Come let's get you to the police station.' This terrified him even more. 'I beg at your feet. Cut my hair if you want. I'll give up begging. Just don't take me to the police station.' It was an offer I could not refuse. I cut his hair and then gave him a hot cup of tea and sent him home.

Now Kitti Adgaon no longer has a kaaran. The Mangs have become farmers in the gaayraan. When I see their fields full of ripe grain, my mind fills with happiness.

At this time, I began to feel acutely how much I needed to know the law really well. And so I took admission for a law degree in the Balbhim College in Beed. The work increased greatly. I had lost touch with studying and so I couldn't study with as much energy and intensity as I used to. This meant that I would pass in one or two subjects each time and this went on for about five years until I had only one paper to pass so that I could get my degree.

But then I decided that I would not clear that paper until the name of Marathwada University was changed. That was because I wanted Babasaheb's name on my law degree. In 1994, the name was changed and I immediately sat for that last paper and passed it. Thus my degree does have Babasaheb's name on it.

*

Around that time, CASA gave me a Suzuki motorcycle to get around. The motorcycle allowed me to travel from Beed to Ahmednagar, Latur, Osmanabad, Nanded and wherever else I wanted. Sometimes I would travel alone, sometimes an old friend like Dongardive would be with me. I would travel all night, sleeping as little as possible. I would meet people, talk to them, try and understand them. I knew what the people in the movement were feeling; I understood their enthusiasms, their joys and sorrows, their successes and their disappointments. I tried to pacify the many people I met who had been forgotten. I wanted to figure out if any of these people could show me the road I should take.

Shankar Sathe, the brother of Annabhau Sathe, had written a novel called *Lakhuji Mangaachi Katha* (The Story of Lakhuji Mang). When I was told that Lakhuji Mang was a real-life character, I decided to seek him out. He was five-and-a-half foot tall with piercing eyes, a droopy moustache, very much his own person. In his youth, he had been a dacoit. He was old now but he would hop on to my motorcycle and travel with me. He would tell me about all the places in Vategaon where he had concealed himself and how in certain areas, even the Marathas did not believe that he was a Mang. He told me about his deeds and doings in

Krantisinh Nana Patil's Prati-sarkar Movement* (Parallel Government). He would tell me how they raided the British government's post offices in order to collect money for the Independence Movement. But he was not acknowledged as a Freedom Fighter. This was because he was illiterate. Many others had spun their own stories, weaving khadi tales of their involvement in the Independence Movement and had secured government pensions for themselves. This had never occurred to Lakhuji Mang. He did not see why, in his old age, he should take on the label of being a safe-breaker, even if the safes had belonged to the British government. Might not the Indian government think he had his eye on theirs? Truly he was his own person.

When I would go into those areas, I would often hear stories of Biru Dhangar. He was popular among the people for he was held to rob the rich and give to the poor. I tried to meet him too, but in vain.

In Kolhapur, there was an Ambedkarite associate called M.T. More. He was the main leader of the Samta Sainik Dal which Dr Ambedkar had founded. I met him too. His children were educated. His house was happy and well-settled. 'All this has happened because of the good deeds of Dr Ambedkar,' he said. During the Mahad Tank Agitation, he had told Dr Ambedkar: 'If you give me permission, I will fill a tank with blood next to this one.' Babasaheb replied: 'What we want is the right to use this water. We have not started this satyagraha to fill tanks with blood.'

When I met these stalwarts, I would feel renewed; a new enthusiasm would fill me. I made it a point to meet people

---

*Krantisinh Nana Patil (1900-1976), born Nana Ramchandra Pisal, was a freedom fighter and later Member of Parliament. He set up a parallel government in the district of Satara.

who had worked for the Mang community: R.K. Tribhuvan of Aurangabad; Advocate Govind Barhalikar of Nanded; Kisanrao Awale, an industrialist from Ichalkaranji; Nanasaheb Katale of Nagpur among others. I would find out what they thought about the community. I would absorb their visions, their views, their anger, all of it. I whirled around as if my heels had wheels. Because of all this travelling, I had become like a ghost. Absorbing all these experiences, the very concept of fear was driven from my head.

*

One day, I was on the road out of Dukdegaon, then an unpaved path. It was so narrow that if two men came face to face, one would have to give way to the other. And there was Parbhu Bade, walking towards me. He was much shorter than me but he had a wrestler's physique. My enemy. The one who had announced that he had a knife hung with ghungroos with which he would kill me. Was he going to give way or was I? As soon as we came face to face, I grabbed him by the collar. I said: 'Where's that knife? Get it out. You want to murder me? Stick it in.' He had never expected me to behave like this. He was terrified and raised both his hands to show they were empty: 'No, no, I have no knife with me.' He opened his dhotar to show me that he had no knife concealed anywhere. As this was happening, some onlookers from the village gathered.

I had totally defeated Parbhu Bade in front of everyone. That was because I had managed to remove every trace of fear from my mind. But perhaps if he had had the knife with him, he might even have stuck it into me.

*

After I began working with CASA, my home had become the regional office. It was somewhat difficult to travel to and from my village because the road was a kachcha one. So I took a room in Majalgaon on rent and began to stay there. I brought the family there to live; it was also easier for the children to go to school there.

Baba was now bedridden. He could not get up on his own. Everything was done lying down. I could not bear to see him like that. He would try his best but the energy was temporary and very soon he would be exhausted. He would remain seated by the door. If anyone came and asked, 'Is Awad-sahib at home?' he would say, 'Aara, what sahib? Say sahib, sahib.' He did not know what was going on around him. We were seeing good days but he was slowly getting to the place where he was not even aware that these were our good days.

Around this time, a new philosophy came into CASA. The idea was to get the women and the young people to organize into groups and to use these groups to become agents of social change. CASA was basically a funding agency; it was supposed to provide economic support to self-help organizations. I took on this new project with great enthusiasm. I had contacts with many young activists who were working in villages. I began to guide them about how to write project proposals, how to account for the money that came in, how to set up an organization. CASA would then approve of aid to these organizations. Many of the organizations that we supported in those days are doing excellent work these days. During the time of this project, I started my own organization. 'Gramin Vikas Kendra' (Rural Development Centre or RDC). Through this organization, I began to do my own work. I started a women's self-help group in Dukdegaon; this micro-credit cell was then a very new idea. However, we began to operate this micro-credit group with the women of Dukdegaon. Subhash would take the meetings with the women's group. So that the women might become aware of how other groups were operating and what social work was being done, we organized expeditions for them. The women of Dukdegaon were getting out and about for the first time. This did not sit well with the men of the village. They opposed these activities and cast aspersions on the women's characters. But the women saw the point of these meetings and these expeditions. They fought their husbands and took part in the organization's activities.

At that time, we had started a movement in Dukdegaon with the women. There was a government clinic at Kuppa. A woman had been bitten by a snake. The antivenin injection is free but the doctor there asked her for seven hundred rupees. He would not even let her enter the clinic without paying this sum. In those days, seven hundred rupees was a vast sum of money. Her husband told me about this terrible thing the doctor had done. I put the issue to the women. They brought the women of Kuppa and Chinchala together and walked in a morcha to the government clinic. The District Health Officer addressed the morcha. The women made the doctor return the money he had extorted.

We started another movement in Dukdegaon. At that time, Dukdegaon and Chinchala had a common gram panchayat. The government had approved funds to build a school in Dukdegaon. The sarpanch was from Chinchala. He had consumed the funds earmarked for the school. When we found out about this, we got the children of Dukdegaon together. We prepared a complaint: 'Our school has been stolen. Could you help us find it?' This was presented by the children to the Panchayat Samiti. The activists organized the school in the middle of the Panchayat Samiti. The children would shout their lessons in the middle of the proceedings; sometimes they would raise slogans. This had an immediate effect. The sarpanch had to start the building work.

Around this time, my organization, Rural Development

Centre, had begun to gather momentum. We took up the cause of the water bodies too. Our experience while working in this area was also interesting. About 20 kilometres from Dukdegaon is a hamlet called Pimparwada, with a population of about 2,500. Most of the village was Vanjari; there was only a single Mahar family. Sahebrao Pawar, the young man of this Mahar family, was known to me. He had once sat on a hunger strike in front of the tahsildar's office. That was when I had met him. The women of this village had to walk 3 kilometres to fetch water. No one wanted their daughters to marry into Pimparwada because of the shortage of water in the village. Sahebrao and I had a discussion. After that, a project for a water body for Pimparwada and the neighbouring Chambartanda village was approved. We started the work.

The men and women of the village began to work on the project. Digging a channel, bunding and preparing gulley plugs began. I chose Sahebrao to supervise the work. He was well-respected in the village. If anyone had to be taken to hospital, it was Sahebrao who would do it; he was also the person who would be asked to sort out any disputes and arguments that might arise. He supervised the construction of the water body extremely well. In a year, the lake began to fill with water. To celebrate this, Anna Hazare, Judge Vahane and Justice Babaurao Tidke were all invited. The meeting went extremely well but this great gathering had a bad result. The Vanjari leader of the village was a stubborn man. He worked with the Hindutva parties. I was a Mang; Sahebrao, a Mahar. He must have felt that he could not work under the leadership of Mahars and Mangs. He began to harass Sahebrao. He even had false cases of theft filed against him. Things got so bad that Sahebrao eventually left the village to which he had brought the gift of water. Till today, Pimparwada does not have a water problem. But this taught me a lesson. I would no longer work with the upper castes. Instead, I worked on many projects that were meant to bring water to the Dalit farmers who were now tilling the gaayraan.

*

Beed district was home to the sugarcane cutter. Every year, more than six-and-a-half lakh workers from this district alone harvested sugarcane inside the state and outside it. People from my Dukdegaon also went sugarcane cutting. Even today, the condition of the sugarcane cutter is not a very good one but then it was a terrible life. A male and female couple of sugarcane workers was called a koyta (a scythe). If there were an underage worker with them, they were called deed (one-and-a-half) koyta. Contractors would take money from the sugarcane factories. If a koyta were to run away, or one half of it were to disappear, or fall ill, the contractor had to bear the loss. This meant inhumane treatment of the workers because the contractors were unwilling to bear any losses. Around August and September, the contractors would pay each koyta around six to seven thousand rupees and during the season he would take them to the sugarcane fields. If the money so advanced were not made up, the workers would be held to ransom, and often beaten up. In a way, this was bonded labour.

One year, seven couples from my Dukdegaon had taken up sugarcane cutting. The contractor was a Mang. Whatever a person's caste status, as soon as he gains a little power, even if it is over someone as weak as a sugarcane cutter, he begins to become arrogant. This contractor took the couples to a factory in Nanded but something went wrong there. He stopped the work. He would neither give them work, nor would he pay them, nor would he take them back to the village. None of them had any money so they were starving to death. There was a woman called Kewal from our village. She had attended one of our camps. She had begun to understand the concept of injustice. She might be illiterate but she was an intelligent woman and a voluble one. Kewal and her husband were among the workers. She had some jowar flour and some money. She distributed the flour among all the workers but it was soon over. Now they were reduced to foraging for berries and wild fruit but still the contractor was not willing to let them go. Everyone called Kewal's husband Captain. No one knew how he had come by this name for he was a docile, straightforward man. Captain and another man managed to get to me and tell me their story.

I sent Captain off with a letter to the tahsildar. This must have been the first letter ever written that described the work sugarcane cutters were doing as bonded labour. The letter demanded that the government use its machinery to end this practice. The tahsildar took cognisance of the letter and went to see the labourers but even before he got there, the contractor had done a deal with him. The tahsildar refused to do anything to free those labourers. I then sent Motiram Bade and Ashok Tangde to free the sugarcane cutters. They managed to find them and loaded them into a truck to bring them home. But the contractor came with them in the truck. He wanted to see how Eknath Awad was going to free his labourers.

The labourers came back to the village. I was not in the village. The contractor decided to wait for me. The workers all went back to their huts. Kewal decided to make some bhakri and since the contractor was also there, she went to invite him to eat with them. In reply he said, 'When I die, I will eat food from your hands in heaven; right now let me take care of the dogs and then I'll see to their master.' In other words, the dogs were the labourers and their master was me. But Kewal was not the kind of woman to take these things lying down.

She took off her slippers and began to beat the contractor. Other workers also gathered there. The contractor managed to get away. When I got to the village, I was told what had happened. The contractor was not just my fellow caste man, he was also a distant relative but that did not prevent me from registering a police complaint against him and getting him arrested. As far as I know, this must be the first case in which labourers were freed from the control of a contractor.

*

Now the village was ripe for change. The young men and the women, the children and the old, everyone was filled with a new enthusiasm. Meanwhile, we kept up the meetings and the camps in the village. My work was beginning to bear fruit. It was as when a couple of showers ripen the earth and now it is covered with green. Next, the wild vegetables begin to sprout as the seeds, long dormant in the soil, come to life. Absorbing the sunlight, the creepers begin to embrace the trees. Taking such support as they can get from available branches, the tendrils of the creeper climb over the trees. The air is filled with a fresh, wild, green scent.

This was the time of my greening.

9

I worked for six years at CASA. Through this time, I tried to bring the ideologies of Phule and Ambedkar to the work I did there. But how long could I do this? When a buffalo settles into a swamp, it does not get out easily. You have to use a stick to get it out. And each time you want to do this, you have to get into the swamp yourself. This was roughly my situation: each time I would drag the bullock out of the marsh and each time, it would head straight back there. Often I would think, 'Either I have to let the bullock go into the swamp and sit down with it there; or I have to walk away from the mess.' 1989 would prove to be my last year with CASA.

There is a certain routine in almost all self-help organizations. The parameters of this routine are defined by sympathy for the poor and the marginalized. You became the generous donor. My personality was not a good fit for this kind of organization. I wanted to start people off on morchas, push for social change. The first time a morcha was ever led by a CASA worker was when I organized one in Mukhed district.

Shalwin was now my direct superior. He did not see the point of raising social issues and pushing for change. He saw our work as helping the poor and giving food to the hungry. This was a humanitarian vision. It is not as if such work has no place. But my life and my experience had taught me that what was needed was a different approach, one that would address fundamental issues and bring about change at that level. The poor can earn their own bread. They need social service organizations to work towards a space where the poor can earn their living with self-respect. No NGO can ever abolish poverty; that is what the government should be doing.

And as long as the poor do not have a stake in society, as long as they do not question the powerful and seek to share the power that they wield, they will stay poor; or such is my opinion. Because of these fundamentally different approaches, Shalwin and I began to have many disagreements.

At my level, there was a young man called Razzak Pathan who was also reporting to Shalwin. Shalwin and he had teamed up. Razzak saw me as his competition but I ignored both of them because I knew the value of my work. But at meetings, these two would find fault with my work. They would say that I had not reported in; or if I had reported there were errors in my reporting and so on. This would annoy me but I would swallow my anger and ignore them. But one day, I was going to explode.

Once there was an activists' training camp at Meraj. During these camps, I would stay with the activists and eat with them. Shalwin, Razzak and the others would stay in a separate hotel and keep a distance between themselves and the activists. Many organizations do not seem to realize that activists are not just employees; they work because of their desire for change but their modest financial needs must be met if they have to work. In my opinion, this was also Shalvin's view of them.

The young men who had come to the Meraj camp were Dalits. They said to me, 'Bhau, mutton at one meal and chicken at another would be great.' I agreed immediately. Where else would boys like these get to satisfy their yearnings for food? They had a great time over those two days.

The bills for the camp went to Shalwin. He said, 'I'm not going to pass these bills.'

I said, 'Why not?'

He said: 'Why did you serve non-veg twice a day? This is not in the rules.'

I replied: 'What rules? These are the young men who do the work in the villages and in the fields. You lot sit in your posh Mumbai offices and stay in posh hotels. You have them stay in ordinary places. So if they eat meat twice a day, what terrible thing has happened? And if it does not fit into your rules, well then cut it from my salary.'

My words must have suggested that I thought that they were a self-indulgent lot. Shalvin was hurt by this. He walked out of the meeting. There was a tension in the air now.

I got on with my work. In a little while, another field officer who worked there, Kishore Gajbhiye, came up to me. Kishore and I were good friends. He said, 'Eknath, you do know what's going on in the office?'

I said, 'No. What?'

He said, 'Arre bhai, Shalvin is going to terminate your services. He's getting your termination order ready even now.'

I lost it. It was evening and there were only a few of us around. There was a teapoy in front of my desk. I gave it a sound kick and broke one of its legs. I picked up the leg and slammed it on the table. Then I said to Kishore: 'Go, tell Shalwin. You go ahead and terminate Eknath and he will terminate your head. The leg of this table and his head are going to meet up soon. Let him come here with my termination order.'

Kishore hopped it to Shalwin's cabin where he gave him a fright. 'Shalwin, you had better not terminate Eknath. He's out there, waiting to break your head.'

Hearing this, Shalwin was terrified. He came out of his cabin. I was sitting there with the stick in my hand. He said in a voice that was close to tears: 'See Eknath, I am not your enemy. We are co-workers. But you have to show me some basic respect. You're always using violence to settle things.'

I said, 'You just try it. Go ahead and terminate me. It will be difficult for you to stay in Mumbai.'

He was even more frightened now. He began his usual spiel: 'See what the Bible has taught us. We humans must not fight with each other.'

I said, 'You follow your Bible. This stick is my Bible. Don't try my patience.'

Shalwin left quietly. After this, he never spoke about terminating me again.

But that did not mean I sat silent either. I began to work on another issue entirely. The grassroots activists were made to work for very low wages. I talked to them about this and they all agreed to support me. They went on strike. The matter went up to the Delhi office but with a good result. At one stroke, everyone's salaries were raised. The activists were delighted with me. This meant that while Shalwin was the official head, I was the leader of the activists. Now Shalwin could not touch me. I began to behave as if I were the king of the organization.

I got deeply involved with the activists. Once, I brought a whole group of them to Mumbai. One evening, we went to Chowpatty beach. The boys wanted to play the games at the stalls there. There was one where you had to try your marksmanship by shooting balloons. The price was three tries for fifty paise but seeing that these were boys from the village, the stallholder tried to dupe them. He said it was ten rupees for three tries. When one of the young men refused to pay, the stall-owner slapped him under the ear. When I heard about this, I went running up. There was a bamboo lying near the stall. I picked it up and slammed it down on the stall-owner's back. He began to howl. His cries brought all the other stall-holders running up. My beard had grown at this time and my head was covered in a gamchhaa.

The stall-owner wailed: 'That Sardarji beat me, the Sardarji.' Ten or fifteen men came at me. I began to whirl the bamboo about and held them at bay. After all this time, thinking about that moment makes me laugh. This was as good as any fight sequence in a film. The police broke it up. We were all taken to the police station and the matter was resolved there.

But these moments brought me activists who were closer to me than brothers. My work began to increase. I only went to the office now to collect my salary. But the thought that I should start something of my own began to pester me. Whenever I went to Mumbai, I would pay Vivek-bhau a visit. At that time, Anil Shidore had just joined the funding agency Oxfam. He wanted to support organizations that were working for the cause of human rights. I would often describe the work I was doing in Marathwada to Vivek-bhau. He introduced me to Anil Shidore. In those days, I would wear safari suits. Anil Shidore looked at me and said to Vivek-bhau: 'Arre, what kind of activist is this? He looks like a sahib!'

Vivek-bhau said: 'Oh, he's an activist all right but one with a different style.'

This meeting with Anil-bhau proved decisive for me and for the direction that my life and work would take. Because of him, I would get a great deal of support from Oxfam for my work in the future.

*

I had been slowly expanding the scope of my work with CASA. Cutting the hair of the Potraj and stopping kaaran sacrifices from happening had given me the reputation of being a leader from among the Dalits. At that time, both the Shiv Sena and the Congress Party had toxic attitudes towards the Dalits. The leader of the Shiv Sena, Balasaheb Thackeray, had opposed the change of Marathwada University's name. Therefore the local established leaders thought of me as their enemy.

Twenty kilometres away from Majalgaon is a village called Telgaon. It has a Laman encampment near it. The Shiv Sena saw this encampment as a nuisance. While the Shiv Sena was seen as a Mumbai-based party that was fighting for the rights of Marathi people, in the villages it had the reputation of being an upper-caste party that was upholding the bitter pride of Hindu casteism. They would earn their money by attacking the poor, the Dalit, the Nomadic Tribes and other marginalized segments of society. The Lamans near Telgaon had borne the brunt of their bad behaviour too.

We had set up a women's savings group in this encampment. Rajubai, an extremely intelligent woman, belonged to this group.

Rajubai would take active part in all the meetings. At these meetings I would often talk about atrocities against and violence to Dalits. In her Laman tongue, she complained about the violence done to her people, how they were often beaten up. They were forced to work free for the upper castes. She asked me to support them so that they could go about their work peaceably. 'If a brave man like you takes up our case, we can work without fear,' she said. In return she was willing to give me two guntas* of her land free.

She had set me a challenge. Her faith that I could handle the criminal element meant a great deal to me. With the land she was offering, I could set up an office of the organization which would benefit her people as well. Later, when the organization had a little more money, we bought an acre of land from Rajubai. But at that time, it was her gift of two guntas of land that made it possible for us to build an office there. It wasn't much of an office, just a temporary shed made of gunny sacks and asbestos sheets on a bypass road where

*A gunta is 101.17 square metres.

no one went in the night for it was infamous for highway robberies.

The office could also be burgled but we had to keep the faith with Rajubai and the Lamans; it was important that we set up our office there.

As soon as we had set up office, the local leaders began to make inquiries. They had decided that by hook or by crook they wanted me out of there. About a week after we had started the office, it disappeared. One night, the whole thing was dismantled, the asbestos sheets were carried away. No one had said anything to me but this was a veiled warning.

My colleague, Motiram, went to the police to complain. The foujdar said, 'What a trifling complaint you have brought.' For him it seemed a trifle, a matter of two or three asbestos sheets. But we insisted on registering the complaint.

Rajubai's son Bhima, my nephew Vishnu and another boy from the village, Arun Awad, began to spend the nights there. One night, there was an attempt to frighten them off. Four or five goondas came and shouted at them. But those three boys did not come running away. Later, a local Congress leader filed fake cases of theft against them.

Whatever party they belong to, established political leaders still maintain close relations with their caste brothers. The Shiv Sena pramukh of Telgaon was a relative of the Congress Party member. This pramukh was the one who was causing all the trouble for the Lamans and did not want me anywhere near them. And so the Congress and the Shiv Sena got together against me. They wanted to frighten me off but I never gave them an inch. I bailed the boys out; later they were proved to be innocent.

One day, the Shiv Sena leader got hold of me. He had a gang of his boys with him. They surrounded me and tried to threaten me. Seeing this happen, my boys also began to gather. I said, 'My office will stay there. If you have the guts come and try and take it down now.'

Not long afterwards, the Telgaon gram panchayat elections came along. We got the Lamans all united and fought the Shiv Sena incumbent. As a result, he lost. The people who wanted to break my office down had been washed out of office by the people's rage but my office remains where it was. It is now a proper office. Hundreds of people bring their problems there every day.

*

We kept on having camps at Dukdegaon and at other villages. The song '*Nahin mhana*' (Say no) began to have a deep effect on the minds of the youth. But actually, the first instance of refusing to do gaavki,* the unpaid labour of the village, happened at Tigaon. Raju Kuchchekar, a thirteen- or fourteen-year-old boy would often come to our meetings. He had lost his father. His mother had mental problems. The Mahars of the village had given up Maharki; the Mangs had therefore taken it over. Raju was a Mang.

In Tigaon, a Maalkari had devoted himself to looking after the temple. The people of the village called him 'Maharaj'. One morning, as Maharaj was making his way to the temple, he saw a dead pig in front of it. Who was to clear it away? The Mahars now refused to do this work. And so Maharaj went to tell a Mang to do this unclean job.

Raju and his mentally ill mother were in their hut. Maharaj arrived and called out to Raju, 'Hey boy, come along, there's

---

*In the traditional caste-based village economy, certain work was assigned to certain castes. Mangs did Mangki, Mahars did Maharki and the whole was subsumed under the term gaavki, work done for the village, which was unpaid but which entitled the do-er to some share in the village produce.

a dead pig in front of the temple. Come and clear it away.' In Raju's head the song 'Nahin mhana' was playing like a mantra. He refused to do this.

His refusal stung Maharaj. He began to beat the boy, saying, 'If you refuse, your mother will have to do it.' So saying, this servant of the gods beat a boy mercilessly. Raju came crying to Dukdegaon.

I took a group of activists and went to Tigaon. We went and saw the place where the dead pig was still lying in front of the temple. Seeing so many people arriving with Raju started some murmuring in the village. We called the police. We registered this as an act of bonded labour, forcing a child to clear away the remains of a dead pig. Maharaj was arrested. At that time, the Atrocity Act was not yet in force. Although a case had been filed against Maharaj, the village did not relent. We knew that we would have to teach it a lesson.

The Dalits of Tigaon would participate in the 'Food for Work' scheme. Rama Awad of Dukdegaon was in charge of supervising the work. He had fallen in love with one of the women who came to work; she was from Tigaon. The girl's parents thought that having a son-in-law who was in charge of this scheme was a good idea. The families gathered for the wedding.

This marriage offered us a way to get the upper castes of Tigaon on the straight and narrow. We announced that the bridegroom would go to Maruti's paara. All the young men gathered to accompany the bridegroom. The people of Tigaon did not understand why the people of Dukdegaon were insisting on the bridegroom going to the paara. The Tigaonkars went off to the police station to complain. They said, 'The Mangs are coming to pollute the paara of Maruti's temple. You must arrest them.'

Their honest opinion was that we were committing an

offence. The foujdar explained things to them: 'We have no power to arrest them. On the other hand, if you continue to protest we will have to escort them to the temple under police protection and we will have to arrest you. You will be thrown into jail and you won't even get bail.'

The villagers were shocked. 'This is a law made for the Mangs and Mahars by one of their kind.' They mumbled and muttered but they withdrew their opposition. And so Rama Awad of Tigaon went in a procession, with songs and music to accompany him, to the paara of Maruti's temple.

*

A young man named Sudhakar Kshirsagar came to this marriage, a member of the bride's party. Sudhakar was a member of the Bahujan Samaj Party's (BSP's) BAMCEF. I knew Sudhakar. He was from the tailoring business. He was a man of strong opinions and a magnificent poet.

Lines from a qawwali of his describe the life of the Dalit:

Subah ki laali Daliton ke lahu ki hoti
Unki Holi bhi Daliton ke lahu ki hoti
Shaam bhi hoti hai Daliton ki lahu se rangkar
Niklo ghar-ghar se tum Bhim ke sipaahi bankar.

The dawn breaks red with the blood of the Dalit.
They celebrate Holi with the blood of the Dalit.
The evening takes its shades from the blood of the Dalit.
Come out of your homes and join the army of Bhim.

When I met Sudhakar, he was in a state of political disillusionment. I asked him: 'Sadhya, what are you up to these days?'

He said: 'The Dalit Panthers folded up. Then we sought an identity in the BSP's BAMCEF. It seemed as if BAMCEF and the BSP would never part ways. But they did. Now I don't feel I should participate in any movement or organization.'

I said: 'I want to bring back the energy and excitement in the Dalit movement. I want the youth to hear the messages of Ambedkar and Phule.'

Sudhakar said, 'But you're always with Brahmins.'

He had heard of my association with Vivek-bhau; that I had worked with the Vidhayak Sansad. And there had been rumours that I had converted to the Christian faith and was converting people to it. Sudhakar was labouring under these misapprehensions.

He added: 'And what's all this about temple entry? Are we supposed to abandon these gods or cleave to them? You're bringing the Mangs back to these gods and temples.'

Only an educated and thoughtful person could ask such questions. That was why I wanted him to work with me. I said: 'I think you're misunderstanding the work I do. Why not join us for a while, find out what we're about and then form your own decisions. We may talk about Dalits having the right to temple entry but we have no truck with god. But we need to awaken the human inside the human being.'

Something I said must have made sense to Sudhakar. Or perhaps he simply thought, 'Let's try this too for a little while and see.' Whatever his reason, he did stay with us and eventually he became one of the most committed activists of our organization.

*

And then the nineties began. This decade would rewrite all the contexts for political and social work. My life too would change dramatically and take a new direction. I was no longer living in poverty. I began a new phase in my life. I had many activist friends who were joining the movement. The youth were forming new groups to fight casteism. At this time, Vivek-bhau toured Marathwada. He was then a consultant to Oxfam. With economic aid from Oxfam, many organizations were running adult literacy classes, teaching women to stitch and so on.

But no one was working on caste issues. Vivek-bhau began to talk to the heads of various organizations. He advised them to put the fight against casteism on their agendas too.

Vivek-bhau's organization was still working with Adivasis on the issue of bonded labour. He saw that Marathwada too had bonded labour as part of the caste system. Any person who was, by writing, by speech or by tradition bonded to his master, who worked under compulsion, who had no right over the produce of his labour, who could not sell the fruits of his labour or use them himself, was a bonded labourer according to the law. By caste traditions, if you were born a Dalit, you were required to work free for the village. By the very fact of birth, Dalits were slaves. They had no rights over the work they did and none over the fruits of their labour. The work they were doing as gaavki was therefore a perfect fit for the definition of bonded labour. This was also a violation of human rights. At that time, this was a novel way of looking at it. Turning bonded labour into a human-rights issue meant it could be brought to the forefront.

Until that time I had seen casteism as an evil practice and as an evil practice, I had fought it. This was around 1989. New winds of globalization had begun to blow across the world. Capitalism and communism had divided the world for decades; now this was ending. The world was beginning to become a smaller place. In the sphere of international politics, boundaries were beginning to blur. The Berlin Wall fell. Similar winds of change began to blow in the Union of Soviet Socialist Republics. The idea of human rights, espoused by the United

Nations, began to spread across the world. The effects of this began to be felt in India too. During the 1970s, the talk had all been about capitalism, communism, socialism, sarvodaya and feminism; now human rights began to gain importance. Whatever the ideological basis of a society, it was to be judged on the opportunities every human being had to live as one. Vivek-bhau had his eye on the international scenario. He began to frame the debate about casteism in Marathwada in the new discourse of human rights.

When I had left Vidhayak Sansad to work with CASA, D.R. Jadhav—otherwise known as D.R. joined the Vidhayak Sansad. D.R. had a strong line on casteism and was an intelligent and energetic activist.

Later, he took a job with the Maharashtra Housing and Development Authority. But the government job did not fulfil him. Vivek-bhau brought D.R. and me together. 'Let us work together to fight casteism in Marathwada,' began to be the leitmotif of our many conversations. I had already been working on these issues. But with Vivek-bhau and D.R., we could put the fight on a war footing.

*

This Marathwada in which we were going to work, what was it like? What was its mindset? And how had this been shaped?

The derogatory word 'Dheda'—used to describe all Dalits—was coined in Marathwada. It had been first been used to describe the Mahars of the Nizam's kingdom. In Maharashtra, a common phrase is 'Mahar-Mang'; in Marathwada, it was 'Dheda-Mang'. If you wanted to insult someone, you spat words like 'Dhedgya', 'Dheda', 'Mangtya' or 'Dhedpat' at them. If you wanted to describe a chaotic event with lots of shouting and screaming, you would say, 'Is this a Dhedgujari (a Dheda market)?'

Marathwada was part of the state of Hyderabad. It was part of the Nizam's kingdom. One year after India gained independence, the Nizam acceded to the State and become part of India. The British had deliberately given the Nizam independent status a year before. That meant the Independence Movement was not as vigorous there as it was in the rest of the country. No political leader, Gandhi included, could enter the state of Hyderabad. Swami Ramanand Tirtha was doing some work under the guidance of Gandhiji but in comparison to the rest of the country, progressive movements were minimal.

The important jobs in the Nizam's state were called Ahd-e Kuliyaan and the unimportant ones were called Gairkuliyaan. Muslims were employed in 95 per cent of the Ahd-e kuliyaan; the remaining 5 per cent were taken by non-Muslims. None of these non-Muslims was ever a Dalit. Some Mahars did have a copperplate stating they had been granted fifty-two rights but these were limited to their rights of baluta. Some of them had even been given gifts of land for services rendered but this land was generally infertile or the kind that would give very little by way of crops.

There were even some Mahar watandars* in Marathwada. Maharki was divided into Jaaglya (those who went around waking up the populace by beating drums) and Watandars. The Mahar-Jaagle were generally the sepoys of the Patils and the Kulkarnis. Their work was not limited to just what the government required them to do; they would do whatever the Patils and Kulkarnis asked of them, too. If an important outsider came to the village, they would have to run errands for him. They were required to report to the Patil or Kulkrani if there were any despoliation of government property or if

---

*The watandar held rights to the land that had been conferred on him by another as watan. This was generally tilled by others.

there were boundary or signpost disputes. They would have to carry the village revenue and taxes as and when required. They had to look after any army platoon stationed near them. They had to arrange for hospitality for visiting government officials, and look after their vehicles. All this fell to the Mahar's lot. The Mang got the leavings and the scrapings. At some places Mahars worked by rotation; in some places this changed at Akshaya Tritiya and at some places on the Amavasya of Bhavai.

There was a little land set aside for the Mahars to do their traditional work; this was called the 'hadke-haduli'. But one was never paid in cash for the village work. The Dalits of Marathwada therefore lived in a state of dependence.

Jobs were hard to come by for the Dalits. The textile mills in the Nizam's territory would not hire Dalits. This was because if the thread broke from the bobbin in the spinning machine, it would have to be rejoined with saliva. This meant that a Dalit would pollute the thread. The Muslims too saw this as pollution. In other industries, they would be given menial jobs that involved physical labour; and there were even Dalit workers to serve the Dalits their tea. Whether in the school or in the factory, the water to be drunk by Hindus and Muslims was kept separate; and then there was water which was supposed to be drunk by the Untouchables. Not even a tumbler was placed near the waterpot meant for the Untouchables. In the restaurants, there were separate cracked dishes and cups and saucers for the Untouchables. Even when the state was abolished, these practices continued.

It was not until 1944 that Dr Ambedkar visited Marathwada. Under the guidance of Dr Ambedkar, B.S. Vyankatrao and B. Shyamsunder began a movement called the Anjuman-e Pashth Akhyaam in the Nizam's state. This movement had the Nizam's protection. The important demands they made were for the Dalits to be given land, that the Nizam should set up educational institutions for them, and that there should be some representation in his government. But there was not much emphasis on the basic injustices of the caste system. In the villages, the relationship between the upper castes and the Untouchables was as toxic as ever. In the matter of a progressive outlook, this was a backward state. It would be a difficult thing to start a movement to fight caste injustice in this state. And after the Renaming Movement, casteism had increased with more atrocities being committed by the upper castes against the Dalits.

Among the Dalits, the Mangs were even more backward. This was the society that we had to awaken. This was the difficult work we had agreed to do.

Vivek-bhau, D.R. and I began to arrive at some decisions. D.R. resigned his government job. I stopped going to the CASA office. I simply took the last three months' salary. And as soon as our work began to pick up pace, I wished CASA 'Jai Bhim' and was on my way.

10

The erstwhile Mahars, who were now Neo-Buddhists, had achieved a great deal of progress by fighting for their rights and holding fast to the principles of Dr Ambedkar. This was how we wanted to work for the Mang community. Outside Marathwada, some Mangs had achieved some measure of awakening but within the area, the Mangs were living backward lives. Educational opportunities were scarce. This meant that lives of self-respect were impossible. And then there was the Mang vs Mahar war. The Mahars saw the Mangs as traitors; the Mangs had equally nasty attitudes to the Mahars.

There was a Minister of Parliament from the Mang community named Devrao Kamble from a village in Pathri Zilla, Parbhani Taluka. As a young man, he had written Dr Ambedkar a letter saying, 'You are a leader of the Mahars only.'

Babasaheb responded to his criticism in a magazine he edited: 'If the Mahars are behind me, that cannot be held to be my fault but if you should ever start a movement among the Mangs, rest assured, I will join you.' This was the appeal Babasaheb made to Devrao.

Devrao Kamble went on to get himself a good education. He became an MP from the Congress Party. But his opinion of the Mahar community remained what it was. His nephew, B.S. Kamble, now works in the movement with me. He was a member of the Dalit Panthers, an Ambedkarite to the core. He fought his entire family to stay in the Ambedkarite movement. Devrao would say mockingly of him, 'He is the child of a Mahar.' Later B.S. decided to get his younger brother married according to Neo-Buddhist rites. Devrao did not approve of this. He refused to come to the wedding mandap. I had achieved some fame as someone trying to bring awakening in the Mang community. I was asked to intervene. When I went to meet him, he was in a temper, refusing to come. I requested him to do so. He refused initially but I sat there, stubbornly. Finally, he agreed but only because it was I who had made the request. But his attitude towards the Mahars remained unchanged.

If this is the mindset of the educated Mang, you can imagine what it is like with the ones who have not had the benefit of education. And it was precisely these communities which we were hoping to bring to the forefront of our struggle. But if we had made this all about the Mang community alone, it would have narrowed our struggle and our minds. We wanted to bring the ideology and principles of Phule and Ambedkar to the Mangs. We did not want to limit ourselves to the Mangs and lose the support of the Neo-Buddhists. And so we began to seek out activists from among the Neo-Buddhists.

Once, Vivek-bhau and I went to meet Gajbhiye, the Deputy District Officer. One of our practices has always been to meet the officers and to get to know them. Gajbhiye was a good officer who had worked his way up from the Dalit community. He showed some sympathy for our movement and its goals. 'There is one Valmik Nikalje who is doing good work in the Aashti Taluka,' he said.

I met Valmik. He had done an MSW from Ahmednagar College; he was a fine aggressive activist. When I met him, he was sitting on a hunger strike on some local issue. I told him about our intention of starting a movement for Dalits other than the Mahars and he immediately agreed to be part of it.

Valmik, D.R., Sudhakar Kshirsagar, Ashok Tangde, Baban Awad, Motiram Bade, Subhash Gaikwad and I comprised the core team. We began to meet many other people. There was a self-help organization called Surya in Nanded. We met

Baburao Aakarbikar from this organization. From the Samajik Arthik Vikas Sanstha (Social and Economic Development Organization) Kerwadi, we met Ramakant Kulkarni. In Latur, we met Onkar Birajdar of the Gramin Vikas Shikshan Sanstha (Rural Development Education Organization) and Pandurang Birajdar and Shivappa Birajdar; also Baburao Dhule and many different people from different castes and organizations working at different levels. Vivek-bhau had good relations with all of them. We began to seek out many activists and exchange ideas with them. We must have met around fifty activists. We called a meeting at the Mahesh Lodge, Udgir. Everyone was seized of the idea of starting a movement in all the eight zillas of Marathwada, of starting a social awakening in the Mang community, of ending Mangki, Maharki and fighting casteist practices of every kind. By 1989, the Dalit Panther movement had faded; Sharad Pawar had given Ramdas Athavale a ministerial position in his cabinet; the Republican Party had split.

The question of renaming the Marathwada University was still alive. Atrocities against Dalits continued. The need of the hour was an aggressive organization that could energize the Dalit community. This was felt by all the activists gathered there. But we also had to bring a discipline to the movement. Many of those who had come to the meeting called themselves activists and wanted to be activists but had no idea of the laws, the legal system, the Indian Constitution, the administrative systems, the machinery of the police. That we all needed to be trained in these things became a common opinion.

The question of what the organization should be called came in for a great deal of discussion. We did not want to set up an organization that would work for a single caste, for a single community, on a single issue and so a name that was comprehensive had to be found. And so it was: Maanavi Haq Abhiyaan (Campaign for Human Rights).

Setting up the Maanavi Haq Abhiyaan was a turning point in my life no doubt, but it also brought about a change in the lives of countless people. A golden age began in my life. I was chosen as the main convener of the organization.

The first of the organization's camps was held at Vasai. Fifty activists from Marathwada attended the camp. We familiarized the participants with the methods of work, the procedures and decision-making processes of organizations. In order to establish our own, we studied the work done by the Vidhayak Sansad; we interacted with their activists to find out how they had discovered the issues that needed to be tackled, how they should be resolved, how people had to be brought on board. Vivek-bhau, D.R., the socialist leader Sadanand Varde, Sangeeta Koparde, Vidyut-tai, Ra Vi Bhuskute, Da Go Prabhu, Shelapkar and I comprised the trainers' team. Many experts came to talk about various laws. We were like fields that had been ploughed and sown and were waiting for the rain.

*

We had primed the activists' memories and we were ready for action. We did not just have the laws down on paper, we had them off by heart. My mind would wander around and finally come back to our list of activists' names: who would be effective at what jobs, what skills and abilities did each have, what were the areas in which they were lacking. I was filled with a kind of creative restlessness that threatened to suck me into itself.

We decided to have an inaugural programme. There would be an exhibition at every tahsil office in Marathwada. The date: 10 December, Human Rights Day. Caste practices were a stain on the nation's human-rights record. This made the day highly appropriate. We would take the lead in attacking and destroying these practices that violated the rights enshrined in the Indian Constitution which should have been available to Dalits as well. We would apply to every tahsildar demanding that gaavki, Maharki and Mangki be brought to an end. We would organize symbolic protests as well.

The first programme got off to a flying start. Now it was essential that the organization should make a ceremonial announcement of its presence. We called it the Nirdhaar Parishad, a meeting marked by our determination. This meeting happened on 17 December, 1989 in Mumbai. More than a hundred activists from Marathwada went to Mumbai to attend it. There were Adivasi activists from the Dahisar–Vasai area, many grassroots activists who worked in the villages. P.N. Bhagwati, retired Chief Justice of the Supreme Court, was the chief guest at this gathering. His name was all over the newspapers then. He was famous for his judgements that took the side of the poor; he was also known for taking action even if someone wrote him a postcard about a social problem. Chief Justice Bhagwati gave us our pledge: 'I will always endeavour to sow in society the values of equality, independence, brotherhood and justice that are enshrined in the Constitution of India. I will not bear atrocities committed upon women in my society. I will dedicate my life to fighting these atrocities.'

An important event took place at the Nirdhaar Parishad. Abhang Londhe and Padminibai Kamble of Pandarwadi village in Latur, who had been doing Mangki, announced that they were no longer going to do it.

*

What must have been going through the minds of Abhang Londhe and Padminibai Kamble as they returned from

Mumbai in a tempo? It was an extraordinary decision that they had made. What happened next?

Abhang Londhe's great-great grandfather, his great grandfather, his grandfather, his father and he, too, would play the sheda at the Maruti Temple. Padminibai's great grandmother, her grandmother and mother and, now, Padminibai would clean the cow dung from the cattle pen. In reality, many more generations than these had been doing this work. And as their ancestors had been given alms in the form of bhakri so were the descendants.

The same work, the same impotent lives. Now with the strength of our organization, this impotence would end; we would crush the idea of gaavki. As they returned to their village in a tempo, what were they thinking? In my head, Annabhau Sathe's lines:

> *Gulamgirichya yaa chikhalaat rootoon baslaa kaa Airavat?*
> *Neegh baaheri, anga jhaaduni…*
> *Ghe bineevarti ghaav,*
> *Saangoon gele maalaa Bhimrao.*
> *Jag badal ghaaluni ghaav, saangoon gele maalaa Bhimrao.*

> Are you still mired in the muck of slavery, Airavat?
> Cleanse your body and come out.
> Take the blow upon your chest
> This is the banner Bhimrao unfurled,
> Strike a blow to change the world.

I felt that even if these were not the precise words in their heads, this must be what they were feeling. For they did refuse thereafter to do the Mangki of Pandarwadi.

Our first struggle was now afire.

*

When the sun begins to set, the cattle return to the village. This is the signal for the Mangs to gather in the front of the temple and play the halgi. Only when they were done with Maruti, Vitthal–Rakhumai, Lakshmi-ai…saluted each and every god, could they go back to their huts. When it was dark, the stoves would be lit. Now the village would have cooked their bhakri; now the Mangs would go, stick in hand, and stand in front of the doors of the upper castes and in a pitiful voice, they would have to beg: 'Please feed the lowly…give me some roti, mother.' If there were Yeskars* in the village, the Mang and the Yeskar would compete in their shouting. Then the woman of the house would give them both something. All his life, Abhang had begged in this way.

Now Padminibai broke with another tradition. In the morning, the farmers would let their animals loose. The enclosures in which they had spent the night would be filled with their shit and piss. It was the Mangs' duty to clear all this up, fill it in baskets and carry it to the dung heap and dispose of it there. Then the pen would have to be washed, the women's courtyard cleaned and the dirt disposed of. Wiping away the sweat, they would set the baskets down by the wall and peer through a window into the house.

'Come in, Madam?' they would ask.

A voice from inside would reply: 'Wait, wait. Take the bhakri…'

Then with the edge of her sari over her head, her eyes fixed on the ground, she would take the stale bhakri. For generations this had gone on: the clearing of the shit, the begging for bread, not raising your head to speak, a life of dependence.

Padminibai had now rejected this life.

---

*Yeskars or Veskars are also Dalits. In his dictionary, Molesworth says a Veskar 'is the person appointed to keep the gate of a village. He is usually a Mahar.'

The village was shocked. 'The Mangs were refusing Mangki…motherfuckers!' they began to say on the paara. Spitting tobacco juice, they would abuse any Mang who happened to be present with sentiments such as, 'These Mangs should be crushed.'

Onkar Birajdar was an activist from the Lingayat community. He was the District Convener of the Maanavi Haq Abhiyaan. The village saw the Lingayats as upper caste but Onkar took on the village. His village was close to Pandarwadi. He announced his support for Padminibai and Abhang Londhe. But a social boycott of the Dalit settlement was announced. They were forbidden from using the village ration shop nor could they bring their grain to grind at the flour mill. They were not given work in the fields. 'We'll let you live if you're willing to do Mangki; otherwise starve to death,' they were told. The atmosphere heated up. Onkar, Shivappa Pandurang and Baburao Dhule were the upper-caste youngsters who helped Abhang and Padminibai. They collected grain from neighbouring villages for them. This was ground and taken to the Dalit settlement. We, too, collected grain, even if it was a handful at a time. The truth about Pandarwadi began to reach every village. 'Today, it's their turn; next, it will be ours,' people said and began to help. Everything from salt to chillies began to reach Pandarwadi. That raised tensions further. The village threatened Onkar with murder. Onkar was naturally frightened. Even two months later the boycott remained in effect. The pressure from the upper castes made his so much as leaving the house difficult.

It was against this background that we held a women's meeting near Pandarwadi. There was a mango orchard one or two kilometres away from the village. In the shade of these trees, we held the meeting. It was Chaitra* and the weather

---

*Chaitra is around March–April.

was hot. Women began to gather with babies on their hips, chanting, '*Aamcha ladaa kashaasaathi? Maanus mhanoon jagnyaasaathi!*' (What are we fighting for? The right to live as human beings!) In this struggle we gained much valuable and vital support. From Sadvijay Arya, for instance, a progressive leader from the Nilanga taluka. Arya was an Arya Samaji. He had a reputed educational institute in the district. He sent his workers from the institute and his D.Ed* students to the women's meeting. When an important man like Arya began to support us, it was natural that other people of note should also help. But if Sadvijay Arya was on the Dalit side, it became clear that Sambhaji Patil was on the side of the upper castes.

Sambhaji Patil was one of the district's rich and well-established men. He was an important leader of the Congress Party. He had a huge wada in Shirur Anantpal. It was said that the walls were so thick that you could drive a bullock cart on top of them. He was considered a descendent of Raja Bhoja in the area. And so a feudal atmosphere had been generated. The Patil had gathered all the upper castes at his wada. We had our meeting close by.

The speeches at the meeting grew heated. 'Aara, we are children of Babasaheb and our chests are made of steel. We will not turn back without teaching you a thing or two about Babasaheb's teachings!'

None of the Dalits gathered had ever heard such language used about the Patil. Slogan after slogan and the decision to stand firm grew.

After my speech I was sent a message from the wada: 'Come and meet us.' The speech had been made over loudspeakers and had probably reached their ears. I left for the wada alone. The meeting continued and tension mounted in the village.

---

*D.Ed stands for Diploma in Education.

I roared up on my motorcycle. Women and children were staring at me from the windows of the houses. 'Will this man return from there?' was the question on every face. I entered the wada. On every Patil face, the thought: *'Kahaan Raja Bhoja, kahaan Gangu Teli?'**

'Why are you inciting people? These people who were living peacefully with each other have begun fighting because of you. Do not let this grow,' was Sambhajirao's tune.

I said: 'Our demand is that the Dalit should get justice. Whatever happens, Abhang and Padminibai are not going to do Mangki again. Our movement will continue. The village will have to back down.'

The Patils began to look angry. They muttered and mumbled among themselves. Taking the opportunity, I said: 'You are here in great numbers. I am alone. But if so much as a hair on my head is harmed, imagine what will happen. If I do not return to the meeting in ten minutes, the folk gathered there will come here.'

That made him play a more peaceful tune. He ordered that I be served tea and so having delivered my message to the Patils, I went back to the meeting.

Even after this, the boycott continued. The Dalits got no daily labour in the village. Then we demanded the implementation of a labour scheme. We led a morcha to the tahsildar's office. D.J. Dande was the tahsildar. He had no idea about the daily work scheme. So he had no way to give us a concrete assurance. He slipped out of the back door. We locked the doors and began a camp about the daily work scheme. We did not let the tahsildar into his office for two days. The

---

*In Hindi in the original. The phrase sums up the class system, suggesting that a royal and famed king and an oil-presser cannot be compared.

tahsildar filed a case against the activists for interfering with and disrupting government work but this incident gave everyone a shot in the arm. News from Pandariwada began to appear in the papers. Vivek-bhau wrote an article, 'Dark Tales from Pandariwada'. Baburao Dhule prevailed upon a journalist to write a story too. The news came on Mumbai's Doordarshan and so questions were raised in the Vidhan Sabha. At that point, Jayantrao Tilak was the Speaker of the Vidhan Sabha.

He ordered that a teacher and the Police Patil be fired. The struggle lasted for four months and only then did the village withdraw the boycott. This victory allowed us to take the spark that had been ignited here to other villages as well.

*

In Marathwada, the halgi was also called the haalki. The Potraj played the haalki but at every festival or village event, the Mangs would play the haalki, the sanai and the trumpet. This music is called Mangbaaj. The Mangs were not paid for their Mangbaajaa. Marriage processions could not happen without Mangbaaj. From the Dalits upwards, if the Patils had to be invited for a wedding, Mangbaaj had to accompany it. At a funeral too, the Mangs had to play. Thus, the village expected the Mangs to play at a series of different events and festivals.

This happened in Hingoli zilla. The baaraatis were dancing and the Mangs were playing. Everyone had drunk freely. The groom's party was from the city. They wanted the newest songs played. 'Ay, pipaanyaa,* play some new songs,' they would shout. The Mang musicians were from rural areas. They did not know the new songs. For this they were beaten inhumanly.

---

*A pipani is a musical instrument played by the Dalits in Mangbaaj. A pipaanya is a derogatory way of referring to someone playing the instrument.

Three or four of them had their limbs broken. One of those so injured was a young Mang, Keshav Avchar, who was in touch with our organization. We filed a case. The entire groom's party was dragged to the police station. The strength of the organization began to be discussed far and wide.

Because of these events which were happening close by, the Mangs began to wake up. In Nanded, Shankar Pawar of the Laman community was an aggressive activist. He and Machchindra Gawale, a Mang boy, got all the Mangbaaj players together. They told them about the injustice in Hingoli and the struggle in Pandarwadi. In great excitement, the Mangs organized a programme for Holi. I was invited for it. And so, the bonfire of Markhel village's musical instruments was set alight. When those beautiful shehnais were burning, I felt bad but it was the self-respect that I could see generated in the Mangs through these flames that was of prime importance.

Other programmes, consciousness-raising meetings, all were based on this idea. When we saw a Mang with a halgi under his arm, we would smash it. I remember an interesting meeting that took place in Jalkot village, Latur zilla. During the Renaming Movement, Jalkot had been established as a sensitive village.

When the University's name had been changed, riots had erupted in the village. During these riots, the upper castes had burned a foujdar by the name of Bhurewar to death; he had been trying to keep the peace. Because the village had been designated as sensitive, we decided to have a meeting there. During the meeting, a man by the name of Raghunath Namwad did an interesting thing. I was giving a speech: 'My poverty-stricken brothers and sisters, let me tell you a story. Dr Babasaheb told the Dalits: "Leave the villages, go to the cities. Abandon the practices of Maharki and Mangki and get jobs. Get an education." At that time, the Mahars and Mangs, paying heed to Dr Babasaheb's words, left for the cities. As a train entered the station, the Mahars would jump in. When the Mangs tried to do this they could not. Why? Aavo, they had their halgis under their arms. The train doors are narrow. How could they get in with their halgis under their arms? The Mangs stayed back in the village to clean the Patils' dung; and the Mahars went to the cities to work as Brahmins work. What do you understand by this? Who lives by the haalki, his caste is halki (of no importance), his language is halki (slight), his gait is halki, his life is halka.'

As my speech ended, Raghunath Namwad came on stage. He said: 'No one plays the haalki as well as I can. Many people have appreciated my art and have given me baksheesh. I too have played the haalki with great enjoyment. But now I give it up. I have understood what it means to play the haalki. In front of all of you, I abandon the haalki.'

So saying, he smashed his haalki on the stage. At this meeting, the sarpanch of Jalkot had been seated on the stage. He said, 'From today, no one will do gaavki in the village. If there is ever any injustice to a Dalit in the village, I will rub my nose on the ground.'

*

Such incidents began to happen, one after another. Now we got no leisure and in the middle of all this, the organization decided to take up the question of Patoda, Khurd village. There Janardhan Gadkar, a Neo-Buddhist, young and aggressive, tried to celebrate Dr Ambedkar's birth anniversary.

The procession started out but the village had its knives and swords at the ready. The Dalits turned back. The procession did not go into the village. The upper castes threatened to kill Janardhan but he did not falter in his opposition to the village.

One day, Janardhan went to fetch water. The Dalits were not allowed to touch the water. Janardhan waited for a long time for someone to fill his vessel.

The upper-caste women would fill their vessels and walk away. They would pour water over their own feet but no one would fill Janardhan's pot. He asked one of the women if she would fill it for him, to see what she would say. She replied, 'That's all I have to do in the world? Go to the river and get your own water.' Janardhan returned home with his vessel empty. The river was where people went to shit. The river was where the buffaloes were shaved. That night Janardhan could not sleep for the thought that the river water was good enough for the Mahar but the well in the village was reserved for the upper castes. His brain began to burn. Janardhan told his cousin Bapu about his feelings. His cousin was also enraged by this injustice.

The next day, Janardhan and Bapu went together to the borewell. It was winter. A line of shivering Mahar and Mang women and children had formed by the well. No one was giving them water. The upper-caste women were filling their pots and walking away. Seeing this, Janardhan and Bapu began to draw water from the well. Fearing a riot, some of the Mahar and Mang women ran back to the settlement. The village gathered. Janardhan and Bapu were beaten up. A boycott was announced of the Dalits. The gaayraan was off limits for their cattle.

Janardhan went to the BSP and the RPI for help. They advised him to withdraw his agitation. Janardhan's sister lived in a village called Ekkurka Road. This was D.R.'s village. The upper castes of Patoda were not allowing their animals to graze. Janardhan and Bapu brought their animals to Ekkurka Road. There they met D.R. and told him what had happened.

We chose 20 March, the day on which Dr Babasaheb had

performed satyagraha at the Chavdaar Tank, Mahad, in 1927 for our agitation at Patoda. Mahars and Mangs from many villages came to participate; everyone was in high spirits at the satyagraha; it caused an uproar. Maanavi Haq Abhiyaan was the name on everyone's lips. Finally the police had to take a hand. Bapu and Janardhan and our organization emerged victorious. During this struggle, Janardhan became an activist who was associated with us and no one thereafter dared to lay so much as a finger on him.

*

Something similar happened to Rama Motewar, who was working as a labourer. We had a meeting at Nanded. Rama Motewar had come to the meeting. When night fell, Vivek-bhau told him: 'Stay the night, go in the morning.'

He replied: 'No, sahib. I stand guard on my master's fields. He comes in the night on horseback. If he doesn't find me in the fields, he will beat me.'

Vivek-bhau saw an issue to tackle there immediately.

'Why will he beat you? What does a single night matter? And if you spend every night at your master's fields, how do you sleep with your wife?'

Rama said somewhat coyly, 'After dinner, I spend some time with my wife and then I go to the fields. I owe my master money.'

Vivek-bhau said, 'Let's see how he dares to touch you. Your slavery ends tomorrow.'

Rama began to plead: 'No, no, I am frightened.'

None of us would let him go. He began to weep out of fear. We calmed him down and kept him with us.

The next morning was a new dawn for Rama. On the one hand there was a tradition that had lasted centuries and left him full of pain and fear; on the other hand was the hope that he might be freed from slavery. We sent Rama on ahead. Behind him, an activist followed on a cycle. We told him, 'Whatever happens, come and tell us immediately.' Gathering all his courage, Rama went to see his master whose name was Iranna. As soon as he saw Rama, Iranna began to abuse him. Our activist returned to tell us and we immediately followed him there. By then, Iranna had Rama on the floor and was thrashing him with a whip. Iranna could not understand who we were and why there were so many of us. But he began cursing and swearing. 'This is my worker. He owes me money,' he said.

Vivek-bhau said, 'How much does he owe? Show us your account books.'

Iranna brought the account books and Vivek-bhau ripped them apart. Actually, we had no business tearing up his account books or threatening him like that. But since what Rama Motewar was going through was bonded labour, we could press charges against Iranna.

We helped Rama Motewar's family find strength. Rama's brother Hanmanta was also present. Iranna protested, 'This family owes me.'

Vivek-bhau asked Hanmanta in front of him, 'Will you do his work?'

Iranna said, 'As if he has he the courage to say no!'

This made Hanmanta clench his fists.

Vivek-bhau said again, 'Look him in the eye and tell him your answer.'

And Hanmanta gathered all the strength he had in his body and said, 'No, I will not do your work.'

Our work was done. We had made the slave aware of his condition of slavery; we had succeeded in making them aware of injustice.

Around this time, in Rajewadi village, Beed district, another instance of bonded labour was brought to our notice.

One of my relatives, an old man called Narayan Awad, lived there. He had taken a loan from the Patil. After he was no longer physically able to work, his grandson, Masoo Awad, had taken over from him and was working off the debt. One day, Masoo was ill but his master insisted he come to work. Illness made Masoo slow. His master got angry at him and began to beat him with a stick. Two Dalit youngsters, Vasant and Vishnu, were witness to this. They had heard about our organization. They came and told me what had happened. I went to Rajewadi with some activists. Masoo's clothes were torn. His face was black and blue and bruised. We took photographs of this and went to the police station.

We took Masoo Awad to the Deputy District Officer. This was bonded labour, we told him, and it was his duty to free Masoo from it. But the DDO had no idea about bonded labour. He began to say that Masoo was a labourer like any other. But when we showed him the law, he issued a certificate that freed him from his bond. His rehabilitation was now the responsibility of the government.

Rama Motewar and Masoo Awad were thus freed from their bonded labour. This must have been one of the first instances in which a caste-based practice had been declared to be bonded labour. This was made possible by the Maanavi Haq Abhiyaan. The organization began to grow in strength.

*

During this time, we would read the newspapers with great care. We were eager to find places where we could intervene. We heard about one such incident through a newspaper in Parbhani. The small news item had a headline that read: 'Sudden Death of a Kotwal'. Immediately we grew suspicious.

If he had been a kotwal, he must have been a Mang or a Mahar. We decided to investigate the incident. It had taken place in Pimpri Deskhmukh village. The very name suggested a feudal society living under the influence of a Deshmukh family. A team of activists set out.

There was no guarantee that we would get sound information in the village. But next to Pimpri Deshmukh was the village of Baabhli. There was a bust of Dr Ambedkar in this village. We felt sure that where there was such a statue, the people would be likely to be able to think in a politically aware manner.

It was here that we thought we should begin our investigation into the death of Ambadas Savne.

But when is it ever easy to investigate a murder? People who have some information are often too frightened to reveal it. So Atmaram Savle began to sing Bhimgeet, standing in front of Babasaheb's statue. People began to gather to hear the songs. In an hour, it had become a solid programme. The people from the Dalit settlement began to feel, 'These are our people.' They invited us for tea. Over tea, we began to talk. And along the way, someone asked, 'So how did the kotwal of Pimpri Deshmukh happen to die?'

An old man who was present said in a whisper, 'What's all this about "happen to die"? "Happen to be killed" is more like it. He was one of us, a Buddhist. He was in a patrolling vehicle on evening duty. A new temple is coming up in the village; there were some Maalkaris playing the cymbals there. When it began to rain, Savne stopped and took shelter in the temple. The cymbal-players got angry and grabbed him and began to beat him. "A Mahar has violated our temple," they said and they killed him by stoning him.'

We had guessed it right: this was a Dalit atrocity case. We went straight to the Dalit settlement at Pimpri Deshmukh.

The Savne family was in a state of grief. When we talked to them, we got more information relevant to the case. Ambadas Savne had been an Ambedkarite, a fearless man. He had been insisting that a statue of Dr Ambedkar be put up in the village. He had even installed a statue in his own home. The villagers had opposed this, for Savne's home was right at the mouth of the village. Anyone entering the village would see that statue. This, the upper-caste villagers felt, was an insult to them.

Now it was clear that the village had been looking for a way to get rid of a man whom they saw as a thorn in their side. That day, Savne had taken shelter in the temple from the rain. This gave them their excuse. The attack began. Savne called for help but none came in the darkness. Ambadas' brother Kachru had heard his cries and gone running to the temple but by then it was all over. The Vaishnav bhaktas had crushed Ambadas' head with stones. Not only that, they had then dipped their hands in his blood and had left their marks on the walls of the temple. Was it their intention to drive home this message: 'A Mahar has despoiled the temple. This is what happened to him. Let he who dares now try to do the same'? An hour earlier, these men had been singing bhajans to Vitthala; how had they turned so heartless in so short a while? This was a baffling question.

Ambadas Savne's mother was lamenting, 'My son was going to set up a statue of Babasaheb Ambedkar in the village... They could not bear to see this... Maaye, they killed my son... Now what am I to do? Who will listen to me? Who shall I tell?... Who has time for the poor? Who will give us justice?' As the old lady wept, she pointed at the statue of Ambedkar. The statue could not reply, so it was up to us in the organization to find an answer to her anguished questions.

We forced the police to reopen the case. We took Kachru Savne to the police along with activists. He was no longer scared. He registered a complaint. The police had filed it as a case of sudden and unexpected death. We forced them to register a case of murder.

*

We brought a contingent of the press down to Pimpri Deshmukh. *The Times of India* put the news on the front page. Questions were asked in the legislature. A storm broke over Maharashtra. The deeds of the upper castes in Pimpri Deshmukh were now known to the world. The upper castes sought the refuge of an MLA. People will go to any extent— they will even eat mud—to protect the image of the caste. And so this MLA, who was from the Shetkari Kamgar Paksh (The Peasants and Workers Party), a 'progressive' leader, took the side of the upper castes. He called a meeting in the village. At this meeting, he said all kinds of negative things. 'There is no need to show Savne so much sympathy,' he said. 'He was a bad character. He had some immoral relationships. That was why he was murdered. The blood on the walls of the temple is that of a dog.'

The press reproduced this statement. A fearless Dalit had been denigrated even in death. His blood was now compared to the blood of a dog.

We did not take this lying down. We held a meeting against atrocities in Pimpri Deshmukh. Thousands of people attended. Pimpri Deshmukh stayed in the news. The Chief Minister was forced to visit the village. He met with Ambadas' family. He announced that they would get government aid. A fact-finding committee was set up by the government. We did not rest until the criminals were brought to justice. This took a year. And when they were sentenced, we publicly installed Ambadas' statue of Dr Ambedkar in a public space.

Today, Dr Ambedkar's statue stands at the entrance to the village.

A visitor ought to ask the statue: 'How does one raise one's voice against injustice?'

I am sure the statue Ambadas brought to the village will answer.

*

Because of this incident, the name of the Maanavi Haq Abhiyaan spread far and wide to areas like Latur, Nanded, Beed, Parbhani, Jalna and Hingoli. For the upper castes, this was something completely new. At chowks, at ST stands, at water bodies, they were saying, 'The Mahars and the Mangs are coming up now,' and 'Maanavi Haq Abhiyaan has given them courage.' We left no question unanswered. There was no talk of compromise. We had descended into the arena, slapping our thighs, ready for a fight. Those who wanted to fight atrocities, the victims of the atrocities, began to join with the organization. Abhang Londhe, Janardhan Gadkar, Ambadas Savne's nephew Pandurang Savne, Vishnu and Vasant Awad, were among the activists who joined us. They brought a firestorm of energy into the organization. After the Dalit Panthers had cooled off, such enthusiasm had not been seen in the Dalit movement. But our movement was well-knit. At every step, in every incident, we planned everything down to the last breath.

11

The movement was gaining momentum. The organization's activists and I had fellowships from Oxfam. I was now seldom at home. I would hand over money to Gaya for the household expenses and I would be off again. I was neck-deep in gheraos, morchas, and a regular at police stations and government offices. When I got home in the night, the children would be sleeping. The family now seemed to consist of Gaya and the children; and Baba of course; I was a guest. I would come home for three or four hours, eat what was left for me on a thali and leave again.

Baba was now bedridden. Gaya cleaned him up. She would wash his soiled bedding and his dhotars. When I was at home, I would heat up some water and then give Baba a thorough scrub-down. Then he would look like a well-washed little boy. He would have some bhakri and lie down quietly. Sometimes he would express the wish to return to the village. Then I would get on to the motorcycle, tie his frail body to my back and ride to the village and leave him there. Satva and Sayabai would clean his shit and piss without a murmur. He was now at the end of his earthly journey…and I was taking my first steps on a new road.

When Baba made his final exit from my life, I was at the Hatta Police Station, Parbhani. Some sugarcane cutters had been arrested and I had gone to get them released. There were no mobile phones then. I did not even have a telephone at home. No one informed me of his death because no one could. Baba had gone in his sleep, quietly, without a word to anyone. Gaya was so involved in the housework that she had not noticed when it had happened. It was only when she found his body cold to the touch that she knew. It was difficult to get word to me. No one knew when I was expected to return home. Gaya and Subhash Gaikwad took the body back to Dukdegaon. I only heard when I got back to Majalgaon. By the time I reached the village, the funeral pyre was burning brightly. No tears came to my eyes. Now I was truly orphaned. Aai had died long ago. Baba's living corpse had been lying at home for years; now that too would be gone. I could not even remember our last conversation. I did not feel I had to cry for him.

I had seen so much suffering in society that the thought 'My father is dead' left me numb.

But with his going, I felt as if a chapter in my life had ended. My three children had grown up; they were going to school. I had no idea how they were doing, what marks they scored or whether they did their homework or not. Gaya was there to handle all that. I had my eyes fixed firmly on the Dalit struggle. That was where I was going to make my mark.

*

At that time the deputy commissioner of Pune was Ashok Dhivare. He had some concern for social movements. He was a supporter of the causes we espoused. One day, Vivek-bhau and I had gone to meet him. In the course of our discussions, Dhivare-sahib gave us some important information. 'The Central Government has passed a great law,' he said.

We turned questioning eyes upon him.

'It is the draft of a law forbidding atrocities on Dalits which has been approved by the Central Government. The Maharashtra government has not made it law yet.'

He gave us a copy of the law. When we read the clauses of the law, we were close to dancing with excitement. We now had a statutory framework on which to base our work.

According to this law, the following acts were criminal offences:

1. To compel a person belonging to the Scheduled Castes and Tribes to eat that which is inedible.

2. To compel a person belonging to the Scheduled Castes and Tribes to do something that would be considered offensive to human dignity like cleaning night soil or carrying corpses or walking naked.

3. To drive a person belonging to the Scheduled Castes and Tribes from their homes or from agricultural land.

4. To compel such a person to do something outside the regular allotted work in an office.

5. To compel such a person either to vote for an upper-caste candidate or to abstain from voting.

6. To submit a false report which would cause harm to such a person.

7. To give false information to government servants and to instigate them to use their powers against the Scheduled Castes and Tribes.

8. To insult a person belonging to the Scheduled Castes and Tribes or to try and frighten them.

9. To assault a woman belonging to the Scheduled Castes and Tribes or to use one's position in an organization to exploit such a woman sexually.

10. To pollute or otherwise dirty a water body used by the Scheduled Castes and Tribes.

11. To forbid the Scheduled Castes and Tribes to use certain roads or public spaces.

12. To compel them to leave their homes, their villages or ancestral lands.*

We had observed all these things happening but we did not have a law with which to fight them. The new law made

---

*The above clauses have been translated as they appeared in the book. For the full extent of the law, please see: http://lawmin.nic.in/ld/ P-ACT/1989/The Scheduled Castes And the Scheduled Tribes (Prevention of Atrocities) Act, 1989.pdf

these things offences and set down jail terms lasting from six months to five years. This law was our touchstone. This encouraged us to teach a lesson to many upper-caste people but the Maharashtra Government knew nothing about this act. The law had been passed in 1989 but if the State Government did not issue a circular, the law could not be enforced.

Sudhakarrao Naik was the Chief Minister of Maharashtra in 1991. We decided that we had to get to him. There was no point in dissipating our energies with morchas and other traditional methods of protest. We wanted to get right to the source, to the CM and get the law implemented quickly. But even this would take a great deal of time. So it was agreed that guerrilla warfare was the only way. We knew someone who worked as a steno at Mantralaya. We learned the lay of the land from him. With only this much information, we devised our plan of getting in touch with the CM. Around thirty workers would arrive at Mantralaya in groups of two or three and gather on the veranda outside the CM's office. We would join the line outside his office and as soon as the last pair arrived, we would begin shouting slogans. Then we would push our way into his office, still chanting. The security measures in those days were not as strict as they are now.

As decided, we gathered in the line. We began with 'Maanavi Haq Abhiyaan zindabad' and then we threw open the doors of Naik's cabin and surged in. The police followed us in, drawing their weapons. Sudhakarrao Naik was discussing something with R.S. Gavai* and Babanrao Dhakne.** At first,

---

*Ramkrishnan Suryabhan Gavai, popularly known as Dadasaheb Gavai, was a politician.

**Babanrao Dhakne was a prominent leader of the Vanjari community, who held various positions in the Government of Maharashtra as well as the Central Government.

he seemed a little surprised but he soon recovered and ordered the police to stop. 'Wait, wait, don't beat these boys up. First, everyone, calm down. What do you want? Why these slogans?'

We quietened down. The slogans stopped. I showed him the copy of the law. 'This must be declared as a law in the state,' I said. 'We want to discuss this with you.'

'Right now?'

'No, give us an appointment and we will come back.'

With a faint smile, he said, 'All right, come tomorrow at 4 p.m.'

He took the copy of the law and told the police, 'No need to beat them or anything. Let them go in the evening.'

The police took us to the Cuffe Parade Police Station and held us until the evening. The next day at 4 p.m. we were back in front of the Chief Minister. By then, Medha Kulkarni, a social worker, had translated the law into Marathi, sitting in the garden across the street from Mantralaya. We gave this to the CM. We would read a clause aloud and he would agree, 'Yes, yes,' and so it went.

He presented the draft in the Vidhan Sabha and the Prevention of Atrocities against the Scheduled Castes and Tribes Act 1989 became the law in the state of Maharashtra.

The CM later sent us the documents relating to the passing of the law and a letter signed by him. We made copies and made sure that they got to every police official. We had a new weapon in our hands. However, the passing of a new law does not mean that caste-based atrocities immediately decrease. What the law accepts as a crime is generally acknowledged as an offence by the offenders. The offenders generally know that what they are doing is wrong, but until those who have been wronged understand that they are victims of injustice, the law is of no use. We did not want to spend our lives climbing up and down the stairs of courts; we had a war to fight. This new law was a weapon; but our real weapon was each activist of the Maanavi Haq Abhiyaan.

*

If this new law were to be implemented, it was important for the social workers to know it well. And so we began to train them. By now they had each clause of the Atrocity Act by heart. The Maanavi Haq Abhiyaan had Marathi copies of the Criminal Procedure Code, the Indian Penal Code and the list of atrocities under the Act. These workers would explain the clauses and contents of the Act to the police. How to collect the proof for a case, how cases had to be registered, what care should be taken when the case is being prepared, all this was rehearsed thoroughly.

The workers of the organization had the following conventions:

1. Each one would have a bag on his shoulder: this was the mark of the activist. Even the ordinary man should be able to tell that this was an activist of the Maanavi Haq Abhiyaan.
2. This bag should contain writing paper, a pen, a stamp pad for taking thumb impressions where necessary. And each worker should have a book to read.
3. The workers should travel by State Transport buses. They should talk to other travellers and get to know them. They should ask about casteist practises in their villages.
4. Once a week, they should go to the tahsil office and help the poor and the Dalit who need assistance. They should attend the weekly bazaar in the areas to get to know people better.

5. The organization had a monthly meeting. At this meeting, each worker would offer a summary of the main points of the book he was reading. In this way, all the workers would hear about forty to fifty books in a single day.

6. At the meeting, each worker would talk about a case that s/he had handled and explain the steps the police investigation had taken, under what the sections the crime had been registered, which sections had not been applied, this would ensure that they would learn from each other automatically.

These were all conventions we had agreed upon amongst ourselves. There was Ambedkarite thought behind these well-planned strategies. We did not want to become the social workers who wore jabbas and pyjamas and did social service. At times of sorrow, these social workers would arrive with exclamations of sympathy, wipe away the sufferers' tears and then leave on the next mission of mercy. We knew this. What we wanted were driven workers; we did not want to wipe the tears of the oppressed; we wanted to bring tears to the eyes of the oppressor. The majority of our workers were Dalit. They had experienced discrimination first hand; they knew what our society's fundamental nature was like. They knew that the enemy did not belong to one caste; it was the caste system itself that was our enemy and this should be fought at every level. Knowingly or unknowingly, this was carved in every worker's consciousness. We never singled out one caste for attack, but we were battle-ready soldiers in the war on caste consciousness. Our strategy during this war was built around the time, the age, the place and the nature of the enemy. But it was only with the support of the law that we could fight. It was more important to get people to stand against the caste system. That we could do now.

But how did this come about?

*

I have already mentioned how we liberated Masoo Awad from the clutches of bonded labour in Rajewadi. This village had a huge fort-like house. The Deshmukhs were huge zamindars. During the rule of the Nizam, they were tax collectors and the fort-like house was the tax office. The village was feudal and casteism had driven deep roots into its collective psyche.

The villagers used to help the Patils in Masoo Awad's case.

We wanted to teach these villagers a lesson. But how? We realized that we had to provoke them to show their true colours. Vasant and Vishnu were two young workers in the organization. They began to make waves in the village.

The village handpump was used by both the high castes and the Dalits; but after the Dalits had filled their water, the upper-caste folk would pour a couple of vessels of water over the pump. This was to cleanse it of any pollution caused by the Dalit using the pump; as much water as had been taken must be spilled. Only then could the upper castes take water from the pump or so their dim-witted beliefs ran.

Vasant and Vishnu had taken up the issue of untouchability and so both of them began to imitate the actions of the high castes at the pump. 'If you think we pollute the pump by taking water from it, then the gods in our homes are polluted by you too,' they would say and as soon as the upper castes had filled their water, they would 'purify' the pump in the same manner. This would enrage the upper castes but they would say nothing. The upper castes gave them no reaction and so their tactics failed.

They decided to start a temple-entry agitation next. On

the day of Dassehra, the villagers would go to the temple for darshan and then distribute the leaves of the apta.* These boys announced: 'On Dassehra, we are going to enter the temple.' There were six of them: with Vasant and Vishnu, Sahebrao and Datta who were both Mang; Ananda, a Mahar; and Gopinath, a leather-worker, a Charmakaar by caste. Dassehra came; the boys wrapped turbans around their heads as shrouds; for they had decided, 'We will die but we will enter that temple.' Playing on the taasha, the boys approached the temple. They entered and then went in a procession around the village. The village folks were furious. The next day they put it about: 'They went into the temple under cover of night. Let them try it by day and we'll show them.'

Women from the Dalit settlement would go into the Patils' fields to work. Their mistresses would tell them, 'The village is furious. Your sons will be murdered. Tell them: better leave the village when they can.' This only strengthened the boys resolve. There was a Gujar bazaar that was held in front of the temple. The boys bought bananas and chivda and these Bhimsainiks went and sat on the steps of the temple, casually munching their snacks. The village saw this but it was quiet. Some time later, the boys were spotted outside the village. The villagers attacked. The boys got away and made their way to me. I went with them to Rajewadi.

In the village square, I began to abuse the villagers roundly: 'My fine gentlemen, hijras the lot of you, ten of you get together to beat one boy up? If one of my boys doesn't smash two of yours to the ground, I'll kill him myself and stick him in the mud here. Come forward, if you dare.'

The whole village had gathered but no one stepped forward. The upper castes of this village were smart. They did not want

*The leaves represent gold, hence prosperity.

witnesses. But we did register cases against eighteen people under the Atrocity Act, based on the attacks on the boys.

There were Shiv Sena workers among the attackers. They were all boys from poor homes. We therefore performed a little sleight of hand. We did not include their names in the case papers; instead we put in the names of those rich leaders who had instigated them.

The local police station dragged its feet and refused to cooperate so I met the Sub-Inspector, at that time a Dalit by the name of Deshbhratar who immediately called the foujdar and asked him in front of me, 'What will happen if I take your uniform away from you?'

He said, 'Sir, I'll lose my job.'

The Sub-Inspector said: 'You understand that, right? So you must register this case.'

Only then did he register the case. For three months, the upper-caste rulers of Rajewadi were in jail. A Mahar would go to the jail to shave the prisoners. He asked them, 'What are you in for?'

They said, 'We had some Mangs beaten up.'

Now that he had learned why they were there, he decided to get his own back. 'That's some big deed you managed,' he said and he poured out all the water he had brought along and scraped the hair off their heads without any water.

Later, all of them were released for lack of witnesses but we devised a good war strategy based on our failures in this case. We learned how to fight.

Another incident. Those who were oppressed had very little idea that they could have recourse to the Atrocity Act or that it applied to their lives; on the contrary, the upper castes often registered fake cases against them and had them arrested. Our workers intervened and atrocities were registered against them in good order.

In the Chakur Taluka, panchayat committee elections were to be held. In the reserved seat, a Dalit was elected from Mohnal village. A Mang called Vaijnath Mhaske had done a great deal of work. When the victory procession began, Vaijnath lead it, dancing in front of everyone. The defeated party was not taking the results well. The procession arrived in front of the temple. There, Vaijnath broke a coconut as an offering to the god. That was it. 'A Mang broke a coconut in front of the temple!' The fact that a Mang dared to break a coconut in front of the temple was taken out of context and the defeated clique began to beat up Vaijnath. He began to run even as the blows fell. He went to the Kasab police station, his attackers hard on his heels. Instead of registering his complaint, the police began to listen to the attackers. Why? By the law, the complaint that comes first must be handled first. The Mang had arrived first, his attackers later. But here who had arrived first was ignored. Because caste trumps all. Who cares about the law? This was the attitude in this area.

'This Vaijnath stole tomatoes from our fields. When we asked him for an explanation, he came to beat us and now here he is at the police station.' This false accusation was placed on record by the upper castes. The foujdar was an alcoholic. He accepted a bribe to register this false case. What could Vaijnath do at that moment? The police beat him too and then he came back to the village.

Even though a false case had been slapped on Vaijnath, the village was still not at peace. 'The Mangs are now taking it upon themselves to complain to the police against the Patils,' they said. The village decided to boycott the Mangs to teach them a lesson. Even after a month, the boycott was still in place. Vaijnath had a flock of goats. The animals had no caste consciousness but the village would give them no pasture. They would bleat their hunger, turning plaintive heads to look at Vaijnath. Finally, he had to sell his animals.

He was not the only one to suffer the boycott. The Mangs of Mohnal began to starve. Tukaram Shinde, a young man, got to hear of this. He had just joined the organization. He met Vaijnath and took stock of the situation. He went with him to the police station.

He registered cases against the village for social boycott, physical violence, registering false cases, giving the police false information, all with the appropriate clause numbers. But this meant the case would have to be registered by the police against themselves too. Tension gripped the police station. And while all this was going on, Vivek-bhau arrived. This made it impossible for the foujdar to refuse to register the caste. He had no clear idea about the Atrocity Act. But because of the pressure from the organization, he was forced to act. At that time, Babanrao Pachpute was the Home Minister. A telephone call went straight from Chakur to the Home Ministry.

The pressure on the foujdar increased. The Home Minister sacked all those involved. The next day, the news was splashed all over the newspapers: 'Police Patil, two teachers and a conductor sacked for boycott, false accusations and unlawful arrest of Dalits.' We had won another victory.

It is vital in any atrocity case to have the case registered: but to get that done one needs to get all the details of the incident. Proof must be collected and kept ready. We learned all this from the incident.

Another incident of the same kind happened in Jawala Khurd, Osmanabad district. And there too we pursued it until we exposed the wrongdoing. 'Accidental death of youth in construction of a well,' said a small news item in the papers: 'The police have registered a case of accidental death when Rajendra Londhe died in the process of constructing a well.

The case is being investigated by So-and-So officer.' This caught the eye of Datta Khandagle, one of our social workers. It seemed suspicious and when he went to Jawala Khurd, he discovered the truth.

Rajendra Londhe was a Mang. He was the eldest child of his family. When his body was found, he had a new topi and koonkoo applied to his forehead. Rajendra was not in the habit of using a topi. And why was there koonkoo on his forehead? We began to investigate.

By an old and particularly vile superstition, a dry waterbody will fill up if the eldest son of a Mang family is sacrificed. The Patils had asked Londhe to drive a crane into the centre of the excavated area. Then they had attached a wire to the crane and electrocuted him. This was a form of human sacrifice and we knew this too. All of this came to light because of our investigation; the difficult part was proving any of it.

The organization decided to take this case on. We registered an atrocity case. We noted that it was an instance of murder by electrocution. The Patils who were accused began to circle their wagons. First they got hold of the engineer at the Electricity Board. They got a statement from him that there had been no electricity that day. The medical coroner who had performed the autopsy had given the cause of death as 'mental shock'. It was said that Rajendra Londhe had seen a snake in the water and the resultant shock had been enough to kill him. This was the case the foujdar had cobbled together. We girded our loins for a fight.

To disprove the engineer's false claim we got a declaration from the area office to say that there had been no shortfall in the electric supply that day. We also got a signed declaration from the flour mill to that effect. We made an investigation into what kind of mental shock would suffice to kill a man. From this we gathered that it would require something truly unexpected, something really out of the ordinary, perhaps even an event that seemed supernatural to cause this to happen. Londhe was a farm worker. It was unlikely that he had spent his life without seeing a snake.

We proved in court that it was a case of human sacrifice. The murderers were punished.

Those were some examples of our successes. Now an example of a failure.

Jalkot Taluka: A Mang called Laxman Jadhav had begun working for the Patil but only after a discussion in which the latter had agreed that Jadhav would be paid. After a few months, when Jadhav found that no money was forthcoming, he stopped working. Two or three days later, he was carrying a load of fodder on his head for his animals. The Patil was sitting in the village square. He began to abuse as soon as he saw Laxman. One of our activists made a complaint at the police station about this.

The case went to court. Laxman was asked: 'What abuses did the accused use against you?' Laxman said, '*Hey Mangtya, tujya maaila…*' In the complaint, the abuse was listed as '*tujya aaila…*'* The case was dismissed and the accused went free.

Despite such strange acquittals, we continued to fight for justice, trying to make sure criminals did not go unpunished and loopholes in the law were plugged.

---

*Aai and Mai both mean mother and the phrase '*tujya aaila…*' and '*tujya maaila*' both have the same suggestion of motherfucker.

12

I have seen countless instances of injustice, witnessed atrocities without number. How many can I count? How many can I tell you about?

A Dalit boy tucks his shirt into his trousers, sets a pair of goggles on his nose? The defenders of caste who have nothing better to do will tear his shirt and smash his dark glasses underfoot. Then they will ask him, 'Will you pluck out our pubes, dheda?'

Is his crime a letter from a high-caste girl found on his person? They will tie him to a pole in the village square and beat the life out of him.

Did you look at one of our girls? Did you wink at her? They scoop his eyes out with a knife.

Does a Dalit want a holiday to celebrate Ambedkar Jayanti? His master ties his feet with a rope and dangles him over a water-tank and swings him around. *Now will you ask for time off to celebrate Ambedkar Jayanti?*

Does a Dalit dare to buy land that abuts an upper-caste farmer's property? *How dare he? Will yesterday's labourer walk around as today's farmer? Here, take that, Mangtya.* And they take a scythe to his skull.

A Dalit girl goes to college… *Look at those goodies! Come with me into the sugarcane fields!* What can the girl do? Who can she tell? Her poverty-stricken father will say: 'Give up your education.' The girl kills herself. And the boy walks free even if accused of a caste atrocity.

The police refuse to register cases. The government does not set up special courts. The judge asks a witness, 'You're an old man. In the dark of the night, how can you be sure that it was this man and he alone who attacked you?'

The aged witness: 'Sahib, this is a boy from the village. I know his whole family.'

The judge's epilogue: 'Your vision is weak so the accused is absolved and may go free.'

It was in such a setting that we took our positions at Maanavi Haq Abhiyaan. The activists began to write songs:

Shaan se jiyo, shaan mein, Maanavi Haq Abhiyaan mein...
Utar jaan maidaan mein, Maanavi Haq Abhiyaan mein...
Bhai tu kis soch mein pada
Nahin koi chhota-bada.
Baat rakho dhyaan mein, Maanavi Haq Abhiyaan mein...

Live with dignity, with Maanavi Haq Abhiyaan
Come fight the good fight, for what is right with Maanavi
     Haq Abhiyaan
What stops you, brother?
No man is bigger than any other!
Bear this in mind, in Maanavi Haq Abhiyaan.

Wherever we heard that someone so much as laid a hand on a Dalit, the Maanavi Haq Abhiyaan would arrive. We registered cases against police officials, teachers, gram sevaks, tahsildars and others. We got several dismissed from their jobs.

This was the time between 1991 and 2008. During this time, the official records pertaining to the eight zillas of Marathwada show 3,529 crimes against Dalits registered. This is the tip of the iceberg. Many cases must have been suppressed in the village. Many must have got to the police station and not been registered. But even so, Marathwada had the highest number of registered cases.

In my opinion, when a case is registered in the police station, a good sign is sent out. Where the Dalits bear quietly the injustice of the caste system and the tyranny of the upper castes, there is peace. When the Dalit begins to discover selfhood and self-respect, she begins to speak out. When she speaks out, there's always a backlash and atrocities happen. This leads to conflict. For four wounds inflicted, only one may be returned, but even this change is very significant. I keep encouraging such change and so the established leaders of the district saw me as Enemy Number One. They went all the way up to the Home Ministry to get me exiled from Marathwada. A request carrying hundreds of signatures to keep me out of Beed also reached the Ministry. But what reason could they give? That I was fighting for justice? That I refused to take insults to my people lying down? So I dug in and became even more resolute, ever more willing to fight. As a result, I had enemies in every village. Death threats followed.

We had also taken up the cause of the sugarcane cutters. When a couple signed up with a muqaddam (contractor) at the beginning of the season, they became his slaves. If a woman were pregnant, she would be expected to get an abortion so as to go to work. In an open truck, ten or twelve couples, all sugarcane cutters, would be dragged through sun and rain and all kinds of weather, from Beed to Western Maharashtra, to Karnataka, Gujarat, Rajasthan—wherever the muqaddam wanted. For the next six or seven months, they would not be so much as allowed to think of their villages.

The muqaddam would take his cut from the factories. He would pay the workers out of this. The agreement would be that so much sugarcane per season should be harvested. The contractor would make agreements with three or four factories. The money would suffice for the muqaddam to build a fine house, buy a car, even acquire some land, while using one bunch of sugarcane cutters in every place.

The number of quintals they had to cut was fixed; the muqaddam would work this into the budget.

When the sugarcane reached one factory, the cutters were off to the next. If the factory owners were to play fast and loose with the contractor, the labourers would suffer. Sometimes the muqaddam would disappear and the factory owners would leave the workers high and dry. It was a vicious circle.

Maanavi Haq Abhiyaan started a bonded-labour liberation movement among the sugarcane cutters. Our idea was to free the groups of labourers who were treated as slaves, to use government help for their rehabilitation and to file atrocity cases on their behalf too. Many of the muqaddams were upper caste. In their opinion, we were destroying their livelihoods. They began to see me as their enemy. Many of them got together and contributed money to pay a hooligan to kill me. This hooligan was one of my relatives. He was known for stealing, beating up people and threatening them. It was now an open secret that he had taken five lakhs as a fee to kill me. My children were now around fourteen or fifteen, school-going and they heard about this too. Gaya too was filled with fear.

One day, an anonymous letter arrived. The threats were explicit. 'We will rape your daughter and your wife, we will break your son's arms and legs, and we will kill you and throw your body away.' This was laced with filthy abuse. I read the letter and for a moment, I was quivering with rage. Then I was calm again. I thought about this threat all night. 'Many people's economic lives have been affected by my work; they feel humiliated by what I have done. It is therefore only natural for them to want the worst possible fate for me. It is possible that I might be killed and my children attacked too. What should I do? Today I live a life of dignity. No one in my family goes hungry. Nor is there any threat of them doing so in the future. We have been through the worst. What can happen now? Let what will come, come...'

And this was the point at which I arrived.

The next day I made several photocopies of that letter. I went to the market at Majalgaon and distributed those copies. I stood up in the village square and announced boldly, 'If anyone has the balls, let him come forward and kill Eknath Awad.'

News of my behaviour must have reached the people who had paid for my murder. That was my intention. I wanted them to know that I was not going to be frightened off and this message must have reached the right quarter in the right manner.

How was a hooligan supposed to terrorize someone who did not fear death? He never so much as approached me.

*

I paid no heed to these threats of violence and death. The workers of the organization and I were on fire with the desire to fight casteism at every level. We did a methodical survey; students from the Nirmala Niketan School of Social Work would often come to work with us for experience. Those students visited ninety-five villages, going into the Dalit settlements and doing extensive interviews. The results were placed before the government authorities.

This was in 1991. The Maharashtra government was celebrating the hundredth birth anniversary of Dr Babasaheb Ambedkar. But what was the situation like in those ninety-five villages of Nanded, Osmanabad, Beed and Latur?

- Seventy-five villages did not allow Dalits entry into the temple.
- Forty-two villages had separate water sources for Dalits and upper castes.
- Ninety-four villages did not allow Dalits to perform the last rites of their loved ones in the crematorium grounds.

- Forty-nine villages practised Maharki.
- Sixty-seven villages practised Mangki.
- Eighty-one villages kept the Dalits from entering the houses of upper-caste people.
- In twenty-four villages the Dalit members of the Gram Panchayat were not given a chance to speak.
- In twenty-nine villages the Dalit members of the Gram Panchayat were treated with disrespect.

Even if a Dalit were elected by democratic process to the Gram Panchayat, s/he was still a Dalit. S/he was made to sit on the ground. Never mind a chair, s/he was not even allowed to sit on the mats. Tea was served to her or him in different cups. All women members of the Gram Panchayat were asked to put their thumb impressions on blank papers. The upper-caste villagers did not seem to think it necessary to tell them what these papers were for. So the question before me was: should I cower and crawl and live my life in mute obeisance or should I fight this injustice openly and with all my strength?

*

We decided to stand against injustice. We sent our research findings to several newspapers. Some printed the findings but many others simply suppressed the story. But who was going to close our mouths? Who was going to stop us?

By the exercise of their 'traditional rights', the upper castes had the Dalit trapped. This was what we had to find our way through. We decided that we would return the compliment and use the rights the law had conferred upon us. This we decided was our stance. We would use whatever means we could to make the upper castes bow down to the Dalits. An example.

Hondal village, Nanded Taluka. A Dalit woman had become the sarpanch in a reserved seat. There were two rival factions in the village. The woman chose to side with one of them. This angered the other faction and they began to abuse her. The woman had bought some land from this group. The deed she signed had not specified that she would also own the trees on the land. These people filed a complaint against her, maintaining that her husband and son had stolen mangoes from the trees. Frightened, the poor woman came running to our office.

Now it was important to teach this perverse leader a lesson. But how could we do this? Our activists had every clause of the Atrocity Act by heart. They decided to use a stratagem. They wrote out a complaint and gave it to her saying that the leader had called her and offered her tea in a separate cup and saucer. When she had asked why, he had said: 'You are a Mang; you eat cattle. Why should I give you a good cup and saucer?' Then he had thrown the cup and saucer at her head and hurt her. The substance of her complaint was that he had hurt her head when he attacked her. We told her: 'Before you go to the police station, make sure you inflict some injuries on your head. Then hand in your complaint.'

The woman was an innocent. The next day she cut her arm with a blade, making a few small wounds and then went to the police station. The policeman read the complaint and laughed and asked, 'Bai, who wrote this complaint for you?'

The innocent woman told them the name of the activist who had done so.

The policeman told her to fetch the man.

The activist came to the station. The policeman asked, 'What is this? What have you written? She's been injured? Her head has been hurt? She seems fine.'

The activist was shocked. But he kept his presence of mind.

'Sahib, this woman is mental. She said that if I did not

write a complaint for her, she would kill herself. So I wrote it up. Never mind, let it go. Come on, Bai, let's go home.'

The worker and the woman came out of the station. When she was distracted, the worker took a stone and hit her on the head. Blood began to flow profusely. The woman began to howl. The worker said, 'Why didn't you do as you were told? Now come back to the police station.'

The woman and the social worker went back into the station.

'Sir, now you can accept her complaint,' said the activist.

The policeman said, 'A-vo, didn't you just say she was a mental case?'

The social worker said, 'A doctor will decide whether she's mental or not. Bai, show the policeman where you've been beaten.' The woman drew the sari down from her head and there it was, the stream of blood. Now you could see only the whites of the policeman's eyes. 'A-bo-bo-bo…' he said. Then he registered the case without further comment. The cunning leader was arrested.

If the activist had lost his head at that point, the woman would have found it difficult to live in the village. Only a Maanavi Haq Abhiyaan activist could have pulled off such a stunt; and this because of the great thirst for justice that each one of them felt. It may also be said that we made false use of the law and therefore committed injustice against the upper castes. This is not true. It was only when we knew that a person was guilty that we used these means. On the contrary, it was often the case that the Maanavi Haq Abhiyaan would have to work to free some upper-caste person when a Dalit had filed a false atrocity case against him.

In Hippalgaon, Shirur Anantpal Taluka, a false atrocity case had been registered. A farmer of the upper-caste Reddys had planted mango trees on his field. He was nurturing these trees, carrying water on his head for them. Just next to his field was the field of a Dalit. The goats belonging to the Dalit got into the field and ate some of the mango saplings. This caused them to have a disagreement. The Dalit filed an atrocity case saying that the Reddy farmer had abused him. The activists of the MHA got to hear of the case. They went to the village to understand what had happened. Even the Dalit farmer's wife said: 'My man complained for nothing. When you have a common border, you're going to have disputes. Why make such a big thing about it? My husband is in the wrong.' The activist went with the woman to the police station. Both the parties were brought face to face in front of the foujdar. The foujdar mediated and the disagreement ended there and the case was withdrawn.

Sometimes when a Dalit was behaving inappropriately, we would correct his ways too. In the taluka of Wadwani, we had a district president who was a Mang. He ran a group of sugarcane cutters and he would cheat them. Not only did I have him thrown out of the organization but I also filed a case against him. Bevnal had a ration shop owned by a Mang. He sold the rations that came into the shop on the black market. Our local activists went on a morcha against him.

What I mean to say is that where there was injustice, we would take it on, regardless of the caste identity of the perpetrator. Of course, it is not always possible to use the law against injustice. Often we would have to mobilize people's opinions by using satyagraha. This was the case in the village of Kharat Mangrul where we had a happy ending.

This was a rich village by a river. Horticulture was practised here. Vilasrao Kharat and Bharatrao Kharat were prominent Congress leaders; they were the Kharats of Kharat Mangrul. In the middle of the village was a wada, spread over an acre, like a miniature fort. The village had two Neo-Buddhist activists, Sudhir Sharnagat and Kalyan Sharnagat. They had decided to celebrate Dr Babasaheb Ambedkar's anniversary. They had posters of the forthcoming event all over the village. But when a poster appeared on the wall of the temple, the village was upset. 'Maruti has been polluted,' they began to say. Sudhir and Kalyan were beaten up terribly. The village decided to impose a boycott on the Dalits.

Sudhir and Kalyan came and told me what had happened. I had a handbill printed.

> My name is Eknath Awad. On such-and-such a night, I had a dream and Lord Maruti of Kharat Mangrul gave me darshan. Having given me a vision of Himself, Marutiraya said: 'Vilasrao Kharat and Bharatrao Kharat have had me locked up inside my temple. I wish to meet the Dalits. Please tell the Dalits and their brethren to come and free me.' Thus on so-and-so day, I am going to come to free Lord Maruti. Please come in thousands.

I had this handbill distributed in every village. It was discussed on ST buses, in the bazaar and in every village of the district. Kharat had been a minister. Now out of nowhere, he was being ridiculed. I did not even mention the attack on Sudhir and Kalyan. The men who had done this were of no significance. They were small fry who felt that their protector was going to save them from the consequences of their actions. I did not take them into account. It was their protector I wanted to get.

Bharatrao Kharat himself came to meet me. He said, 'Cancel this programme.'

'You are important people. Since you have come to see me, I welcome you. But what happened in the village was not right.'

Bharatrao said, 'I admit that what happened was a mistake.'

'How can a programme that has been announced be cancelled? Instead, you should grace the occasion yourself,' I said.

Bharatrao laughed. He was a pakka Congressman. He offered no further opposition.

On the day announced, Marutiraya was freed from the confines of the temple. Bharatrao himself was on stage. He placed coconuts in the hands of a line of nearly four thousand Mangs, Mahars and Bhils who had come to enter the temple. In the line, the Dalits would cry out, 'Dr Babasaheb Ambedkar vijay aso' (Victory to Dr Babasaheb Ambedkar) as they went forward to liberate the Lord.

After the programme, Bharatrao said to me, 'Come and have tea at my place.' I was in the mood to pull his leg a little and I said, 'How can I come alone? Look at all these Dalits with me. Will you have enough separate cups and saucers?' He took us all back to his mansion with him. There he said, 'Eknathrao, these are the same cups and saucers we use at home. No separate ones for you.'

That Dalits should be given tea in such a grand mansion was unthinkable. It was my first time in such a grand house as well. The 'Free Maruti Agitation' resulted in the boycott of the Dalits being lifted. And a new energy was infused into the Dalits of Kharat Mangrul.

Another great protest of the same kind. Bamni village: the Dalit settlement faced the Maruti temple. The settlement had a blue flag in front of it. The villagers got angry and threw the flag away. There was an attack on the Dalit settlement. That's when we got involved.

'If one blue flag defiles Maruti, let us bring thousands of blue flags for darshan. Let us see if our defilement turns his red colour into blue,' we announced.

On the agreed date, thousands gathered at Bamni. There were young men with blue bandanas tied to their foreheads. 'Babasaheb cha vijay aso' (Victory to Babasaheb) roared thousands of old men, little girls and women too. Bamni was flummoxed. A long line formed in front of the Maruti Temple, all waiting with blue flags in hand.

The upper-caste villagers had a group of women, a bhajan mandali, sitting in the temple. They expected something to happen, riots to be instigated perhaps. But our volunteers were satyagrahis; all they did was to enter the temple with their blue flags. Maruti stood there, silent. His colour did not change despite the 'defilement'. But the village became a sea of blue. That the village had also allowed women to enter the Maruti Temple in order to make things difficult for the Dalits was another incidental revolution that we managed.

Beed zilla, Dalegaon village. Another protest that went well. The village had a dozen or so Mang households; the rest were upper caste. That the Mangs were now farmers did not sit well with the rest of the village. These mumblings exploded on the festival of Bail Pola.

Before Bail Pola, the Patils' cattle were gathered in front of the Maruti Temple. The Mangs were playing traditional music. After the Patils' cattle had left, the Mangs' animals were gathered. The Mang buffaloes were in fine shape. They looked healthier and fitter than the Patils' cattle. This upset the Patils. They attacked the Mangs. The Mangs of Dalegaon came to me. I got a leaflet printed.

> Ever since the Mangs of Dalegaon were attacked, the cattle have stopped feeding. Unless they are fed naivedya of puran poli, they are not going to give up their fast. And so on 2 October, Gandhi Jayanti, we will celebrate Dalegaon's Mang Pola. Come with your buffaloes to Dalegaon and take part in the feast.

Even the idea of Mang Pola was supposed to be humorous. Where the Patils of the village had been unable to bear the sight of a couple of healthy buffaloes owned by the Mangs, the animals of the entire district were going to be paraded. The village was seized by a storm of gossip. The police were tense because they did not want anything untoward happening on Gandhi Jayanti. The police came to me. 'Please don't come to the village. We will do exactly what you say. If you want we will arrange police protection for the procession.' I didn't insist. In the middle of the night before Gandhi Jayanti, we celebrated our Mang Pola. And the pride of those who would maintain caste differences suffered a setback.

*

On the one hand, the movement was gaining momentum, but on the other, my enemies in the village were becoming active. Aasruba Patil and Parbhu Bade had joined forces. A Shiv Sena board went up. The Republican Party of India opened a branch. My opponents wanted to put forward their own people to show that there was opposition to me and to my activities in the village. Our MLA was from the Shiv Sena. He was instigating this.

Every day fights began to erupt in the village. Every day the police had to be summoned. Dukdegaon was becoming notorious for its violence. Once the headlines read: 'Dalits Attack the Upper Castes'. Of course, this was no mistake. The Dalits had resorted to violence in order to get the upper castes in line. The upper castes burned the huts of the Dalits and called this a response. This had become commonplace in Dukdegaon.

On my side I had a bunch of young men, I had only to say the word and they were ready to hit out. There was no telling when the enemy would attack. So the boys were always in a state of readiness. There was an oafish Vanjari in Pimparwada.

He had bought land in Dukdegaon. He styled himself 'Tight*
Vanjari'. This demonstrated the pride he took in his caste and
in what he thought was his spirit. As he went on his way, in
a snow-white dhotar, black jacket and moustaches massaged
with ghee, he would snaffle a hen here and a goat he found
untended there. He molested any woman he could lay his
hands on. As he walked through the village, he would say: 'I
will buy your women for a paayli of jowar. They call me Tight
Vanjari. I have filled all the cradles in the village.'

In other words, he was responsible for all the pregnancies in
the village! That kind of rot. He was a man of base character.
My opponents felt: 'Good he's come to the village. He will
put Eknath in his place.'

One day, this Tight Vanjari was sitting in front of me. He
saw me and said, 'Hey, c'mere you.' His tone was arrogant. I
went over. He said, 'I am Tight Vanjari.' It was important to
put him in his place right there. I said, 'Right. You're tight
but I'm vaait.** Come on boys, let's felicitate him.' I let loose
with the first blow. Then my boys stepped in and gave him a
sound thrashing. He had never had such a beating before. He
stayed out of my way after that. His reign of terror also ended.

*

But even so there were still murmurings and mumblings against
me in the village. Once they even made low accusations that
I had molested some women and stolen their mangalsutras.
There was a Maalkari, Pandu Maharaj, in the village. My

---

*This is an untranslatable epithet but I suspect it has its origin in Indian
English phrases like 'one tight slap'. This is a forceful and controlled
slap, generally to the face, and perhaps this made the Vanjari think it
a suitable self-descriptor. It is unlikely that he thought of himself as
drunk when he applied it to himself.

**Vaait is bad; here the meaning is not one to be fooled with.

opponents got hold of him. He began to make all kinds of wild accusations against me. The police ignored him so he took his complaints to the MLA. I told him in front of the MLA, 'Don't talk big just because you're in the MLA's house. Think of what comes next.' Half an hour after he got to the village, he was beaten up by the boys.

I decided to flatten my opponents. There was a cruel moneylender in the village. He was usurious and unforgiving. The Dalits and those farmers whose land was not irrigated would often fall into his hands.

There were two types of loans on offer: the didi (one-and-a-half) and the savai (one-and-a-quarter). During the month of Ashadh, the poor went hungry. There would be nothing to eat in their homes. They would then borrow jowar from the moneylender. If you took six paaylis of jowar on the didi scheme, you would have to pay nine to clear your debt, or half as much. On the festival of Sati, this money had to be repaid. This would be in the month of Margashirsha*, the time when cotton, tur, bajri, beans and groundnut are all ripe. The jowar had to be repaid in these crops. If you failed to pay, then the interest would be compounded. And this was to be paid at the next harvest at Gudi Padva, in Chaitra. That would be jowar, gram, safflower and wheat. Once again if the loan were not paid, the interest would be compounded. The moneylender would then take anything he could lay his hands on: the livestock, the tin sheets from the roof of the house, the land, everything. A cash loan would mean ten rupees to the hundred added every week. He would also hand over only ninety rupees out of every hundred he loaned; he would withhold ten for a drink for himself. But at the time of repaying, a hundred and ten rupees would have to be repaid.

---

*November–December, the beginning of winter and harvest time.

This was the money-lending system by which Dukdegaon operated. The moneylender was not above trying to lay hands on the wives of the indebted farmers too. This caused a great many lawsuits. I decided to put an end to all this and began to investigate all the cases that had been brought up against him. I petitioned the police to exile him from the village. Because usury is a crime, he was so exiled. This reduced the amount of debt incurred. And no one had the nerve to speak against me in the village.

Finally, my opponents decided to give up the ill-will they had harboured against me. Dukdegaon was to be made an independent gram panchayat. The villagers thought it a good idea to put me in charge of it. Many people intervened and a compromise was sought. Many people said, 'You can stand unopposed; only let these disagreements stop.' I was not interested in becoming sarpanch. I put another proposal before them: 'Instead, let us elect a woman sarpanch and choose all the other panches from among the women as well. Not a single man. Let the affairs of the village be run by the women.' No one opposed my idea but one of the opposition suggested: 'Awad-sahib, let your wife become sarpanch. At least listen to us in this one instance.' I agreed and for the last fifteen years Dukdegaon has had a female sarpanch.

A village that had been in a political quagmire was now taking its first steps towards progress.

*

I started a cooperative society in the village: the Ramabai Ambedkar Bigarshethi Sahakari Patasanstha (Ramabai Ambedkar Non-Agricultural Cooperative Society). Women from the Vanjara, Maratha, Laman, Muslim and Mang communities participated in the work of the organization. This must be a rare example of a rural organization named after Dr Babasaheb's first wife in which a number of women of different castes took part. The population of Dukdegaon was a thousand, but this cooperative had, by 2010, affected the lives of twenty lakh families. This began when women from the neighbouring four or five villages began to become members. They used the money to start small provision stores; they began animal husbandry or bangle-selling enterprises; they took to selling fish or dealing in livestock and setting up small paan stalls.

The very villages that had opposed me because I had wanted the Marathwada University renamed for Babasaheb were now all part of a microcredit society named after his wife. What more could I want? In a socially backward district, the upper castes were now celebrating Babasaheb's birth anniversary. Who would have ever dreamt it? But this is now an annual event.

Our work had transformed the village. And the movement was expanding in scope. The Maanavi Haq Abhiyaan had become the representative of Dalit pride. Many lives had been transformed by it. With me, other activists had grown and developed. Their faces pass before me now. I have seen their lives turned right round. So many have made huge strides and they have taken the movement forward with them.

Rajasthan Kale: A well-educated boy from the Pardhi community. No one would give him a wife in his community until he stole a mangalsutra himself and proved his worth. He joined the movement. It was his idea that our flag should be red as well as blue. He introduced the salutation, 'Jai Bhim' to the Pardhis of Ahmednagar. Today he runs an independent organization of his own among his people. He works to free them from the stigma of crime.

Valmik Nikalje: A Neo-Buddhist working to take Mang society forward. He is the Secretary of the Maanavi Haq

Abhiyaan. His is the word that carries the most authority after mine. My closest friend. Today he educates rural Dalit boys and girls and gives them computer education so that they may find their feet in society.

Bajrang Tate: A Mang, he was once a player in a band. Today he runs a school for the Pardhi community.

Motiram Bade: My chief opponent in Dukdegaon, Parbhu Bade? His blood brother. He is from the Vanjara community but has been with me from the very beginning. His caste brothers refer to him slightingly as a 'Mang Vanjari' and imposed a caste boycott against him but he has never wavered in his support of the Dalit movement.

Abhang Londhe: Mang. He would beg after having played the sheda for the gods in front of the temple. Today he has ration shops in ten villages.

Keshav Avchar: Mang. Because he could not play new tunes, he was beaten up when he was a musician. He joined the movement. He studied and finished his MA and his LLB. He is now the chairman of the society of his village. He runs the village ration shop.

Arun Jadhav is from the Kolhati community*. His mother was a dancer in a tamasha-sangeetbari troupe. Because he did not want his sister to take up the profession, he was thrown out of his home. He joined the movement with Valmik. He graduated and is now the sarpanch of his village.

Antikabai Karad is from the Vanjara community. She ignored opposition from the village and was active in the women's cooperative.

---

*The Kolhatis are listed as a Backward Class in the Maharashtra Gazetteer. They are a community involved in dancing.

Radhabai Survase: Mang. Earlier, she had a liquor distilling business. She took the lead in celebrating Babasaheb's birth anniversary in the village of Sadola, known for its fascist opinions. She closed down her liquor business. She bought land. She began to fight against atrocities committed against women.

Shankar Pawar: From the Laman community. A militant activist. He began to spread the movement in Nanded. The police arrested him as a threat to national security. To free him, the organization wound tricolour bandages around their mouths and went on a silent protest march on 26 January. He was later released.

Machchhindra Gawale: Mang. He joined the movement as a little boy. He now offers a version of marriage based on Mahatma Phule's Satyshodhak Samaj*. If a Mang gets married according to Neo-Buddhist rites, it is felt that the couple has become Mahars. This explains the importance of the Satyashodhak ceremony. It is also important to dispense with the old ways. For instance, some of the sugarcane cutters practice child marriage. A husband-and-wife team is seen as a unit, a koyta. And so a fourteen or fifteen-year-old girl and a boy whose moustaches have just begun to sprout will be married off. This means taking a loan from the muqaddam. The newly-married couple is immediately drafted into the work of cutting cane in order to pay the wedding debt. In order to stop this practice, we began to organize mass marriages. Hundreds of Mang, Mahar and poor Vanjaras were married according to Satyashodhak rites.

Now there was no need to take a loan from the contractor.

---

*These are simple rites that do not require the presence of a Brahmin priest.

The couple would also get married at an appropriate age. It was Machchhindra who offered this direction. He himself organized the weddings of hundreds of young Mang couples.

Sunita Bhosale: She was a twelve- or thirteen-year-old Pardhi, still in a parkar-polka when she attended the Ahmednagar conference. Today she takes up the cause of the Pardhis in Shirur. She is one of the few women activists from the Nomadic and Denotified Tribes.

Manisha Tokale: She is an upper-caste Yallam woman. She fell in love with Ashok Tangde and got married to him. She joined the movement and is now the head of the Maanavi Haq Abhiyaan's women's front.

Madhukar Kamble: Mang. Earlier he played the trumpet with a band. He would, in the past, also pick pockets at the ST bus stand. He has given up a life of crime. He is now the district head of the organization's Majalgaon operations. He lives a life of dignity.

Baban Kasbe: Mang. As a bridegroom, he dared to touch the feet of the deity and so he was beaten up. The organization took up his case. Now he is the sarpanch of the same village where he was once attacked.

Radhika Chincholikar: Mang. She was a housewife. She became active in the movement. Now she sits on the Panchayat Samiti as a Congress candidate.

Madhukar Londhe: Mang. Not just a Mang, a pakka old-style Mang. He would drive a three-wheeler, an autorickshaw. Then he set up a paan stall. When I greeted him with 'Jai Bhim', he would respond with 'Jai Lahuji'*. He was an

---

*Lahuji Raghoji Salve (1794–1881), activist, thinker, social reformer and Mang.

activist with the narrow-minded Akhil Bharatiya Maatang Sangh. He abandoned his false caste pride over time. He is now the president of the Beed district of the Maanavi Haq Abhiyaan. His son first salutes Babasaheb's photograph and then sits down to his studies.

Gangadhar Pol: He too was a dyed-in-the-wool Mang. He took pride in calling himself a Matang or a Mang. He belonged to a narrow-minded organization. He became an activist with the Maanavi Haq Abhiyaan. He abandoned his Mang identity. He wrote fine songs like: *Julmavarti tootoon pada re/ Annabhaucha girva dhada re...* (Fall upon crime wherever you see it/Follow in Annabhau's footsteps...)

Shivaji Dhavale: Bhil. He came to one of our meetings in a ragged state. He joined the organization and found direction and inspiration. Today he runs the Bhil Samaj Sanghatana on his own.

Balaji Kamble: Mang. A tailor. He joined the organization and is now the head of the Latur district operations. He is the chairperson of the Ausa Panchayat Samiti.

Gaya: My wife. She took part in the movement as an activist. She has kept me going over the years.

Milind: The upper castes attacked him because he was Eknath Awad's son. Later, he went to Pune to study. He joined various organizations there. After taking thought, he became an activist too. He has a doctorate from Jawaharlal Nehru University on the Aesthetics of Dalit Literature. Despite his higher education, he has not abandoned activism.

So many activists from so many castes...Nandu Bangar and Maruti Bansode were Dhangars; Uttam Tikhe was a Charmakar; Raju Phulpagar was a Dhor; Umakant Dersetvar

was a Komati; Pandurang Birajdar was a Maratha; Mehrunissa
Sheikh, Bismillah Pathan, Ajamuddin Sheikh were Muslims;
Asha Pawar was a Gujar; Savita Kulkarni was a Brahmin.

This was like a garden blooming with a variety of flowers.
So many people from so many different caste backgrounds,
from such different life experiences and religions, all coming
together to work for this cause.

Truly, I was rich.

*

1993. The earthquake at Latur. Our cause was the self-respect
of the Dalit. What had we to do with an earthquake? It was
possible for someone to think: well, this was the very land that
had thrown up the horrors of caste; let it be laid low. I am
tough-minded but I am not vicious. As news came in of the
earthquake, I began calling my activists. The rain was coming
down steadily. In the morning, we left for Latur. Ashok and
I were in the jeep along with as much bread and biscuits as
we could load up.

Killari village. Huge crowds. Radio and television crews.
People had come from far and near, all those who had heard
the news. The epicentre of the quake was Killari. That meant
everyone was coming there. The rain kept everything wet.
All the aid workers, all the amateurs and thrill-seekers who
wanted to study the destruction caused by the quake were in
a hurry to get to Killari. And in the other direction, those
who had survived the destruction were hurrying to the city.
Traffic jams. No one seemed bothered about anyone else.
We went to the government clinic at Killari. There were no
patients there; only corpses and moving among them, their
faces drawn and haggard, the survivors who were trying to
identify the dead.

The injured were being taken to Latur. Eight thousand

people died that night in eighty-one villages. Thirty thousand were injured. Many were wounded. The necessities of life began to vanish. Empty-faced people were everywhere, dragging the corpses of the dead. 'This is my corpse,' they would say and it would be noted down.

Then the corpse would be taken away for burial. The relatives would follow the body. The earthquake had forged a bond between the dead and the survivors. This was the first time I had seen so many dead bodies. What relationship did I have with them? Ashok, who was with me, burst into tears. I was dry-eyed. Inside my head, a voice: 'An activist does not weep.'

Near the clinic a JCB earth mover was digging a pit, a long pit. Into it went women, men, little children…of what caste had they been, what religion had they followed? Now they were all corpses. When one section of the pit was filled, the JCB would shovel a pile of mud over it. Over this, the tuneless screams of the mourners. There were no words, just screams drawn from the depths of grief. No one to sprinkle so much as a handful of earth as offering. One pit filled, another dug. What were we to do with the biscuits and bread we had brought with us? Who had the desire to eat? We left Killari and headed for the outlying villages.

The villages had been levelled. The rain had turned the ground into a morass of mud. People were carrying corpses out and laying them on the tarred roads. There was a queue of the dead, 3 or 4 kilometres long, all wrapped in white. One or two confused and dazed people were waiting by the corpses. Animals, let loose from their enclosures, were wandering around aimlessly. The cows and buffaloes lowed their dismay. Everywhere, a feeling of helplessness. What can man do when faced with the might of Nature? Many people were still buried in the mud; I decided that digging them out would be our main job.

By the evening, workers from many self-help organizations had arrived in Latur. A Relief for the Earthquake-Affected Committee was formed. Different organizations took on different responsibilities. Some took on caring for the injured; some provided food; others fed the livestock or set up temporary shelters and tents. We had more people on the spot than most organizations. We chose to dig out the dead bodies.

Our tempo went to the market places of various villages. Announcements were made: Come and help the earthquake-affected. Three hundred people responded. Meanwhile, the rain continued to come down. Each worker was given a tarpaulin. They swathed themselves in these tarpaulins as they worked and sat on them when they rested. We divided them into teams of fifteen or so. The young men got to work. If it was impossible to bring the corpse out of the mud, then sticks were piled upon it and the last rites were concluded there. The bodies we rescued were burned on common pyres.

For the first eight or ten days, the Maanavi Haq Abhiyaan workers only dug bodies out of the mounds of mud. That year it rained well, rains of the kind that had not come down for several years. People began to say: 'Now we will have a good harvest. This is the rain of dead people. Death rain.' Farmers believe that when Nature wreaks havoc upon a place, it also offers compensation later. To each his own way of thinking. After the fourth or fifth day, the corpses that were still in the mounds, began to rot. A terrible stink erupted. Flies and worms gathered everywhere. We distributed such bottles of perfume as we could lay our hands on. Our workers would drench their handkerchiefs, wrap them around their noses and go back to digging out the bodies. Somebody would come up, wailing, 'Here, this is where my son lies buried.' When we saw a hand or a foot, we would grab hold of it and pull it out. Later, the corpses began to swell up. If you grabbed a hand, it would come off at the wrist.

In Haregaon, one of our activists pointed out a mound and said, 'This was my home. My wife and one-year-old daughter are sleeping inside.' We began to dig out the mound. Underneath we found the dead body of a woman. Her left arm was protectively draped over a baby, who was sleeping by her side. Under that arm, the child was alive. She was breathing. How had she survived, this little mite? Her name was Priyanka. Later, we bought a cow and gave it to this little girl who had lost the protection of her mother.

*

The aid workers began to find their rhythm. We got a great deal of assistance from Oxfam. We set up ten base camps in different villages. Different kinds of aid began to arrive. Lines formed and of course, there was much pushing and shoving. This was to lay hands on what was available, but there was also a caste aspect to all of this. The houses of the upper castes had been large and spacious; these had been razed to the ground and the people within them had been killed. In comparison, most of the Dalit homes were small and so not as many Dalits died inside their homes. There were not as many injured. The upper castes felt that since they were the ones who had died, the assistance was meant solely for them. They would shove their way into the Dalit lines. And so we simply stopped those lines from forming by not giving out anything. The activists would scour the countryside to find out what was needed and where. They would make lists and come back in the evening to the main camp at Latur and give them to the workers who would then see about fulfilling those needs.

'Aid' brings some strange creatures out of the woodwork. Some would come with laddoos and distribute them and have photographs taken. Some would distribute grain and again they would want photographs taken. The people grew tired of these self-publicists. When any assistance arrived, they would ask for it to be delivered to the Maanavi Haq Abhiyaan camp.

When grain came from the government, it would be distributed after the sarpanch had signed for it. But some sarpanches began to hoard the grain in their godowns. They distributed the grain according to their whims and fancies. Of course, this meant that the Dalits were cheated. The villagers came to me with their complaints. Tukaram Shinde, Ashok Tangde and Manisha Tokale, our activists, were supervising all the work at our camp. They brought these things to the attention of an army officer. This man threw these godowns open to the people and the Maanavi Haq Abhiyaan was given the right to distribute grain to the people.

For the next three years we were involved in the assistance programme to earthquake survivors. Tearing down traditional rural structures and ending caste-ridden practices was also part of our work. This could have become the positive aspect of a natural calamity, a way of deriving some social benefit from a terrible happening, if we could have rewritten caste practices. And so we wanted the new villages that came up not to be based on old patterns of caste. But the government had other plans. The government was going to use the old zamindari records to distribute the land. Those who had more land were going to get plots of 750 square feet. Those who had had less would get 500 square feet and those with even less, 350 square feet. All the 750-square-foot plots belonged to the upper castes. They would have a separate settlement. The Dalits would be segregated.

The common people suffer when there is an earthquake but those who rake it in are the dealers in steel and cement. This is because so much new construction happens. Laurie

Baker is a world-famous architect. He believes that one can build earthquake-proof homes using cheap and easily available local material. We sent a request to the government with two major demands. The first: the new houses should not be spaced according to caste. The second: the new homes should be built on Laurie Baker's principles. Because of the entrenched nature of caste prejudice and capitalism, our demands were ignored. Many industrialists made the most of the situation after the earthquake. They would assist only those villages that were by the main road so that they could advertise their charitable deeds. The companies even named these villages after themselves.

The earthquake threw up many questions. One of these was the question of abandoned women and widows. The government only handed out assistance to the unit it recognized as a 'family'. But to which family did an abandoned widow belong?

People began to abandon women by the roadside. Old men who had lost their wives in the quake began to marry young women. Some old men got as much as twenty to twenty-five lakhs as compensation. With an eye on that money, the fathers of young women began to give their daughters in marriage to these old men. Many of the women who were pregnant lost their children. Those who got pregnant afterwards, found it difficult to find medical help…these questions were all around us.

The arrogant leaders had no idea about these problems. We went on a morcha about these issues. There was a tahsildar called Phulari. He registered false cases against Ramakant Kulkarni, Ashok and Manisha for taking part in the morcha. He accused them of bringing the morcha into the government office and destroying it. All three refused bail. If they accepted bail, it would have been made out to seem that they had actually done those things. These young people suffered eight days in jail but kept their zeal alive.

The Maanavi Haq Abhiyaan worked on the rehabilitation of eighteen villages. Because of this, our basic work suffered. Some of the activists left; some of them developed bad habits such as alcohol and womanizing. Others started new organizations. And so I began to feel the need to work on the revitalization of the Maanavi Haq Abhiyaan.

13

If every movement has a period of intense activity, it is also natural for it to have a period of stagnation. But how does one infuse spirit into it again? Only those who began the movement can answer the question, we decided, and agreed that we would go to the people and set the problem before them. We would walk the 650 kilometres between Ahmednagar and Nanded, meeting and talking with Dalits along the way. We would bring the ideas of the movement back to the people. We called this padayatra, the jaagaryatra or the walk of awakening.

We started in the Khandala village of Nagar district on 24 September, the day on which Dr Ambedkar signed the Poona Pact. This pact had an adverse effect on the political status of the Dalits of the nation. If Ambedkar's demand for a separate electorate for the Dalits, through which they could elect their own Dalit representatives, had been passed, the political situation of the Dalits would not be as dire at it is today. Today, it is the entrenched political parties who decide who the leaders of the Dalits will be. They choose those who are likely to be pliant. This has caused an increase in the number of tame Dalits and an increase in sycophancy too. The bootlickers among the Dalits are chosen by these political parties. It is obvious that the system will not allow any real Dalit leader to rise. Even if a Dalit is elected in a reserved seat, his behaviour is governed by the upper castes. This is a vicious circle. A split was inevitable in the Dalit castes.

Because I was born a Mang, the main Dalit parties offered me stepmotherly treatment. It was as if only one caste had the right to use Babasaheb's name. I did not think it right that we had trapped Babasaheb's ideas in a caste ghetto. And so our jaagaryatra began in the Pardhi community. I kept a diary of this padayatra. Some pages from the diary:

Ahmednagar. Khandala. Pardhi Settlement

Forty or fifty activists gather. The blue and red flag of the Maanavi Haq Abhiyaan flutters. A Pardhi woman flags us off, a first for her. This causes a great burst of enthusiasm in the Pardhi community. These people have always been seen as thieves, criminals and beggars. They have always been treated savagely by society. This is the first time so many well-educated people have gathered in their settlement.

Lunch: bhakri with pitla and onions. The women and girls are somewhat worried as they serve the food. 'Will these people eat food from our hands?' you can see these questions in their body language.

An old Pardhi man took the flag of the Maanavi Haq Abhiyaan on his shoulders, and shouting 'Jai Bhim', the padayatra sets off for Aarangaon.

Third day: Towards Nimboda Village

Thirty to thirty-five kilometres done. Everyone tired. No one has eaten. A small stall in the military camp. The activists fall upon his bread and tea. An excited welcome at the Nimboda village. Will they have enough cups and saucers? They serve us in steel plates. Some Mang leaders arrive... Two or three of them are somewhat intoxicated... They oppose us but a Mang Police Patil sets up a small meeting at the village square. Before us, the representatives of the Republican Party of India have come and gone... They had told the people to offer no support or assistance to our padayatra. Why would they do that?

The Neo-Buddhists are proud of Babasaheb. But why trap him in a single caste identity? Would they obscure the sun for their own narrow sectarian goals? Seen from one perspective, they could be the false inheritors of a great man's legacy. They have locked him into these statues and images of Bhim… Such thoughts arise in my mind.

Fifth day. On the road to Dhanora

On the way, three or four Mahar homes in the village of Dashmi Dhavan. An old man with a tulsi mala; on his face a network of wrinkles. On his forehead a saffron teeka. That we are taking Babasaheb's ideology from village to village fills his eyes with tears. He is illiterate; he was a carpenter by trade. Though we kept refusing, he insisted on organizing tea for all of us. Such was his respect for Ambedkar. How does this affection, this respect, vanish from the hearts and minds of the city folk? And why?

The Maratha community is not the enemy of the Dalits

It has rained. The tarred roads are wet and mucky. Waglooj village. The Dalits have no time for us but the Maratha community's Gund Guruji welcomed us. He organized sleeping quarters for us in the gram panchayat building. A cold night. The activists curled up and slept as hens tuck their heads into their wings on a chilly night. Our welcome at the hands of the Gund Guruji left me thinking—had the Maratha community begun to become aware of the teachings of Ambedkar? And if this happened, would the Maratha community find common cause with the Dalits?

Do the Mangs disrespect Babasaheb?

A Mangwada next to a rock-sugar factory. The settlement came out to welcome the padayatra. The meeting began. There was no image of Babasaheb at the meeting. I asked why. They replied: 'The Mahars harass us. If they did not exist, we would accept you as our own. You have descended into the arena using Babasaheb's principles so they probably feel their leadership is threatened. But don't you let go of Babasaheb. He is a sun that shines down on all of us, a father to us all. Fights between siblings can be sorted out. Eventually all these disagreements will be resolved. Does anyone bear a grudge against his own father?'

Who allowed this grudge to fester? The Mangs? I know so many Mangs who are followers of Ambedkar's principles. Who let them down? Were they forced back into a Mang identity? Who disrespects whom? The Mangs see the Chambars as a lower caste, the Chambars look down on the Dhors, the Dhors on the Pardhis…this is also casteism.

How do we change human nature?

A musical welcome at Jamkheda. We garlanded the statues of Mahatma Phule and Annabhau Sathe. When we went to garland an Ambedkar statue at a Mahar settlement, we faced opposition from the activists of the Republican Party who were also drunk. Before this, I had helped one of them during a time of difficulty. He himself put a hand on my shoulder and said, 'If you garland Dr Ambedkar's statue, it will start a fight.'

Such helplessness.

It was in this village that we cut the locks of a seven-year-old Potraj.

If they tease me, I beat them mercilessly.

On our way to Osmanabad. Near Pathrud, children going home from school. A little boy, schoolbag on his back, tossing his long plait as he walked. I asked him his name.

He said: 'Navnath Adagale.'

One of the activists asked him, 'Aren't you ashamed of this plait?'

He said, 'Yes.'

'Do the boys of your class tease you about being a girl?'

To which the little fellow said, 'Who has the guts? If they tease me, I beat them mercilessly.'

The boy had self-respect, it was evident.

'Do you want your hair cut?'

'Go on then, cut it,' he said.

That night, in the presence of his father, we cut the boy's hair. The boys played the harmonium to accompany the programme. The rain had turned the ground into a morass but the theatrical programme drew a crowd despite that.

A programme in Annabhau Sathe Nagar

The village of Jambphata, Varud. We were welcomed into the Maharwada but this was because the people of Sathenagar felt that if we were taking Babasaheb's name, we must be Mahars. The Mang settlement had a dispirited air. But we worked hard at preparing the people of Sathenagar. The Maharwada programme was full of energy. We explained the principles of our organization to the youth.

Along the way a member of the Charmakaar community took great care of all of us.

A Masanjogi presides

At the village of Kalamb, a band comprising members of the Nomadic and Denotified Tribes along with Masanjogis, the Neo-Buddhists and the Mahars welcomed us with music. We had a meeting on the road between Kalamb and Bhum. The chairman of the meeting: Vyankappa Shenure, an uneducated Masanjogi. On his head, a crown made of tin surmounted by a peacock feather; in his hand, a bell; a piece of black cloth over his shoulders. He was from a Nomadic Tribe that ekes out an existence on cremation grounds. When Shenure was put into the chair, he was on top of the world. He felt as if he were sitting on a throne. No one had ever asked him to come forward or sat him upon a chair, nor had he ever been asked to make a speech. And so he stood up to make his first speech. Somehow he managed a couple of words: 'This makes me happy. Jai Bhim.' And then he ducked his head and tried as inconspicuously as possible to mop up his tears of joy.

Aamhi nighaale Bhimaachya vaatene...tumhi ya ya ya

(We've set out on the road marked by Bhimrao...come with us, come, come)

Singing these songs, our padayatra set off for the Aambulaga Sugar Factory. A man on a motorcycle stopped. 'Here is a hundred rupees for tea and snacks,' he said. He had a refrain: 'This is my duty.' At Aambulaga, Mang, Mahar, Maratha, Hatkar, Dhangar and other activists of other castes showed up. They collected contributions and offered these as assistance to the padayatra. A good meeting. There was also a folk theatre group.

Salutations to Babasaheb

The Muslim settlement in Vadavana (Buldhana). People refer to this area as 'Pakistan' contemptuously. The people who live there, returning contempt for contempt, named the area 'Pakistan Gully'. The Shiv Sena opposed our programme there. Jalilbhai Golandaz, a Muslim activist, welcomed us. The Muslims of the settlement gathered to hear songs expressing Babasaheb's philosophy. The Muslims made great arrangements for our stay. As we left, I said 'Jai Bhim' to Jalilbhai. He said, 'Insh'Allah, milte rahenge... Khuda hafiz... Jai Bhim.' (God willing, we will meet again. God go with you. Jai Bhim.)

Vijayadashami at Nanded

Three months in. Six hundred and fifty kilometres all on foot. Vijayadashami at Nanded. A festive day and a festive spirit. We offered a garland to Shivaji Maharaj's statue.

Dr B.D. Chavan of the Laman community was enthusiastic in his welcome. Garlands, bouquets, felicitations. The poor people organized a good meal for the activists.

*

What was the outcome of the Jaagar Padayatra? We brought the message of the organization to a variety of castes. We found that the Nomadic and Denotified Tribes and the poor Muslim community could also respond to the message of Babasaheb. We discovered afresh how strong the caste system was in some villages and reminded ourselves of how important it was to break it and how many people agreed with us about that. We saw once again the need for an organization of this kind. The divisions among the Dalits had to be resolved. We found new inspiration. And the Maanavi Haq Abhiyaan was up and raring to go again.

*

14 January 1994. Makar Sankranti. Sharad Pawar, the Chief Minister, gives a speech over the radio.

'Today is Makar Sankranti, an auspicious day. Today we distribute til gul*, a symbol of our mutual love of each other. Let us seek answers to our complex questions and try to start afresh in this new spring. On the occasion of the new year that has just begun, I speak first of all to you. Today the state has decided to change the name of the university to the Dr Babasaheb Ambedkar Marathwada University. The State truly belongs to the subjects. It is important for the State to pay more attention to the poor and the marginalized, the oppressed. They must be given justice, for this is what Shivaji Maharaj has taught us.'

I had spent the night in the police station. To keep the peace after the change in name, it had been decided to intern the Dalit and the upper-caste leaders. I was delighted that the name of the university was being changed after a struggle that had lasted fourteen years; but on the other hand, the government had named the new university at Nanded, the Swami Ramananda Teerth Marathwada University. That caused me some regret. The upper-caste demand for this name had been sanctioned overnight. How much the Dalit must suffer... exile from one's village, the destruction of standing crops, self-immolation, murder, riots, hunger strikes, processions, long marches and only then this change in name.

In 1992, Uttar Pradesh elected a government that was formed by the Samajwadi Party and the Bahujan Samaj Party. This was the first blow to the Congress. The Bharatiya Janata Party took up the cause of the Ram Janmabhoomi and began

---

*Laddoos made out of sesame and jiggery; On Makar Sankranti, Maharashtrians give them to friends and say, 'Til gul kha aani gode bola' (Have some til gul and say some sweet things.)

to dig in. It was now important for the Congress to keep the Dalits voting for them.

In Maharashtra, Sharad Pawar had announced in November 1993 that he would seek a referendum on the name change. We got angry with this submissive political policy. The Maanavi Haq Abhiyaan sent a nine-page letter to the President. How many issues are you going to have referendums over? Will you have a referendum over the issue of self-determination for the Kashmiris? Will you have a referendum over the demand for an independent state for Jharkhand? If this is the solution to such issues, why have a State Legislature at all? Why have democratically elected representatives? These were the questions we raised. I have no idea whether our letter had any impact at all, but within four days, the announcement was made that the proposal for a referendum on the change of the name of the university had been dropped.

The name was changed. There were celebrations in large cities such as Aurangabad. In Mumbai, Ramdas Athavale went in a procession, singing and dancing to the Chief Minister's house to felicitate him. Sharad Pawar was overwhelmed with slogans such as 'It was only because of you that this has happened.' All over Maharashtra, the police were at the ready, policing every crossroad. In Marathwada, more than fifteen thousand police corps were on full alert. At eleven p.m., the entrance archway to the university was being painted over. The board began to look beautiful. The name began to shine: Dr Babasaheb Ambedkar Marathwada University. Many illiterate women who had never been to college had come to look upon it. With their ragged saris drawn over their heads, they began to perform aarti. 'My Babasaheb now has a university named after him,' they said.

But news of riots also began to come in. Attacks at railway stations, the burning of property, stabbings. It was a contemptible attempt to raise the bogey of 'Marathwada Burning' again. In Rudrapur and Pimpri villages of Beed, the lives of Dalits were devastated. In Pathrud, Bhoom Taluka, the houses of Dalits were burned. There was rejoicing in Dalit settlements but there was also fear.

Our activists began to gather information—this area was burned, that area was tense. I got the organization's jeep out and went towards the troubled areas. With me were Valmik, Sudhakar, D.R. and Ashok.

We got to the village of Girgaon in Parbhani. A two-storey house in the Dalit settlement had been burned. The children's schoolbags and schoolbooks, the bedding and the clothes, the grain, the furniture and the cupboards, all reduced to ashes. An old woman was staring at the burned shell in stunned silence.

I went up to her. She looked at me from behind thick lenses. Her eyes were bright with tears. Just to say something, I said, 'Aai, what a lot of damage...'

The old woman began to speak as if possessed: 'What of it, son? What does it matter? Let it burn. Let my home burn, let my money burn...let my crops burn... But what of the self-respect Babasaheb has carved into my heart? Who can burn that away? Who has the courage? No one can burn down his achievements...'

She was speaking with her hand on her heart. My eyes filled with tears. I said: 'Aai, that is the truth. No one can burn our Babasaheb... I will come back to your village one day... Jai Bhim, Mai.'

In comparison to 1978, the riots and the arson were limited to a few villages, but the Shiv Sena still wanted to make political capital out of the change in name. It was on this issue that they had gained strength in the rural areas of Maharashtra. They cut down the trees along the Kalamb-Dokhe Road and threw them across the road. In Shakud, the upper castes came to the Dalit area in a procession, playing musical instruments like the dhol, performing lezim dances and then attacked. We went and saw ten to fifteen such villages that had been attacked.

My mind was filled with sadness. It was important to send some help to those whose homes had been burned. We got to Arun Jadhav's home at Jamkheda. There we managed to eat a few mouthfuls. From an STD booth, I made a call to Anil Shidori of Oxfam: 'Anil-bhau, so much has been destroyed. We need to help immediately.' Anil-bhau asked: 'How much money does your organization have?' I said: 'About two lakh rupees.' Anil-bhau said: 'You start buying whatever is needed. I'll send you more money.'

Through the dark night of abandoned streets, we left Jamkheda. It seemed as if a Trax vehicle was following us. Perhaps someone had heard me talking on the phone and so was following us to loot us; or it was someone who heard that we wanted to help the Dalits and was angered by this. Out of the windows we could see swords and batons protruding. At the Santad Ghat, the vehicle began to gain on us. Our driver, Shiva, was at the wheel of our jeep. He drove off the road at high speed and descended onto the verge. The episode ended there. We managed to distribute jowar, rice, vessels, clothes and spices to those who had suffered in these attacks.

During the course of the movement, there have been many such moments of physical danger. I was alert and survived, but some of our activists lost their lives. Baban Misal was one such marvellous activist out of Jamkhed, Songaon. He moved on from the struggle to enter politics. He became the speaker of the Panchayat Samiti. Then he became a member of the Krishi Utpanna Baazaar Samiti. He always fought for the Dalits. He closed down the liquor shops in the villages. The grant-in-aid to the Dalits' hostel had stopped.

He fought the sand-mining lobby that was ravaging the Khairi Lake.

The rich folk were stopping the flow of water into the lake so that they could take the sand at the bottom for construction. This affected the farmers' supply of water. Baban took the matter to court. He won his case. Delighted with his victory, Baban got on to his motorcycle and went to give the farmers the news. A Maruti van cut him off. Seven or eight men jumped out. 'You're going to close the liquor shops, you son of a Mang? You're going to stage rasta rokos?' As they abused him, they attacked him with sticks and knives. His head was beaten to a pulp. There was blood and brain everywhere…

As he died his clenched fists raised above those streams of blood…it still causes my hair to stand on end when I think about it. We raised a hue and cry. The murderers were arrested. One of them was a member of the Panchayat Samiti; another had a brother who was a corporator in Mumbai.

It is extremely difficult for a Dalit activist to work in the rural areas. The murder of Shyam Thorat of Gungurde, Hadgaon, Jalna district, is evidence of this. Shyam was an Ambedkarite and a Mang. He was a militant activist. If someone slapped a Dalit, Shyam would extract rough justice by returning slap for slap. He had the village walking in fear of him. In a feudal village this was very disturbing. The villagers began to file false cases against him. He was exiled from the village. He came in contact with me. 'Eknath Awad is behind him,' it was said and the village was frightened.

Shyam's exile hearing was to come up in two days. And it was during this time that his wife gave birth to a baby. Impatient to see his child, Shyam entered the village in the dead of night. He saw the child, talked to his wife a little and then slipped into a farmer's cattle pen and went to sleep. In his excitement, he had also drunk some alcohol. Emboldened by the drink, he threw himself down to sleep without taking any precautions. Someone tipped off the upper castes. They took their chance; Shyam was murdered in his sleep. So that no one should find out, his body was cut into pieces. This was the ultimate cruelty of the feudal order.

Most farmers construct a firewood trap in store for the rains. Everyone's courtyard will have a firewood trap. Shyam's body was cut into pieces and thrown on to this firewood. The pieces of his body were burned and the whole affair was hushed up.

But word got out. Our activists told me what had happened. We went to the village. We found half-burned pieces of Shyam's body still lying in the wood. We got after the police to register a panchnama. Thousands of people gathered in the village. We held a meeting about this atrocity. Ramdas Athavale attended. The murderers were brought to trial and were sentenced.

There were attacks on me as well. Stones were thrown at me in Ambevadgaon. There was a Mang named Hanmant Adagle in the village. He was a Potraj. I got him to abandon his Potrajki. Faced with the question of how to fill his stomach, he began a liquor business. I had not paid much attention to this. In my view, it was of primary importance that he was no longer begging. In a little while, Hanmant bought himself a motorcycle. Now a gold ring gleamed on his finger. Then he closed the liquor business and opened a flour mill. That this beggar Hanmant should now be seating his wife on a motorcycle and driving around in high style began to sting the upper castes. They decided to drive him out of the village. 'He has become arrogant because of the money he made on alcohol. We don't want him living in the village,' they decided in the gram sabha.

Hanmant's son told me about the gram sabha's decision over the phone. I got the jeep out. Motiram, my assistant, was with me. I went and sat down in the sabha. The villagers began to talk among themselves. What does this outsider have to do with our gram sabha? They wanted to know. I sat where I was. Then someone stood up and said: 'We don't want these disgusting Harijans in our village.' I rose to my feet and said, 'Why are you only targeting Dalit houses?' Hardly had the words left my mouth when the riot began. Everyone got up and started shouting abuse. I, too, jumped at someone to beat him up. The villagers retreated and began to throw stones from a distance but the Dalit women formed a protective shield around me. There was an old Neo-Buddhist woman called Bhojne in the village. She spread the edge of her sari over my head. She said to me: 'I won't let anyone or anything touch you. I'll die before I let them lay a hand on you.'

Some people ran off in the direction of Hanmant's house. They began to attack him there. Just then the police arrived. They fired four shots and that saved Hanmant.

The riot ended. I escaped unhurt. The Vanjari boys got me back to the jeep. I got out of the village. Hanmant still lives in that village today, and he lives a life of dignity there. He is now a member of the gram panchayat. One of his sons is studying for the Public Service Commission examinations. The other two boys have jobs as conductors and are leading lives of dignity too. His younger brother has been elected a corporator in Mumbai.

In the village of Rajur, effigies had been made of four other activists and me. The villagers had burned a Dalit's chappal shop. Since we had offered the Dalit our support, these effigies were supposed to frighten us. When one has such foolish enemies, those who take pride in their caste, it increases one's pleasure. In that village we had an Aatmaahuti Parishad, a meeting in which we declared our willingness to die in a good cause. 'We are ready to be burned,' we said.

'Come forward if you have the guts.' At that meeting, I also heaped abuse on the upper castes, attacking their ideas of humanity, using words such as they must never have heard before. All this over the loudspeakers. But no one had the guts to set those effigies on fire.

*

If you want to stand against injustice, you have to be ready to take what comes. Once, I fell foul of a powerful politician who had achieved minister status. I, too, played the poisonous game of our enmity. I am deliberately not naming names here. For this, too, is a tendency. It doesn't matter what name you give it. Politics can take you in any direction; that's all I wish to note here.

This politician called himself a Mang leader but in reality his Mang identity was merely a political stratagem. Though he had been voted to power on a Mang ticket, he never gave Mangs any jobs in his many educational institutions. The head of his party got in touch with me and asked me about his personality. He asked about and understood the issues facing Dalits, their problems and our movement. This made the Mang politician insecure. He began to see me as his political rival. This leader who worked among the Mang community was part of a narrow-minded organization. This organization gets hold of young Mangs and uses them for its political ends. It had become active in my sphere of operations. I had worked hard to bring Ambedkar thought and philosophy to the Mangs. This organization wanted to keep the Mang in the Hindu fold, under Hindu control, to teach the Mang to accept his helplessness and dependency. I lost my temper.

The excitement of the elections was upon us. I proved that this politician was no Mang at heart. There was an open revolt against him. As a result, he had to accept defeat in the elections. This must have been a body blow. Twenty-five years of political life was now at stake. I began to receive threats. He even called me himself to threaten me. But I had heard the like before. I was unafraid.

The morning of 4 June, 2004. This day is truly unique in my entire life. This is one of my most painful memories. For it was those who I had helped, members of my own caste, who attacked me. In truth, I had always stood up to the upper castes and opposed them, but they had never threatened my life. They might have paid others to kill me but they had never laid a hand on me. But this day brought the realization that my own people, my caste members, those I had always sought to help, could seek my life. And it was all over in a matter of minutes.

As always, I went in the morning for a medical check. An activist would come with me. This was to prevent an attack on me. This precaution often annoyed me. 'Boys, stop hovering. Go away, don't follow me around,' I would say and send them off.

I returned from the clinic. Annabhau Sathe Chowk, Majalgaon. I met a couple of professor friends, a lawyer or two. All of us went to a restaurant called Rangoli Corner for tea. We were chatting and joking. Suddenly someone began to throw stones at the restaurant. The shutters began to be pulled down rapidly. I got up to see what was going on outside. One of our activists, Raju Ghode, was struggling with an unknown man. The man had a sword in his hand. I was about to go forward when five other men appeared in front of me, all with swords and daggers in their hands.

In a second, I grabbed hold of one of the plastic chairs from the restaurant. I whirled it in the air, slamming their heads with it. Using it as a shield, I bore down on them. Now I could recognize my assailants. I hit one of them. He fell out of the back window. The ones in front of me attacked again. Once again, I raised my chair but the swords tore through the plastic and now they were beginning to cut me.

A sword slashed at my chest. Another got me on the shoulder. A third came at me from behind. But seeing that I was not retreating and that people had begun to gather, they decided to run for it. My shirt was soaked in blood but I ran out into the road after them. I gave chase until a car drove up and I jumped in and we followed my assailants. One of them came into my grasp and I told the driver: 'Run the car right over him.' Anger and rage were roiling inside me. I was like one possessed. The assassins ran towards the police station.

There they got themselves into the lock up. When I got to the police station, the doors had been closed. I kicked them open. Behind me were my activists. News had spread like wildfire. The MLA arrived at the station. My activists were now talking of burning down the police station. That was when I came to my senses. I did not want my movement to acquire this kind of reputation. I had no alternative but to calm down so that I might calm them down, and that is what I did. The police carried out some first aid and got me to the hospital. Outside, my activists and workers had gathered. They were all angry. I told them that they had to calm down. I was admitted to the Civil Hospital in Beed.

Meanwhile Majalgaon was in turmoil. Shops were looted, buses were burned. No one knew who they were supposed to attack to express their anger. And so people began to hit out at anonymous enemies, throwing stones at random. The names of those who had attacked me came to be known. Their homes were in Majalgaon. A mob formed and went to their homes. They were empty. Their families had left. All this had been planned in advance. Those empty houses were set on fire.

Until the time I got to the hospital, I was fine but after

that I began to feel dizzy. Meanwhile, people began to gather. I was in the ICU. My blood pressure rocketed. I wanted to talk to people but I lost consciousness…the saline drips, the bottles of blood…the windows of the hospital, the medicines being applied to my wounds…the bandages…the sudden sting of the wounds that I had paid no heed to up to then… the smell of medicines in the hospital…the blood running from my nose and drying in my beard…the smell peculiar to my own blood…the police afraid that seeing me wounded would enrage people again…someone sobbing…Gaya… where is she? Someone outside raising angry slogans…calm down, boys…I'm falling asleep…outside the hospital, many groups of people.

The next day it was in the newspapers: Attempt on Eknath Awad's life…a total bandh… In Beed, a mixed response…the homes of the assailants burned down…great tension…in the afternoon, a morcha. People were eager to see me. I made an appearance in front of that public gathering. It touched me deeply that people had come from far and wide to see me. These poor people might have run riot if they'd got the wrong ideas in their heads. My body, my nose, my hands were all swathed in bandages. One of my arms was strapped to my chest…but in this state, I went before the people. I had to go or they would not have been quiet. I said, 'I have faith in my country's Constitution, the Constitution that Babasaheb has given us. The enemy wants us to lose control, to give in to rage. Do not bring shame to our movement. I am healthy and fit. I have the strength to withstand ten such attacks. Be calm, be peaceful. Do not lose your balance. Jai Bhim.'

And then I went back to the hospital.

All day long people came to see me. Leaders, politicians, activists, friends…they came and went all day. In the night, the pills put me to sleep. But just before I fell asleep, memories of the attack would come back…the face of my first assailant. He was the one who had a business of selling weapons… he supplied pistols, swords and other weapons. The second assailant was his brother. I had not wanted him to follow the criminal path his brother had taken and so I gave him a job in the organization, a post. Some time ago he had demanded a bribe from a government servant and had attacked him. I had dismissed him from the organization… Was that the cause of his rage? No, that wasn't it… After I had dismissed him, he had been made district head by the politician who was my opponent. That leader had come to meet him the day before the attack. What if Raju had not been there? He just happened to be around. Seeing someone advancing on me with a sword in his hand, he had confronted him and grappled with him. Their plan must have been to have an unidentified assailant attack me as I sat there. Raju had brought that plan to nought. The others must have been there to frighten off other people. But they had been forced to take a hand. I had not retreated a single step. Had I shown fear, it would have emboldened them. Since I kept advancing, they were forced to retreat… and as I went over all this in my head, I would fall asleep.

This was my first stay in a hospital and I was beginning to feel depressed and helpless. On the second and third days, more activists arrived. People came in a steady stream. A Vanjari woman came to meet me with a boy of five or six, holding on to her finger. The woman folded her hands but the boy continued to regard me steadily, without blinking… innocent eyes, free of all attachment, straightforward… I do not know what happened to me then but I began to weep. When my mother died, I had cried a little. My father's death had left me dry-eyed. So why had I been moved by this little boy? Why was I weeping? The boy clutched his mother's hand, his eyes shining…my throat was getting choked. It became difficult for me to swallow. For two or three minutes, I wept unrestrainedly. No words came. Why had this happened? I still do not understand.

At the hospital, Doctors Vijaya and Chandrakant Kante, a married couple, were looking after me. Dr Kante was the Civil Surgeon of Beed. He would say to his wife, 'We are treating a tiger.'

I would want to laugh. A man who could burst into tears at the sight of a toddler clinging to his mother's finger? Who, me, a tiger?

I did not register a police complaint. After the attack, everything was chaotic. The police registered a case on their own. It was clear now that the attack had been paid for. My assailants had admitted as much to the police. Afterwards, I thought about it: My attackers were Mangs. They had criminal backgrounds. But they had had no success in their attempt. I had been saved. But now they could in turn be murdered. If something happened to them, if they were killed, I would be held to blame. If I were to register a complaint, that would be used against me. It would be said that I had got angry and ordered them killed in retaliation. And the real sutradhar would remain hidden. And so I did not register a case against my attackers. I did not feel the need to. People seek answers to questions like why, who and what in the newspapers. This is why the dailies are filled with the news of accusations and counter-accusations. But I was not interested in that kind of thing. I knew all along that something like this was going to happen. And one day it had. Death came close, brushing by me as it went. And this is the way I would like Death to present itself: with a naked sword in its hand. I do not want to go in a hospital bed, my life supported by medicines. I have always fought the good fight. I am a human being and I wish to fight until the end for the dignity of other human beings.

Through the night my mind would be filled with questions. Who am I? This universal question would haunt me. I was born Eknath Dagdu Awad. My parents were Mangs, Hindus by faith. The men who attacked me were also Mangs, Hindus by faith. It does not matter who is standing in front of you, Partha,* pick up your weapons and kill or be killed. This is your fate. I decide what is righteous and what is not... This is what Hindu dharma teaches, it creates a dharma that keeps people in compartments and marks some as slaves.

This was the dharma that kept my mother and father in a state of deprivation. This was the dharma that had kept my community away from education and so forced us into lives of crime. I had refused to accept that path. I had followed my own path and reached this place. I had fought with the members of my caste; I had fought those outside my caste. I had become an activist, a leader. It was my own drive that had brought me thus far. So what had turned my attackers into criminals? Why had their lives not turned out as mine had? Was it only a question of the need for money? They were always going to be kept in their place as Mangs. But who was doing this 'keeping in place'? The structures in our society. Even the Neo-Buddhists had not accepted the Mangs. Because their behaviour was different, they had been rejected. So what was the right way forward for us, the path to liberation? Truly Babasaheb's direction was the right way. Where did that road lead? To the Buddha.

And so the thought began to come to mind—should I accept Buddhism?

I was already half a Buddhist in my head. In 1978, when I had named my son Milind, it was out of a Buddhist belief.

---

*From the *Bhagwad Gita*, Partha or 'son of Pritha' being a way of referring to the Pandavas, this one presumably Arjuna.

Later when I cut my father's hair, when I had thrown the family idols into the river, what had been my dharma? Buddhism. What does it mean to become a Buddhist? Does one stop performing pooja of Rama and Krishna and start offering the same worship to Buddha? Is truth to be found in statues and images and caves? Was Bodh Gaya now a tirtha? Was a banteji the equivalent of a bhatji? No, not at all. The Buddha is also known as Tathagatha. This means he has been born in a special stage, free from anger, greed and lust, temptations and jealousy. That is what being the Buddha means. He is an active thinker.

Babasaheb has given us the Buddha as a positive attitude to life. He looked at the problems of society and the ways in which they could be resolved, by the Middle Path. The Buddha is humanity, in its fullest, most-realized form, which is why the Buddha is represented as seated on a full-blown lotus.

The Buddha is not to be found in temples, not in pilgrimage spots, nor in caves. The Buddha is to be found within the self. Just as the entire plant lies quiescent in the seed, the Buddha is within each one of us. Each seedling will be different. To care for one's children, to ensure their safety, to direct them to the right paths to take, to live a contented life in poverty, to abstain from alcohol and other intoxicants, to fight for justice, to erase inequality from society, to develop wisdom, character and compassion—all this is to awaken the sleeping Buddha within one. The majority of the Mahars had taken this route and were firmly on the road to progress. Why should not the Mang take this road too?

It is not as if it is given to everyone to become a Tathagatha, but if one could try and walk His road one might become a good human being. My attackers had followed the wrong route. How many Mangs did much the same thing, trying to score over others? They would set up matka booths and liquor dens and destroy themselves. It was only because I had been thinking along Buddhist lines that I was having these thoughts at all. When Dr Babasaheb Ambedkar had given his followers dhammadiksha he had made them take twenty-two oaths.

1. I shall not think of Brahma, Vishnu and Mahesh as gods nor shall I worship them.
2. I shall not think of Rama and Krishna as gods nor shall I worship them.
3. I shall not believe in Gouri–Ganesh and other gods and goddesses of the Hindu religion nor shall I worship them.
4. I do not believe in the incarnations or avatars of gods.
5. Buddha is not an avatar of Vishnu.

These I had already accepted in my mind. Even when I had been physically hurt, the expression, 'Arre Deva' (Oh god) had not crossed my lips. I had seen much pain and suffering but I had never felt any need to argue about it with any god. I had no belief in the entity called the atma (soul). I also believed that death was the end of human existence; no trace of us remains thereafter.

6. I shall not indulge in ancestor worship by performing shraaddh, nor shall I give pind-daan.
7. I shall not practice anything which is inconsistent with and contradicts Buddha's Dhamma.
8. I will not have a Brahmin preside over a ritual.
9. I believe that all human beings are equal.
10. I shall work to establish equality.

I had never participated in any Hindu rituals. When my father was alive, I would say to him, 'You can say what you want. After you die, I will perform no rituals. I will feed no crows.' Baba would only laugh at this.

As for fighting for equality, that had always been my battle. I had not retreated in the face of violence nor had I ever raised a hand on the weak. I had fought for the weak. I had never resorted to violence. I had all the raw material needed to become a Naxalite but I had never seen that as my way.

11. I shall follow the Eight-fold Path of the Buddha.
12. I shall practice ten paramitas (principles) of the Buddha.
13. I shall have compassion for all living beings.
14. I shall not steal.
15. I shall not lie.
16. I shall commit no sexual misconduct.
17. I shall not drink liquor.

Theft, lying, sexual misconduct. Had I indulged in these, my life should have been worthless. I had not and so ordinary people saw me as an elder brother.* Because I had no vices, people had offered me their love and respect.

18. I shall lead a life based on the Buddhist precepts of good character, knowledge, wisdom and compassion.
19. I renounce the Hindu dharma which holds some people to be lower than others.
20. I believe that Buddhism is the only true faith.
21. I believe that I have been reborn.
22. I swear that I shall live according to the teachings of the Buddha.**

---

*This is a reference to the honorific, Jija (senior uncle) that was bestowed on Awad by common use.

**These represent the sum and substance of the oaths that Dr Babasaheb Ambedkar had his followers swear.

I had never taken an oath like this. I had followed many, if not all twenty-two of these principles. Without knowing it, I had already been walking the Buddhist way.

*

And out of the oaths that Babasaheb had constructed, I found my answer to the question: who am I? I was a follower of the Buddha. My mind was flooded with light. I had experienced the cold touch of death. But now I was experiencing the warmth of life again. I had been reborn. Tukaram said:

> *Meechee maj vyaalo. Pota aapuliya aalo.*

> (I was born of myself. I came into my own womb.)

The saint must have felt he had scaled the peak of realization. Would I ever be able to conquer such a peak? Those were the happy pains of birth. I decided to publicly accept the Buddhist faith. I came out of the hospital and began a new campaign— *Chalo Buddha ki ore* (Let us make our way to the Buddha.)

This was not an easy campaign. Conversion must be undertaken with a sense of responsibility.

The twenty-two promises of Babasaheb were no hollow ritual for me. They represented the steps I felt we must take to bring about a social revolution in the country. In 1935, Babasaheb said at a meeting at Yeola: 'I was born a Hindu but I will not die a Hindu.' And from then on, until 1956, he began to work on preparing public opinion, on ensuring that his followers were prepared for this. And when the time was right, he converted to Buddhism. It is not possible to compare my own activities to those of Babasaheb. However, it was important to prepare people mentally.

Dadasaheb Kshirsagar was a friend of mine from the Vidarbha. He was also a Mang. He had long recognized the need for Mangs to accept Buddhism. Dadasaheb was working with the Nomadic and Denotified Tribes. The two of us began this conversion drive. My son Milind was at the forefront of the drive. He organized a number of dhammaparishads at various districts, where the dhamma of the Buddha might be explained. At each one we would get a thousand or two thousand people. Sometimes there weren't as many. That didn't matter. We did not want people accepting the Buddhist faith blindly.

Dadasaheb began to travel around the villages with a begging bag. He went to the Mangs and said, 'Up to now, you have been going around begging. *De de daan, sutate graahan* (Give alms and end the eclipse) and the alms of your helplessness would be dropped into your bag. Now I have come to ask you for alms. Give me the gods from your devhara. Cast aside your helplessness. And take to the Buddhist way.' This was an effective strategy. Many Mangs did give up their gods and took dhammadiksha.

Some Mangs would say, 'Why should we take up Buddhism? Who will give our sons Buddhist girls?'

This was a valid objection. I knew an activist who had insisted on getting married according to Neo-Buddhist rites but no one would give him their daughters. Another Mang who had earned his MBBS wanted to marry a Mang girl but by Neo-Buddhist rites. This friend could not find a girl until the age of thirty-five. A Mang father who had turned Neo-Buddhist had a similar story. When his daughter came of age, he began to look for a groom. Mang families would come to see the girl. They would see the pictures of Gautam Buddha and Dr Ambedkar on the walls and would refuse the match. The Neo-Buddhists would say, 'So what if he's a Buddhist? They're still Mangs.' The girl could not bear her father's disappointments. She wrote a letter: 'With the Bodhi Tree as my witness, I am ending my life. Should I fail in my attempt and the police come to arrest me, I would request them to arrest Gautam Buddha. This is not my suicide; this unfortunate death is to be attributed to Bhagwan Buddha.' The girl did live. And Buddha was not arrested.

Now many Mang boys were falling in love with Mahar girls. Many Mang–Mahar marriages were taking place. I have often performed the role of the priest at these ceremonies. When a Bauddha girl enters a home, she brings with her a certain culture; she understands the value of education. Well-educated Mang boys began to recognize that. Neo-Buddhist girls also began to marry Mang boys. We would explain all this to the people. Some of them began to get it.

But well-educated Mangs were opposed to my conversion. And in one way they were right. In their experience, educated Neo-Buddhists did not give educated Mangs the appropriate respect. This was also my experience. But this was also one of the psychological side effects of the caste system to which we had all been subjected. When we could give it all up, this caste system, the politics that it had generated, the benefits that accrued from it, only then would these differences be erased. But if we were all to take up caste positions and throw mud at each other, nothing would be achieved. Some people accepted his reasoning and some did not.

Other reformers took up other stances: 'There are many issues plaguing the Mang that need to be tackled. When we have dealt with questions like education, employment and intellectual awakening, we can consider conversion to Buddhism. Let us fight on for the next ten years and then we can convert to Buddhism.'

I did not argue with this position but I did feel that conversion to Buddhism would offer a leg up and, seeing this, others would also begin to move.

*

At around this time, Laxman Mane announced conversions from the Nomadic and Denotified Tribes. 'Let us convert together,' I told him. Some people said, 'Will you follow the lead of someone from a Nomadic Tribe?' Of course what they meant was, 'We are above them in the caste hierarchy.' When those on the lowest rungs of the so-called social hierarchy offer intellectual leadership, how will we be able to feel any sense of relief from following in their footsteps? By what standards were the Mangs above them? All of us had been victims of the same society. Pardhis, Kaikadis, Bhils and others were among those with whom we entered Buddhism. This happened on 2 October 2006.

*

Bhante Surai Sarsai of Japan gave us diksha.

Buddham saranam gachchaami.
I seek refuge in the Buddha.

Dhammam saranam gachhaami.
I seek refuge in the Dhamma.

Sangham saranam gachhaami.
I seek refuge in the Sangha.

I had now made a tripartite salutation to the Buddha, the Dhamma and the Sangha and a tripartite surrender to them. But where were these three centres? They were within me. 'God is in your heart,' they say. Is that what I mean? No, that isn't it. Many parts of my mind had not been purified. But those were areas only I could improve. It is not only the sight of a bar or liquor shop that makes a man want to drink; it is also something that happens inside his body that makes him crave alcohol. Watching the self and its excesses is also a requirement of the Buddhist way of life. To make oneself worthy of one's own respect is to be a Buddhist. And so I became a Buddhist.

*

Religion fulfils a human need. In the social environment in which we live, religion gives us meaning. But what about the carnal/physical questions? Conversion does not provide all the answers, nor does the battle end. It offers a theoretical basis for it but the struggle does not end and only when the scenario changes—along religious, social and political axes—will the Dalit struggle end. Unless we address the fundamental causes, we will never secure respect for the Dalit.

The word Dalit means people who have been crushed. Who crushed them? In what mill were they ground up? It was in the rural economic and social setting that the Dalit was crushed. The entire rural economy is based on land and its ownership. All questions and issues can be traced back to the land. We had been fighting for the rights of the Dalit to the gaayraan from the beginning. When an atrocity happened in a village, we would go there and encourage the Dalit to claim their rights aggressively to the common land. Different parties, organizations and groups had made different attempts to fight this battle in their own ways. We opened a new front in this war when we started a Campaign for the Landless.

Marathwada is in south-western Maharashtra. In 1760, the Peshwas of the Maratha Kingdom and the Nizam fought a war here. The Nizam lost and both sides signed a treaty by whose terms the Marathi-speaking areas between the Godavari and the Tungabhadra and the Sina Rivers were ceded to the Marathas. Wada means 'area'; Marath-wada, therefore means 'area given to the Marathas', but because of sloppy administration, the area remained under the control of the Nizam. In all this confusion, it was the Dalit who suffered the most. On the one hand, the caste system was strengthened and its hold intensified by Peshwa rule; on the other, the secondary or even tertiary status accorded to the Hindu in the Nizam's territory meant that the Untouchable Dalit was the slave of a slave.

In 1944, Dr Ambedkar came to Marathwada. In his discussions with the Nizam, he reminded him, 'In the princely state of Hyderabad, the Dalit rendered you a great service. In return you should make over the gaayraan to them.' The Nizam's government made over the common lands to the Dalit. The order was passed, but few Dalits benefited from it.

Gaayraan means the land reserved as pasture for cattle around the village. A few Dalits began to till the land here. For the most part, they did not take charge of the land. For one thing, they did not have the means with which to farm the land: the capital, the bullocks, the plough, etc. And for another, there was the attitude of the village. A spectral question began to haunt rural Maharashtra: 'What if these Dalits became farmers?' The upper castes were particularly worried. 'The Mahars and the Mangs depend upon us to live. They eat when we give them bhakri. Tomorrow if they begin to earn their own bread and eat it, they will want to sit next to us, thigh to thigh. They will not labour in our fields. And then how will we till the hundreds of acres that we own?' This free labour would be lost to them; this worried the landowners. And so they did not let the Dalits so much as set foot in the gaayraan.

India's political system has ensured that power remains vested in the hands of the land-owning class. After Independence, there was an attempt to reform the patterns of land ownership...laws relating to the ownership of family property were passed, the abolition of zamindari, the

Agricultural Land Ceiling Act. But these laws were not put into practice. The government redistributed just 1 per cent of the arable land. Out of the 45.5 crore acres in the possession of the government, it only distributed 45 lakh acres to the poor and the landless. And even in this distribution, how much land went to people who already had enough is a question still to be answered. Out of the land earmarked for this under the Eighth Five-Year Plan, 36 lakh acres of land are still to be distributed.

'The question of landlessness can only be solved in three ways. The first is the law. The second is compassion. And the third is barbarity,' said Vinoba Bhave. The law was just ignored.

The Land Ceiling Acts were subverted through a series of subterfuges. Even before the act was passed, the chicanery had already happened. This meant that the law achieved nothing. Vinoba himself tried to use the mode of compassion. During his Bhoodan Movement, Vinoba received thousands of acres of land as charity but he himself stopped the movement abruptly. Untillable land was usually given as bhoodaan. Vinoba received 42 lakh acres of land; 12 lakh acres went to the landless. The rest was not distributed.

So much for compassion.

That leaves barbarity.

The Naxalbari movement demonstrated this version of the struggle over land. But the government behaves like Kumbhakarana, feigning sleep. One can awaken those who are asleep; how can one rouse those who are feigning?

Since 2004, the Maharashtra government has been working on the Karmaveer Dadasaheb Gaikwad Sablikaran Swabhimaan Yojana (Empowerment and Self-respect Scheme). It was expected that Dalits would get land under the scheme. But since 2010, the government has distributed only 16.9 per cent of the land available under the scheme. 83.9 per cent has been held on to by the government. Why? The answer is simple: caste politics, caste-based administration.

After Babasaheb Ambedkar achieved mahaparinirvan, Karmaveer Dadasaheb Gaikwad took over leadership of the Dalit movement. Dadasaheb also raised the issue of the landlessness of the peasants. His slogan was: 'He who holds the plough, holds the title to the land'. Dadasaheb started an eye-opening movement. And so 'Land to the tiller' became the law. The Maharashtra government, spurred on by the movement, issued circulars on 14 August 1972, 27 December 1978, 20 October 1993, 14 April 2001 and 29 November 2003. According to these, land was to be given to the landless. These successes have been attributed to the Republican Party, to the Leftist parties and to the Dalit Panthers. But did the landless really become the owners of the land? No. Because they were all stuck in a caste-ridden, reactionary bureaucracy. The Shukracharyas got in the way of the Dalits getting their rights.

Whenever there was an attack on a Dalit basti, during the Marathwada University Renaming Movement, the Dalit movement had made it a practice to go there and strengthen the movement. But after the University's name was changed, the movement quietened down. The question of landlessness was also dropped. The Dalit movement attached itself to larger political parties. The desire for positions and profit defanged many activists. This was the background against which 2001, the birth centenary of Dadasaheb Gaikwad, dawned. Taking this as a pretext, we started the Gaayraan Parishad. We invited 500 activists to the meeting.

We had two days of debate and discussion on the issues of landless peasants. And the Zameen Adhikaar Andolan (The Land Rights Movement) began. This was our theme song:

Karoo nirdhaar, padeek saara gaayraan peraaycha. (2)
Maalak karaaycha,
Ya…bhoomiheenaalaa maalak karaaycha…
Nako maadi kunaachi, nako gaadi kunaachi,
Aaamhi mooleech maagit naai shetivaadi kunaachi.
Swaabhimaanana jagnyasaathi maaga na saraaycha, (2)
Maalak karaaycha,
Ya…bhoomiheenaalaa maaalak karaaycha…
Peek aamheech pikvaava, tyaachya vaadyaat taakaava.
Maalkaana thaataat te baazaari vikaava…
Doosryasaati raabraabooni koothvar maraaycha? (2)
Maalak karaaycha,
Ya…bhoomiheenaalaa maaalak karaaycha…

We are determined that every pasture be sown (2)
Chorus: We must own the land.
      The landless must be made masters.
We ask for no one's coconut trees,
We ask for no one's carts,
The landless must be made landowners.
We ask to live with self-respect; we won't turn back. (2)
(Chorus)
We harvest the crop, he sells it in the market.
How long shall we slave and die on another's land? (2)
(Chorus)

In the villages, the term maalak, landowner, was not just
a word, it was a way of life. A person's view of herself or
himself changed once s/he could lay claim to a piece of land,
however small. When an upper-caste person could say he had
20 or 25 acres of land, he acquired wings. White clothes, a
motorcycle under his butt, gold at his throat and wrist. At
least one trip to the taluka every day. Paan in his mouth, or
gutka. And a stream of caste-based abuse when he opened

that mouth. When he saw a Dalit, he would call out, 'Hey Dheda, Hey Mangtya, hey Kamblya'—always referring to the Dalit by his caste.

The upper-caste women were no different. They would refer to Dalit women as 'Here comes the Mangin; there goes the Maharin, that Chambhaardi'...to their faces. No one thought this odd. For they had the power of the land behind them and the Dalit had no land, and so, no power at all.

We had decided to break the bonds of this slavery through the Zameen Adhikar Andolan. The population of Marathwada was sixteen million then. One fifth of the people were Dalits. This meant that landlessness affected about 32 lakh people in the district. But the government had nothing to say about the issue.

In Marathwada, the Lokvikas Manch and the Maanavi Haq Abhiyaan (Campaign for Human Rights) were both fighting for Dalit access to the gaayraan. Oxfam Intermón, the aid agency, brought us together. They made our working together a condition for their economic support. Vishwanath Todkar's Paryaay, Sudhakar Kshirsagar's Sankalp, Mangalatai Daitankar and Ramnath Bhise's Janavikas, B.P. Suryavanshi's Kalapandhari and Bajrang Tate's Lokhit Samajik Vikas Sanstha, among others, came together and took up different responsibilities to set up the framework of a well-organized movement.

We divided this into three sections:

A: To help those who had already gained access to the gaayraan and whose names were registered.

B: The Dalits were farming the gaayraan but their names were not on the saat-baaraah.

C: The villages which had gaayraan but had not given the Dalits access to it. These would be the villages in which the caste system would be deeply entrenched. We would have to encourage them to become self-respecting farmers here.

The question of landlessness is always a political one. 'How can these self-help organizations do anything about it?' people would ask. We let them say what they wanted and quietly set out to work. And what was that work precisely? There were many aspects to our work, many things that we did, but let a story about a brave woman activist suffice as an example.

Baijabai Ghode was the daughter of a Potraj. Her father went from village to village begging. He would return home late at night. He would fling off his abraheen as if he were throwing a cockroach off his body. Then a deep sigh. Next a beedi. Then he would mumble to himself, 'This fucking life!' He had to look after seven children on what he got from begging. But he put his children into school. Maanavi Haq Abhiyaan organized a bonfire of the symbols of Mangki: the halgi and the saaj. Mari-Aai departed from his body and the winds of change began to blow. He gave up Potrajki and began to till the land. That was the kind of father Baija had: tall, burly, fearless. Baija joined the organization. As an activist, she travelled from village to village. She had not been adequately educated, but she knew every government document there was and where it could be found. She began to take up leadership of the Land Rights Movement. Those who had lived with their heads bowed in front of the upper castes were afraid to claim the gaayraan. Baija would stand on the borders of the land and encourage the people.

Jamb village, Parbhani: Baija encouraged the Wadar people to claim the gaayraan for tilling. There was a meeting on the issue. Baija presided over the meeting. It was decided that the Wadars would make this a cooperative enterprise; they would clear the land of weeds and stones and make it ready for sowing and they would plant together. Even the decision on what to sow would be taken jointly.

Baija was carrying out these investigations and gathering

this information. Then a hundred or a hundred and twenty-five villagers turned up there. One of the upper castes said, 'Don't you do these things in our village. This woman has come from outside and is instigating everyone to get above themselves. Get her.' One of them grabbed her hair, one took her arm and began to drag her away. Clods of mud began to rain down on her head. Abuse, blows, kicks, all of it.

The Dalits who had come with Baija to take possession of the gaayraan began to plead with the attackers. 'We came to take hold of the land,' they said. 'Leave this woman alone.' One of the attackers said, 'It's because of her that you lot have got above yourselves. We should tear her apart.' He set upon Baija with an axe. At that point an old woman threw herself in the way and took the blow to her head. Blood began to stream from it. Now the attackers were afraid that she might die, so they all hurried away. Baija went to the police station. The villagers had also arrived there. Both sides accused the other of violence. The case came to the courts.

Baija is standing now in front of the judge. An officer of the court presents her with a religious book and says, 'Repeat after me, I promise by god to tell the truth, the whole truth and nothing but the truth.'

Baija replies: 'I have no belief in god. I will swear by the Constitution of India. I swear by it that I will tell the truth and I will not lie.'

The judge is angry. 'Are you here to give speeches?'

But then he calms down. When the hearing is over, he calls Baija and says, 'Bai, you spoke your mind in the court today. These days, one does not meet people who have the courage to speak out honestly. I was very happy to hear you.' Taking her life into her hands, Baija managed to prepare proof of the violation of the gaayraan tillers' rights with this case.

That was Baija. Since she did not know when another

such incident might happen, she always kept a packet of chilli powder close to hand. Since she was behind those who were fighting for the gaayraan, there were threats to her life too.

But Baija was not turned from her slogan: '*Zameen aamchya hakkaachi, naahin kunaachya baapaachi*'. (The land is ours by right/It's no one's hereditary property).Our movement had many Baijas who kept up the slogans. '*Jo zameen sarkaari hai…*' (The land that belongs to the government…) one of them would begin and the people who were supporting them would reply in a roar, '*…woh zameen hamaari hai*' (…belongs to the people). It was the responsibility of the government to ensure that laws governing the maximum land ownership and the Land Ceiling Act were effectively deployed. But instead, they had simply kept their mouths shut.

So why could the land that was in the government's hands not go to the Dalits? The Dalit could contribute a great deal to the national output using land that is fallow. This was one of the strands of our argument. To get the poor and the Dalit to be declared owners of the land they tilled, we held dharnas, morchas and conferences, keeping the atmosphere charged. We fought this battle as if it were for our lives. It is possible to set down any number of incidents, but let me just note one.

Aarajkheda is a village in Latur. It was in the then Chief Minister's constituency. This village fought a noble battle for the gaayraan. There were twenty-five Dalit families in the village. All were landless. There were 95 acres of land around the village. A river ran through it, so the land was fertile. The upper castes had laid claim to the gaayraan. When the Dalits tried to till the land, the village exploded. Over loudspeakers, they asked people to get ready to suppress the voice of the Dalits. The dispute between the Dalits and the village worsened. There were riots. The village cut off economic support to the Dalit settlement. Under any small pretext, Dalits were beaten up.

Even the bread-and-butter man was not allowed to go into the Dalit settlement. If someone ground flour for a Dalit or let a Dalit sit in an autorickshaw, a fine of five thousand rupees was imposed.

The Dalits were being boxed in. The Zameen Adhikar Andolan stood by them. Then the Dalits got ready to fight. Now the tension reached the pitch you might expect at the India-Pakistan border. The upper-caste villagers would not give the Dalits work. The Dalits sought work outside but would not abandon the gaayraan. Why? Because to do so would mean they would have to leave the village, and that would mean going to the city and washing vessels in someone's house or scavenging garbage. So they had decided that come what may, they would become farmers. This hope was kept alive in the Dalit settlement.

Then the gram panchayat elections came around, and this time, the sarpanch's seat was reserved for the Backward Classes. A woman from the Dalit settlement was elected but she could not become the sarpanch, because no one was ready to propose and second her. But somehow she did manage to become sarpanch. Now a Dalit woman was sitting in the sarpanch's seat. The upper castes could not bear this. They would force their way into the office of the gram panchayat and abuse her. They tried to drive her from it with their filthy abuse. Their aim was to prevent her from taking her rightful place.

But the woman would not be budged. She was a Mang but she was also the sarpanch. She began to sit there in high style beneath a photograph of Babasaheb. She assigned the contract to cook food for the anganwadi to a Dalit woman's savings group. But the upper-caste women would not allow their children to eat this nutritious food. Why? 'How can our children eat food cooked by Mangs and Mahars?' they asked. Eventually the Dalit women's group stopped cooking the food.

This struggle lasted for more than ten years. The Aarajkheda case went to court. The court gave its decision—'The gram panchayat cannot stop the Dalits from tilling the gaayraan. The gaayraan belongs to the State. The village authorities cannot interfere in what happens between the Dalit settlement and the revenue department of the government.' The Dalits of Aaarajkheda won. They began to till the land in the gaayraan. They did this as a cooperative. Since they could not afford hybrid seeds, they decided to opt for organic farming. The Zameen Adhikaar Andolan gave them training in organic farming and gave them loans for the materials needed for farming. We established the Savitribai Phule Mutual Benefit Trust for these tillers of the gaayraan.

Today under the leadership of the Zameen Adhikar Andolan, 70340.22 hectares of land have been brought under the till. We are still fighting to have the land put in the name of those who till it. As a rule, one needs seventeen different pieces of paper to get a saat-baarah for the land. With great difficulty, we have accumulated these proofs in 50,000 cases and sent them on to the government. If one member of each family has his or her name so registered, and one assumes about five people in each family, two-and-a-half lakh Dalits will benefit. The question of the Dalits' survival has been taken up by the Zameen Adhikar Andolan.

Those who once had no homes in the village and no fields in the gaayraan, now till the land with great self-respect. In a hundred villages, approximately 940 acres of common land are being tilled. In homes where there was not a grain of food, now there are mounds. Dalit women now tell upper-caste women: 'Don't talk to me if you don't want, but don't call out to me with "Ay Mangin" when you do.' Now that Dalit women are tilling the gaayraan, they are called Kaku (Aunty), Jiji (Elder sister), Vahini (Sister-in-law), Tai (elder sister).

There was a settlement of about a hundred or a hundred and fifty fakirs at Didhala village, near Aunda Nagnath, Hingori Taluka. For ten months of the year, this group would travel to Gujarat, Mumbai, Nashik, Pune and Nagpur to beg. In the rains, they would return to their villages. That was the time of Dadasaheb Gaikwad's movement. In 1964, members of the Republican Party of India came to their village to talk to them. The Dalits of the village took over the gaayraan and began to till it. But at this time, the fakirs had not understood the importance of claiming the land. Only one family from among them came forward to till the land. Even today, these farmers who have possession of the land, do not have the saat-baarah in their names. The rest of the fakirs continued to wander about begging for alms. In 2002–03, the workers of the Zameen Adhikar Andolan explained the importance of the land and encouraged the fakirs to till the land. These wanderers who covered great distances spread the message wherever they went. Wherever it was possible, the community would enter the village and begin to cultivate the land. Now all the fakirs have become farmers. The very fakirs who would go from door to door to beg in pitiful voices for a little grain, now have so much grain it does not fit in their houses. Their children have begun to go to school.

It was not just for the gaayraan that the Zameen Adjikar Andolan fought. Some land had also been set aside as 'god's land'. This was supposed to be for the maintenance of the deity of a temple. God did not till the land, of course, so we encouraged the Dalits to do so. When they did, the land blossomed. The Dalits proved to be better farmers than the deity.

In this fight for the land rights of the Dalit, sometimes,

there would be administrative problems too. The land where the Dalits had their cremation ground was not marked down as such. The man who acquired a saat-baarah for this land, refused to allow the Dalits to perform their final rites there. We began to take on these issues as well.

The land on which dead cattle was stripped was also in the same situation. The Dalits no longer strip cattle, but the village had it down as Dalit land. There is another place on the banks. This means that when water in a stream begins to dry up, it is brought up here. We claimed this land for the Dalit as well. The Zameen Adhikar Andolan also took up a wide variety of issues, including the land given as a reward and the land given as a watan.

One of our beautiful songs ran:

Karoon kaam an' gaaloon ghaam,
Gaayraan aapla kasaaycha,
Jodine sajane raahoon aapan,
Mulaabaalaana shikvaaycha.

We will work and we will sweat,
And we will till our land.
We will remain together, friend,
And our children will go to school.

This was one of the things that the Zameen Adhikar Andolan insisted upon: that children should go to school. But the condition of the Dalit was very bad. Many of them were forced to humiliate themselves by begging in front of the moneylender. They had no idea of the market and so had no money to pay their debts. It was often not possible to live on the yield of the gaayraan. They had to do some side business to get by. It was this realization that made us set up the Savitribai Phule Mutual Benefit Trust on 10 December 2009. Our original intention was to focus on the women who tilled the common land for this savings group. In the first level, the scheme had a favourable response in five districts. And then we did something that had never been done before in the fight for the rights of the landless: we set up a bank for landless women labourers.

In economic terms, what is the role of the Dalit? Unskilled labour sums up the Dalit identity. The Maharashtra government was trying to increase employment opportunities among the Dalits. Annabhau Sathe and Mahatma Phule Backward Classes Economic Development Corporation gave them loans. But these corporations gave priority to traditional occupations. Making brooms or baskets was a Dalit occupation and so that was what they would support. Their policy was that Dalits should still be doing this work. They would give subsidies, but this often took two or three years to process. And then there were the agents. Generally, in a zilla, in two or three years, fifty to sixty proposals would be approved. When you get charity in the guise of loans, everyone knows about it. The Dalits who got them were mocked as being 'the sons-in-law of the government' (*shaasanaache jaawai*) or the 'subsidy community' (subsidy jamaat).

Why does that happen? Because the Dalit leadership have no time to spare from brokering government deals. This is what the Establishment has always wanted. 'We are your saviours' was their attitude. A new vicious cycle emerged. The energy of the movement was lost. Into this chilling silence, we brought the voices of the landless Dalit women. We set up Anik Financial Services Private Limited for landless women.

We bought out a Mumbai-based company and merged the Savatribai Phule Mutual Benefit Trust into it. We took expert advice from Basic, a company that dealt in loans. We got economic assistance from Oxfam to start the company. What was all this for? So that tomorrow, a Dalit woman, who had spent her life clearing shit in the villages, might say proudly to a Patil, 'Aara, go on with you. You may be the chairman of a company but I am the co-owner of a bank.'

And shortly this dream became a reality.

The landless women's saving group began to grow. The women got loans from the bank. Every year, 95 per cent of the money borrowed was repaid. This is because no one will lend money to the landless in the market so the women knew that if the bank of the landless was to go under, they would go down with it. In Bangladesh, Dr Yunus Mohammed's Gramin Bank has been praised all over the world. With small sums, he has encouraged the poor. These small sums of capital can make a marked difference to the standing of the owner in the market. Those who had no standing were given one. This was also what made us unique.

In Sailu Taluka, Rajamati Kale of Khavne Pimpri was an uneducated woman. She came to a meeting with the recoveries of ten to twelve different savings schemes. She was late for the meeting. The women had made a rule: whoever was late had to pay a ten-rupee fine. Rajamati said: 'I'll pay it, but after the meeting I'll tell you why I got late.'

After the meeting, Rajamati revealed her reason for being late. She had three-and-a-half lakh rupees with her, the recoveries from those ten or twelve savings schemes. To get to the meeting, she went to a crossroad where a jeep was parked, waiting for passengers. Rajamati took the front seat. Then the sarpanch arrived. The driver told Rajamati, 'Go sit in the back.'

Rajamati asked, 'Why?'

The answer: 'Let the sarpanch take the front seat.'

She said, 'I am not going to sit in the back. I give my money same as the sarpanch. Why should I sit in the back?'

The driver said: 'Get down...take another vehicle.'

Rajamati got angry. She said, 'Tell me how much your vehicle costs. I'll buy it from you right now. I will go in this jeep and I will sit in this seat.'

Then she showed him the money in her bag. The sarpanch had to go and sit in the back and Rajamati travelled to the meeting in the front seat.

This is just an example of the self-respect awakened among these women. But it is only direct economic progress that makes this experiment successful. A woman who used to work in a brick kiln now owns one of her own. Those women whose children wailed for milk are now buying their own buffaloes and starting their own milk-production units. These are some of the many small businesses that the women set up. These Dalit women are now entrepreneurs.

It was not as if the only things discussed at the savings scheme meetings were matters of profit and loss. The domestic violence women faced, the rights of women members of the gram panchayat—these were also matters that were discussed. And so the women began to be elected to the gram panchayat and even became sarpanch. Their husbands would often insist on accompanying them. The women would tell them: 'Wait outside. I'll get this meeting done and be back.'

In the movement, we often invoke the names of Babasaheb, Phule and Annabhau. And this gives us a certain thrill. But when the subversive ideas of these great men reach the borders of the village, then a boycott is imposed on the Dalits. They are hemmed in on every side. Their grain will not be ground into flour; they will not be hired, no credit either. But in the villages where banks for the landless have been set up, the Dalits have their own flour mills and ration shops. Babasaheb's dream was that no one in his society should have to beg by virtue of birth, no one should have to become the vehicle of the goddess' possession. We work to make this dream a reality. We have taken Babasaheb's thought out of the Dalit settlement and to the Lamans and the Pardhis too. The Lamans, the Hatkars, the Pardhis, Ghisadis, Kaikadi and Muslims, all those heads that sport the proverbial eighteen head-gear that make up the diversity of the state, have all been included in this experiment. Of the women in the Landless Women's Bank, 60 per cent of the shareholders are Dalit tillers of the gaayraan; 20 per cent are Dalits who have no access to that either and 20 per cent are from other castes.

Anik will soon carry Babasaheb's name. There are some bureaucratic issues that need to be sorted out. There are 1,685 savings schemes under its aegis. It will reach another 2,500 villages and 6,000 savings schemes. Approximately Rs 2.75 crore worth of loans have been disbursed. Soon we will receive permission from the Reserve Bank of India to become a bank. By then this bank of the landless will have affected the lives of ten crore families. Fifty per cent of the directors of the bank are women. Soon they will all be women.

*

When I look back to see where I started out… '*De daan, sut- te girhaan*' (Give alms so the eclipse may end)… I was born a Mang, the community that begs when the eclipse happens. And then a full moon burgeoned into my life. It was as if my life had been a dark terrible night and now a luminous moonlight had flooded it.

I did whatever I thought was needed in the Dalit movement. I fought the 1996 Lok Sabha election. Kanshiram of the Bahujan Samaj Party told me I should stand. I did not contest the elections for a personal victory, but rather to clear one more obstacle from the path of Dalit success. If you yank an elected leader off his seat, he will try his best to get to the next best position he can manage. Once there is a certain prestige attached to the seat, then the importance of the Dalit would increase in the national political scenario. This was Kanshiram's idea. He said, '*Tum* victim *bano. Ladke haarna aaj ki zaroorat hai. Hum aaj haarenge to kal ki jeet hamaari hogi.*' (Become a victim. It is important to fight and lose right now. If we lose today, we can win tomorrow.) On the same election symbol that Babasaheb had fought the elections—the elephant—I went into mine. That election proved decisive for me. Even up to the time of writing, in our district, no election can be fought without seeking my help in getting people together.

What would have happened if Baba had dedicated me to Mari-Aai? Aai was proud that I was going to school. That was how I got a chance to study and get this far. But neither parent is here today to see my happiness.

Baba, I abandoned your Potrajki. After that, I cannot remember how many halgis I have broken, how many times I have burned the paraphernalia of Mangbaaj in bonfires.

Aai, I thought it was not a respectable profession for a woman to go and clear the cow dung at the Patils'. Aai, how many women like you have been freed from slavery.

Now times have changed. The Dalits who once worked free in their masters' fields now ask to be paid before their sweat has dried. The Potraj is not such a common sight. No one plays music unless they are paid. The practice of gaavki exists in small pockets. That too will soon become extinct. Mangki and Maharki are now frowned upon. No bloody pimp has the courage to insist on these practices.

But the fight is not over. What do the statistics of the National Crime Records Bureau show us?

Every hour, three atrocities are committed against Dalits.

Every day, four Dalit women are raped, two Dalits are murdered, eleven Dalits are attacked.

Every week, five Dalit homes are burned, six Dalits are stripped of their clothes.

Which is why I am still fighting. Until the Dalit can live a life of self-respect, I will keep on fighting.

*

I am browsing at a bookstall. An old woman, who looks illiterate, comes up. She examines a book that has Babasaheb's picture on the cover. The stall-owner says, 'Aaji, you won't be able to afford that book; put it down.'

She says, 'Baba, what does it cost?'

The stall-owner says, 'Two hundred and fifty rupees.'

The old lady takes out a cloth purse she has folded into the edge of her sari. The stall-owner says: 'Aaji, give me two hundred. For you a fifty-rupee discount.'

The old lady says: 'Am I going to haggle over my Babasaheb's book, child? I can't read. But I'll get my grandson to read every word, every single word in this. Take the money.' And she left.

I kept looking after her… These are the golden moments in my life.

I think of how much has happened. I have started a school for the children of sugar-cane cutters. I have established a trade union for poverty-stricken labourers. I still have much to do. The Dalits must be made the owners of the land they till. Dalit women must be brought together, must set up industries. I dream that one day the daal from their mills will be sold in the malls of London.

I am still at the bookstall, lost in thought, dreaming while still awake.

Into my head comes the thought… When my father begged he would cry, 'Jai lakhpati Laxmi-ai. May that which is one stay united, may five become fifty, may your cattle increase and multiply, may your creeper climb up its trellis…'

I made Baba's words come true in another sense. I was alone. I benefited from the hundreds of activists who joined me in the struggle, I have been enriched. Just as a child who is teething wants to taste everything on the floor, I have experienced every facet of the Dalit's life.

A seed of the thoughts of Phule and Ambedkar was planted in me. A vine grew in my head. From that seedling, a peepal tree began to grow. Around that tree many activists twined themselves as creepers do. Those vines I had planted at the huts of the Backward Classes and Nomadic Tribes have begun to climb their trellises…